The Silence of Entropy or Universal Discourse

*New York University Ottendorfer Series*
*Neue Folge Band 21*

unter Mitarbeit von

Helmut Brackert (Frankfurt/M.),
Peter Demetz (Yale), Reinhold Grimm (Wisconsin),
Walter Hinderer (Princeton)

herausgegeben von
Volkmar Sander

PETER LANG
New York · Berne · Frankfurt am Main

Arlene Akiko Teraoka

# The Silence of Entropy or Universal Discourse

The Postmodernist Poetics of Heiner Müller

PETER LANG
New York · Berne · Frankfurt am Main

Library of Congress Cataloging in Publication Data

**Teraoka, Arlene Akiko, 1954–**
The Silence of Entropy or Universal Discourse.

(New York University Ottendorfer Series; n.F.,
Bd. 21)
Bibliography: p.
1. Müller, Heiner, 1929–   – Aesthetics.
I. Title.   II. Series.
PT2673.U29Z92      1985        832'.914        84-15431
ISBN 0-8204-0190-0


CIP-Kurztitelaufnahme der Deutschen Bibliothek

**Teraoka, Arlene Akiko:**
The Silence of Entropy or Universal Discourse:
the Postmodernist Poetics of Heiner Müller /
Arlene Akiko Teraoka. – New York; Berne;
Frankfurt am Main: Lang, 1985.
  (New York University Ottendorfer Series;
N.F., Bd. 21)
  ISBN 0-8204-0190-0

NE: New York University: New York University . . .


© Peter Lang Publishing, Inc., New York 1985

All rights reserved.
Reprint or reproduction, even partially, in all forms such as
microfilm, xerography, microfiche, microcard, offset strictly prohibited.

Printed by Lang Druck, Inc., Liebefeld/Berne (Switzerland)

## ACKNOWLEDGMENTS

This study was supported in part by a Whiting Fellowship in the Humanities. In addition, a travel grant from the Department of German Studies and the Office of Graduate Studies and Research at Stanford University enabled me to work briefly in the German Democratic Republic.

I wish to thank Russell Berman and David Wellbery, whose insightful comments and criticisms have helped to give this project shape. My parents, Tetsuo and Doris Teraoka, have provided moral and financial support throughout my graduate study, and I dedicate this to them as a small token of gratitude. Finally, without Don Nonini, whose love and wisdom continue to be a source of strength, I would not have finished in such good time, and in such good spirits.

# TABLE OF CONTENTS

Introduction    9

Chapter I: The Poetics of a Revolutionary Postmodernism    17

    Orpheus Under the Plows    17
    "Literature is an affair of the people"    19
    The Project of the Self-Expropriation of Talent    21
    "Art Without Strain"    25
    The Hope of the Third World    31
    The Disappearance of the Author    38
    The Silence of Entropy or Universal Discourse    47

Chapter II: The Critique of the Enlightenment: *Leben Gundlings Friedrich von Preussen Lessings Schlaf Traum Schrei* (1976)    51

    Jacob Paul Freiherr von Gundling: Scene 1    52
    Friedrich II: Scenes 2-7    55
    Heinrich von Kleist and Gotthold Ephraim Lessing: Scenes 8-9    69
    The Enlightenment Dialectic    76

Excursus: Lessing, Hegel, and the Model of Bourgeois Drama    81

Chapter III: The Entropy of Bourgeois Drama: *Die Hamletmaschine* (1977)    87

    Scenes 1 and 5: The Dramatic Hero and the Undramatic Victim    89
    Scenes 2 and 4: Two Attempts to Reject a Role    97
    The Hamlet Scenes: The Failure of the Intellectual    104
    The Ophelia Scenes: The Revolutionary Gone Underground    110

|  |  |
|---|---|
| Scherzo and the Play as a Whole | 112 |
| "Im Rücken die Ruinen von Europa" | 119 |

Chapter IV: The Emergence of an Alternative Discourse: *Der Auftrag: Erinnerung an eine Revolution* (1979) — 123

|  |  |
|---|---|
| The Overall Structure of the Text | 125 |
| Scenes 1-3: The "Auftrag" of Remembering | 127 |
| Scenes 4-6: The Donning of the Masks | 135 |
| Scenes 7-9: The Theater of Revolution | 143 |
| Scene 10: A "Walk into Oblivion" | 151 |
| Scenes 11-12: "Das Schauspiel ist zu Ende": The Betrayal of Forgetting | 156 |
| The European Revolution(s) and the Third World | 165 |

|  |  |
|---|---|
| Conclusion | 171 |
| Notes | 183 |
| Works Consulted | 219 |
|   I. Works by Heiner Müller | 219 |
|     A. Collections | 219 |
|       1. West German publications | 219 |
|       2. East German publications | 219 |
|     B. Singly published works | 219 |
|       1. Dramatic texts | 219 |
|       2. Lyric texts | 221 |
|       3. Prose texts | 221 |
|       4. Speeches and essays | 221 |
|       5. Interviews and discussions | 223 |
|       6. Reviews and journalistic articles | 225 |
|   II. Works on Heiner Müller | 227 |
|     A. Scholarly works | 227 |
|     B. Theater reviews | 231 |
|   III. Other Primary Works | 232 |
|     A. Literary works | 232 |
|     B. Theoretical works | 235 |
|   IV. Other Secondary Works | 237 |

# INTRODUCTION

A recent interview published in the glossy West German weekly news magazine *Der Spiegel* introduces the East German playwright Heiner Müller as "der im Ausland erfolgreichste und angesehenste DDR-Dramatiker seit Brecht, im eigenen Land wohl der umstrittenste."[1] "Dort [in the German Democratic Republic] wie hier [the Federal Republic of Germany] oft angefeindet und doch respektiert wie keiner seit Brecht,"[2] honored in mid-May of 1983 by a Heiner Müller Festival in The Hague, ten productions of ten plays by theaters from East Germany, West Germany, Bulgaria, the Netherlands, and Belgium, Heiner Müller has definitely "arrived" as the most significant playwright since Brecht to emerge out of East Germany, if not out of *any* of the German-speaking countries of post-war Europe.

For the fifty-four-year-old Müller (born in 1929), both popular and academic recognition come relatively late in his career. Heiner Müller's thirty plays span in terms of their dates of origin over thirty years of East German political, economic, and cultural history. Scholars generally define three major phases in Müller's oeuvre:[3] from the early 1950's to the early 1960's Müller dealt with contemporary problems in industry and land reform in the developing East German socialist state; plays such as *Der Lohndrücker* (1957), *Die Korrektur* (1958), *Die Umsiedlerin oder Das Leben auf dem Lande* (1961, revised as *Die Bauern,* 1964), and *Der Bau* (1964) explored the contradictory adjustment of German workers, Communists as well as former National Socialists, to the new collective work system. The cancellation of further performances of *Die Umsiedlerin* (directed by B.K. Tragelehn) after its premiere in the student theater of the Hochschule für Ökonomie in Berlin on September 30, 1961, was followed by Müller's expulsion from the East German Schriftstellerverband. This event, and Erich Honecker's denunciation of *Der Bau* in the 11th Plenary Session of the Central Committee of the SED in December 1965, placing severe restrictions on aesthetic representations of socialist "reality," mark the beginning of the second phase in Müller's work.[4]

For ten years following the cancellation of *Die Umsiedlerin*, East German theaters would mount only a handful of productions, with the exception of Müller's *Macbeth* in Brandenburg in 1972, of relatively "minor" works: Sophocles' *Ödipus Tyrann* (based on the Hölderlin translation, completed in 1966), *Drachenoper* (with Ginka Tscholakowa, the libretto to Paul Dessau's opera *Lancelot*, based on the play *Der Drache* by Jevgenii Schwarz, 1968), *Horizonte* (with Benno Besson and others, the first scene of an adaptation of the play by Gerhard Winterlich, 1968), and *Weiberkomödie* (based on the radio play *Die Weiberbrigade* by Inge Müller, 1969).[5] From the mid-60's to the early 1970's Müller's completed projects consisted largely of radical re-workings of Greek and Brechtian plays.

In *Philoktet* (Sophocles, 1964), *Prometheus* (Aeschylus, 1968), *Der Horatier* (Brecht, 1969), *Mauser* (Brecht's *Die Massnahme*, 1970), and *Zement* (Fedor Gladkow, 1972), Müller examined the ideologically problematic relationship of the individual to the collective cause in a socialism that is no longer the optimistic vision of the future, but the contradictory reality of the present. In stark and boldly experimental verse and in the abstract situations of mythological and literary models, these plays present political-philosophical discussions of the conflict between the immediate claims of the individual and the sacrifices required by the daily process of building a socialist state.

The change in official cultural politics since the 8th Party Congress in 1971, which allowed for "die

Ausprägung individueller Schreibweisen im Zusammenhang mit der Reflexion und Formulierung divergierender poetologischer Programme" throughout the 1970's, prepared the way for Müller's "breakthrough."[6] The Berliner Ensemble production of *Zement*, premiering in October 1973 and directed by Ruth Berghaus, represented the first production in a leading East Berlin theater since 1958 of a major work by Heiner Müller. In 1975 the East German publishing firm Henschel made available a collection of nine plays including *Der Lohndrücker, Die Bauern, Der Bau, Philoktet, Macbeth,* and *Zement,* followed two years later by a second volume containing *Die Schlacht, Traktor,* and *Leben Gundlings Friedrich von Preussen Lessings Schlaf Traum Schrei*. In West Berlin, Rotbuchverlag began publication in 1974 of a now seven-volume series of Müller's collected works. Thus Heiner Müller literally exploded onto the theater scenes of both East and West Germany in the middle of the 1970's.

Müller's artistically most complex, and politically perhaps most controversial and perplexing work comes in this third phase of his playwriting career. From the mid-1970's to the present, Müller has composed historical-mythological-literary "montages" which explore the philosophical and psychological causes for, and the consequences of, the failure of the revolutionary German intellectuals and the demise of the working-class movement in Germany. In plays such as *Germania Tod in Berlin* (1971), *Die Schlacht* (1974), *Leben Gundlings* (1976), *Die Hamletmaschine* (1977), *Der Auftrag* (1979), and, most recently, *Verkommenes Ufer Medeamaterial Landschaft mit Argonauten* (1982), Müller investigates the issues of cultural colonialism and the exportation of revolution, the role of the intellectual in the revolutionary process, and, specifically, the role of the European socialist intellectual in the contemporary struggles of the Third World. My dissertation deals with three of these later plays.

11

Much of the literature on Müller's works appearing in the West treats the East German playwright, as Marc Silberman observes in his excellent *Forschungsbericht,* either as a dogmatic Marxist and defender of the German Democratic Republic, or as a linguistically and artistically gifted writer whose political engagement is of secondary concern.[7] Müller's plays are either deciphered as reflections or veiled allegorical depictions of East German society, while their poetic achievement is effectively ignored, or they are interpreted within the context of nihilistic, apocalyptic, "existentialist" avant-garde literature, as East German siblings of Beckett's *Endgame.*[8] Political and aesthetic elements are thus never successfully linked.

A second shortcoming of the scholarly literature on Müller is the lack of detailed analyses of individual plays. The two monographs on Heiner Müller which present interpretations of individual plays within the context of a thematic overview of Müller's oeuvre often fail to move beyond basic presentations of historical and political background and descriptive summaries of action to an integrated critical analysis of the texts.[9] Leftist scholarly discussions, which avoid the artificial separation of the realms of art and politics and treat Müller as "den Vertreter einer anti-bürgerlichen Theatertradition, der sich jedoch bewusst von den mechanistischen Widerspiegelungstheorien des offiziellen sozialistischen Realismus entfernt,"[10] have devoted their energy to exploring general lines of development (for example, the critical relationship to Brecht) or specific problems or themes (the concept of history, the role of women) in Müller's works.[11] While these investigations represent some of the most insightful and intelligent scholarship available on Müller, the plays as individual works remain largely unexamined.

The present study undertakes detailed studies of three plays from the most recent phase of Müller's work: *Leben Gundlings Friedrich von Preussen Lessings Schlaf Traum Schrei* (1976), *Die Hamletmaschine* (1977), and *Der Auftrag* (1979). I treat these plays not against the background of their specific political or economic East German "context," but rather in terms of Müller's poetic project as a postmodernist artist in a post-capitalist world system. As such, my study is primarily aesthetic or poetological rather than political in its focus. However, I avoid the error of totally separating the realms of the aesthetic and the political by exploring the specifically political or ideological significance of Müller's aesthetic categories.

I hope to demonstrate that *Leben Gundlings* and *Hamletmaschine* work to deconstruct certain central norms of the German Enlightenment (the concept of rational authority, the integral rational individual/hero, the rational teleological process of historical development, intersubjective rational discourse) as these are manifested in the model of bourgeois drama formulated by Lessing and later Hegel.[12] Further, I argue that an *alternative* order to the European Enlightenment (the dominance of reason) is suggested in these plays, as the order of the colonized and oppressed "Third World." In my discussion of *Der Auftrag* which deconstructs the opposing socialist model of the Brechtian *Lehrstück,* I hope to show how this thematic alternative of the Third World represents at the same time a *poetic* alternative to European models of drama.

I begin with an analysis of Müller's essay on postmodernism from 1979, in which the playwright provides a dense and cryptic statement of his revolutionary "postmodernist" aesthetics. Defining and aligning himself within an anti-literary tradition in modern literature which works toward the liquidation of aesthetic autonomy and the dispossession of the author, Müller identifies two productive strategies for the revolutionary author engaged in the project of his own "disappearance": "das Schweigen der Entropie oder der universale Diskurs, der nichts auslässt und niemanden ausschliesst."[13] In a way my endeavor in this study has been to understand the significance of "entropy" and "universal discourse," and to make them fruitful interpretive concepts for approaching the difficult, yet immensely compelling works of the most important German playwright since Brecht.

Auch wer das Unglück hat, in
einem Land mit grosser Literatur
geboren zu sein, muss in seiner
Sprache schreiben wie ein tsche-
chischer Jude im Deutschen oder
ein Usbeke im Russischen: schreiben
wie ein Hund sein Loch buddelt, wie
eine Maus ihren Bau gräbt. Dazu ist
erst einmal der Ort der eigenen
Unterentwicklung zu finden, das
eigene Kauderwelsch, die eigene
Dritte Welt, die eigene Wüste.

    Gilles Deleuze/Félix Guattari

# CHAPTER I
# THE POETICS OF A REVOLUTIONARY POSTMODERNISM

Heiner Müller's essay "Der Schrecken die erste Erscheinung des Neuen" was written for the forum "The Question of Postmodernism" moderated by Ihab Hassan at the 93rd Annual Convention of the Modern Language Association, held in New York City from December 27-30, 1978.[1] It represents the most complete and most concise statement of Müller's understanding of his place and role within modernist and contemporary European literature. My aim in this first chapter is to sketch the outlines of that project and that role.

## I

### Orpheus Under the Plows

Müller's contribution to the academic discussion of postmodernism begins with a retelling of the Orpheus myth which takes direct issue with Ihab Hassan, one of the foremost theoretical spokesmen of postmodernist literature and literary criticism.[2] Hassan's major work, *The Dismemberment of Orpheus,* takes its central and unifying image from Ovid's *Metamorphoses*: the Maenads, furious because the singer has turned to the love of young boys, tear him limb from limb; Orpheus's head and lyre, drifting down the Hebrus River, continue their mournful song.[3] Hassan interprets the dismemberment of Orpheus in terms of the modernist crisis of language and culture. The singing poet whose song draws the trees, the beasts, and the stones to follow (*Metamorphoses* XI.1-2) represents a universal harmony between man (consciousness) and nature; after his dismemberment a "lyre without strings" is left to the moderns, whose poetry denies the mediation of language. As I understand Hassan, the severed head of the poet which continues to sing after death presents a poetic image of the postmodernist authors who "exemplify, in some hieratic order of despair, the sovereignty of the void."[4] Thus the central, paradoxical metaphor of a literature of *silence,* an anti-literature separated from nature, reason, history, society, working through the subversion of forms towards the self-repudiation of art: the dismembered poet continues, impossibly, to sing.

Müller's remaking of the Orpheus myth focuses on a detail that Hassan ignores. Ovid writes of a group of farmers, plowing the field with a team of oxen, who flee before the wild onrushing Maenads. They leave behind them hoe, rake, and mattock, with which the Maenads kill and dismember the oxen before rushing back to murder Orpheus (*Metamorphoses* XI. 31-39).[5] Müller's version reads as follows:

> Die Verschmähten jagten ihn: mit Waffen ihrer Leiber Ästen Steinen. Aber das Lied schont den Sänger: was er besungen hatte, konnte seine Haut nicht ritzen. Bauern, durch den Jagdlärm aufgeschreckt, rannten von ihren Pflügen weg, für die kein Platz gewesen war in seinem Lied. So war sein Platz unter den Pflügen. (94)

What is for Hassan a nonessential action in Ovid's account takes on central significance for Müller. While in the *Metamorphoses* the Maenads overcome the softening, calming power of Orpheus's music by drowning it in the noise of trumpets, drums, and howls, the poet in Müller's retelling is vulnerable only to the plows of the peasants. Orpheus is buried under the plows which had had no place in his songs: the principle of the artist as an individual with privileged insight or power gives way under the weight of the material realities and needs of the masses, which hitherto had had no place in the realm of art. The aesthetic ideal of a harmony between the self and the world achieved through the medium/

illusion of art (the stones, beasts, rocks follow Orpheus's song) gives way to the concrete reality of a relationship of *work* (the farmers plow their field). Müller, in the opening paragraph of his essay, takes issue with the critic Hassan whose analysis of postmodernism remains within the bounds defined by a bourgeois concept of art. The severed head of Orpheus continues to sing, the "Artist" lives on. Müller's myth, in contrast, shatters the bounds of traditional art to encompass the reality of the working masses; the plows of the peasants, brought to the foreground, redefine the concepts of art and artist. Müller states his thesis:

## II

"Literature is an affair of the people"

The quote from Kafka is found in the long diary entry on December 25, 1911, where Kafka speaks of the value and productive power of "kleine Literaturen" which lack writers of great talent.[6] One central task of these literatures in their work to create and maintain "das einheitliche Zusammenhalten des im äussern Leben oft untätigen und immer sich zersplitternden nationalen Bewusstseins" is the formulation of the literary history of their past writers.[7] In this context, Kafka writes, "Es werden zwar weniger Literaturgeschichtskundige beschäftigt, aber die Literatur ist weniger eine Angelegenheit der Literaturgeschichte als Angelegenheit des Volkes, und darum ist sie, wenn auch nicht rein, so doch sicher aufgehoben."[8]

The provocative passage from the diaries provides the impulse and main theoretical statement for Gilles Deleuze and Félix Guattari's *Kafka: Für eine kleine Literatur,*[9] a brilliant and radical rereading of Kafka that, Müller admits, has been of great importance for his own writing.[10] The authors develop - somewhat tendentiously - the political ramifications of Kafka's concept of the "small literature": it is the literature of a minority group that makes use of a major, dominant language (as, for example, the literature of a Jew in Prague writing in German); it is a literature in which every separate, individual event is immediately connected to a larger political sphere; finally, and most importantly, it is the literature of a collective.[11] It is in this third characteristic most of all that Deleuze and Guattari radicalize the import of Kafka's diary statement and move beyond the accepted understanding of the author:

> Gerade wegen ihres Mangels an grossen Talenten fehlen ihr [der kleinen Literatur] die Bedingungen für *individuelle Aussagen,* die ja stets Aussagen des einen oder anderen "Meisters" wären und sich von der *kollektiven Aussage* trennen liessen. Somit erweist sich der relative Talentmangel durchaus als günstiger Umstand: Er gestattet, etwas anderes als eine Literatur der grossen Meister zu konzipieren.[12]

In place of a literature of master-pieces by great individual talents, Deleuze and Guattari, through the mouthpiece of Kafka, call for a "small" literature "der die Rolle und Aufgabe einer kollektiven, ja revolutionären Aussage zufällt."[13] The affinity to Müller's own thought is clear: the plows of the peasants bring Orpheus's song to an end. The collective, revolutionary statement replaces the privileged self-expression of a genius; literature, to borrow from Kafka, is an affair of the people. Müller quotes, I believe, not directly from the diaries, but from the radicalized, revolutionary interpretation presented by Deleuze and Guattari:

> Die literarische Maschine bereitet den Boden für eine kommende revolutionäre Maschine, nicht als vorauslaufende "Ideologie", sondern weil sie als einzige dazu berufen ist, die ansonsten überall fehlenden Voraussetzungen einer kollektiven Aussage zu erfüllen: *Die Literatur ist eine Angelegenheit des Volkes.*[14]

## III
## The Project of the Self-Expropriation of Talent

In their discussion of "small" literature, Deleuze and Guattari define the nature and function of the revolutionary artist, the artist who works within a dominant (and dominating) literary and cultural tradition of oppression while subversively striving to end all oppression. The following statement is particularly striking in light of the significance of the Third World in Müller's work; the adjective "small" qualifies:

> ... nicht mehr bloss bestimmte Sonderliteraturen, sondern die revolutionären Bedingungen *jeder* Literatur, die sich innerhalb einer sogenannten "grossen" (oder etablierten) Literatur befindet. Auch wer das Unglück hat, in einem Land mit grosser Literatur geboren zu sein, muss in seiner Sprache schreiben wie ein tschechischer Jude im Deutschen oder ein Usbeke im Russischen: schreiben wie ein Hund sein Loch buddelt, wie eine Maus ihren Bau gräbt. Dazu ist erst einmal der Ort der eigenen Unterentwicklung zu finden, das eigene Kauderwelsch, die eigene Dritte Welt, die eigene Wüste.[15]

"Gross und revolutionär ist nur das Kleine, das 'Mindere,'" Deleuze and Guattari state in a later passage; "Hass gegen alle Literatur der Herren. Hinwendung zu den Knechten, zu den kleinen Angestellten."[16] The revolutionary artist must write from the standpoint of the "small" and the "minor" within the large and dominant structure; he speaks from the position of the Third World within the colonialist, imperialist, oppressive regime, his voice from the desert is directed against the metropolises of the world, his language is the subversive jargon at the periphery of the standard grammar. The artist as revolutionary must work to erode the position of the artist as one of power and privilege; he is an Orpheus who must sing of the plows, not to charm and dull their revolutionary force, but to inspire them and to throw himself down before their onrushing attack.

Müller goes on in the third section of his essay to establish a clear political and international context for his redefinition of art and the artist. The "Third World" which Deleuze and Guattari momentarily invoke in their discussion of the "small" literature is not merely a metaphor for Müller, but the concrete reality of Africa, Asia, and Latin America in a world system divided into capitalist and socialist blocs. The "small" literature has international import. Müller describes above all the role of the *socialist* writer: "Schreiben unter Bedingungen, in denen das Bewusstsein von der Asozialität des Schreibens nicht mehr verdrängt werden kann. Schon Talent ist ein Privileg, Privilegien müssen bezahlt werden: der Eigenbeitrag zu seiner Enteignung gehört zu den Kriterien des Talents" (94).[17] Elsewhere Müller speaks of the consciousness of the asocial character of writing in terms of the "bad conscience" of the socialist author, who must write with full consciousness of his privileged existence:

> Weil Kunst bei uns [in the GDR] doch nicht so eine Ware is wie hier [in the FRG], entsteht zunächst, vielleicht auch viel mehr als hier, ein schlechtes Gewissen bei den Produzenten. ... das schlechte Gewissen, das man hat, wenn man eine halbe Nacht damit verbracht hat, einen Reim zu finden oder was immer, und man sieht, wie Leute die Nacht gearbeitet haben, eben für mehr oder weniger als einen Reim. ... man muss sich bewusst bleiben, dass es ein Privileg ist, dass man eine Arbeit machen kann, die einem Spass macht, während die Mehrheit der Bevölkerung Arbeiten machen muss, von denen es wirklich unmöglich ist, auf die Dauer Spass zu beziehen, die man macht, damit andere ihren Spass haben. Und in diesem Widerspruch schreibt man, glaube ich, bei uns mehr als hier ...[18]

In a society that claims to abolish all privilege, the author, privileged by virtue of his talent, has the social task of working toward his own self-abolition. In Müller's words, one of the criteria of talent (in a socialist society) is its contribution to its own expropriation. The concept of property, of the art work as the "private" property of its wholly "individual" creator, belongs to an economic system that has been overthrown: "Mit dem freien Markt fällt die Illusion von der Autonomie der Kunst" (94); the autonomy of works of art ist, Müller writes, the "Produkt ihrer Unzucht mit dem Privateigentum" (97).[19] In the "Planwirtschaft" of socialism, in contrast, art is "zurückgenommen in die soziale Funktion. Bevor sie aufhört Kunst zu sein (eine im Sinn von Marx borniert Tätigkeit), kann sie daraus nicht entlassen werden" (94-95).

The "Widerspruch" in which the socialist writer finds himself is due to the fact that the "planned economy" is not simply and neatly established in its entirety by the fall of the free market, but contains within itself elements of the previous system. Marx's schematic separation of capitalism, the division of labor, and the artist as specialist, on the one hand, and socialism, collectivization, and the overcoming of exclusive specialization, on the other, has not (yet) been realized in the modern socialist state. According to Marx:

> Die exklusive Konzentration des künstlerischen Talents in Einzelnen und seine damit zusammenhängende Unterdrückung in der grossen Masse ist Folge der Teilung der Arbeit. ... Bei einer kommunistischen Organisation der Gesellschaft fällt jedenfalls fort die Subsumtion des Künstlers unter die lokale und nationale Borniertheit, die rein aus der Teilung der Arbeit hervorgeht, und die Subsumtion des Individuums unter diese bestimmte Kunst, so dass es ausschliesslich Maler, Bildhauer usw. ist und schon der Name die Borniertheit seiner geschäftlichen Entwicklung und seine Abhängigkeit von der Teilung der Arbeit hinlänglich ausdrückt.

> In einer kommunistischen Gesellschaft gibt es keine
> Maler, sondern höchstens Menschen, die unter anderm
> auch malen.[20]

As Müller explains, artistic activity in East Germany today is still carried out by specialists. Marx's analysis did not - and could not - consider the stupefying effect of mass media, which works to broaden the base for culture, but at the expense of the cultural niveau: "Im Smog der Medien, der auch in dem Land, aus dem ich komme, den Massen die Sicht auf die wirkliche Lage nimmt, ihr Gedächtnis auslöscht, ihre Fantasie steril macht, geht die Verbreitung auf Kosten des Niveaus" (95).[21] The consequences are serious ones for the author: "Im *Reich der Notwendigkeit* sind Realismus und Volkstümlichkeit zwei Dinge. Der Riss geht durch den Autor" (95).

Müller's pointed and cryptic formulation draws upon an important passage from Volume III of *Capital* where Marx speaks of a future condition of creative leisure brought about by the proletarian revolution and the advances of modern industry; this "realm of freedom" lies beyond the "realm of necessity" in which labor is still required to produce necessary goods:

> Das Reich der Freiheit beginnt in der Tat erst da,
> wo das Arbeiten, das durch Not und äussere Zweck-
> mässigkeit bestimmt ist, aufhört; es liegt also der
> Natur der Sache nach jenseits der Sphäre der eigent-
> lichen materiellen Produktion. ... Die Freiheit in
> diesem Gebiet kann nur darin bestehen, dass der ver-
> gesellschaftete Mensch, die assoziierten Produzenten,
> diesen ihren Stoffwechsel mit der Natur rationell
> regeln, unter ihre gemeinschaftliche Kontrolle
> bringen, statt von ihm als von einer blinden Macht
> beherrscht zu werden; ihn mit dem geringsten Kraft-
> aufwand und unter den, ihrer menschlichen Natur wür-
> digsten und adäquatesten Bedingungen vollziehen.
> Aber es bleibt dies immer ein Reich der Notwendig-
> keit. Jenseits desselben beginnt die menschliche

> Kraftentwicklung, die sich als Selbstzweck gilt, das
> wahre Reich der Freiheit, das aber nur auf jenem
> Reich der Notwendigkeit als seiner Basis aufblühen
> kann.[22]

In the "realm of necessity" work is determined by material necessity; in the "realm of freedom," man's activity is an end in itself, the development of his human capacity. Müller postulates a similar ideal for art: the realm of freedom, which lies for Marx beyond the sphere of material production, is for Müller "jenseits der Privilegien" (97), beyond the artist as privileged specialist. In the realm of necessity, realism and popular culture ("Volkstümlichkeit") are separate; in the realm of freedom, they become one.[23] Müller goes on in the rest of the third section to clarify this ideal.

### "Art Without Strain"

Müller begins by addressing, criticizing, and rejecting the academic question of postmodernism: "Ich stehe, was die Bedingungen meiner Arbeit angeht, zu Ihrer Fragestellung zunächst einmal quer" (95). As a socialist author engaged in the project of his self-expropriation, he rejects the roles of Polonius, who argues with Hamlet over the shape of a cloud,[24] and of Lorca's gypsy, who turns with his absurd answers the interrogator of the Civil Guard into a screaming bundle of nerves.[25] The comparatist Polonius demonstrates, Müller says, "am Elend des Vergleichens das wirkliche Elend von Machtstrukturen" (95). Once again we can use Müller to illuminate Müller; in an essay from 1979 he writes:

> Eugen Gottlob Winkler ... schreibt 1936 in einem
> Text über ERNST JÜNGER ODER DAS UNHEIL DES DENKENS:
> Zwischen der Verschiedenheit zweier Erfahrungen kann

es kein Streitgespräch geben. Bei dem Versuch, für
Leser in Frankreich etwas wie einen "Kulturbrief" aus
der DDR-Hauptstadt zu schreiben, geht mir die Wahrheit
dieses Satzes auf. Das Unternehmen hat den Schwierig-
keitsgrad einer Beschreibung der erdabgewandten Seiten des Mondes. Die Sozialismusklischees der Medien
von Dissidenz und/oder Dogma greifen an der Wirklichkeit vorbei. Sie wohnt nicht in den Extremen. Was für
die Eliten Geschichte, ist für die Massen noch immer
Arbeit gewesen. Die Klischees bedienen den Appetit
auf Signale von Verrat aus dem Lager jenseits des Ka-
pitalismus, garantieren das gute Gewissen des Kon-
sums, den Frieden der Korruption.[26]

Comparisons are made (can be made) only with clichés
which fail to grasp reality; they are the concern
of the elite who, like Hamlet and Polonius, debate
the shape of a cloud. The reality underlying all
comparisons, however, is the *single* reality of the
working masses; the misery of comparing, the misery of power structures, lies in their separation
from this reality. The gypsy also cannot be Müller's role. On one level, of course, Müller is
simply and with tongue in cheek promising not to
torment the members of the panel on postmodernism
(and us!) with his own surrealistic response. More
significantly, Müller, unlike Lorca's clever gypsy,
is not seeking the nervous collapse of an oppressive, external "other," but rather the collapse of
his own identity as privileged author. The author
himself, like the Lessing figure in *Leben Gundlings,* must be brought to scream.

The question of postmodernism is rejected on the
basis of its underlying politics. "Ich kann die
Frage des Postmodernismus aus der Politik nicht
heraushalten. Periodisierung ist Kolonialpolitik,
solange Geschichte nicht Universalgeschichte, was
Chancengleichheit zur Voraussetzung hat, sondern
Herrschaft von Eliten durch Geld oder Macht" (95).
Under present conditions, efforts at defining pe-
riods of literature (a "postmodernism" as distinct

from "modernism," for example), like Polonius's comparisons, are the affair of the elite; the question of postmodernism is a privileged one. As long as oppression exists in the world, the issue to be dealt with is an entirely different one: not the shape of a cloud, but the revolution of the oppressed. Müller stated in an interview from 1981, "ich glaube schon, dass wenn ich eine Vorstellung habe von Kommunismus, dann ist das Chancengleichheit; und solange es die nicht gibt, ist Revolution eben die Hauptfrage. Ich rede nicht von Deutschland und nicht von Frankreich. Aber niemand kann mir erzählen, dass das Problem Lateinamerika lösbar ist ohne Gewalt."[27] The aesthetic ideal of the "realm of freedom" is intimately tied to the revolution of the Third World:

> Vielleicht kommt in andern Kulturen anders wieder, bereichert diesmal durch die technischen Errungenschaften der Moderne, was in den von Europa geprägten dem Modernismus voraufging: ein sozialer Realismus, der die Kluft zwischen Kunst und Wirklichkeit schliessen hilft, die *Kunst ohne Anstrengung, mit der Menschheit auf Du,* von der Leverkühn träumt ... Die Literatur Lateinamerikas könnte für diese Hoffnung stehn. (95-96)

Müller's aesthetic ideal, we have seen, is one in which the author as privileged creator, and art as "private property," the creation of an individual, no longer exist. It is, to borrow from Marx, a society in which art is no longer a product of the specialization of labor, but instead belongs to the activity of every person; Müller speaks of his belief in the "Marxschen Projektion von der Aufhebung der Kunst in einer Gesellschaft, deren Mitglieder unter anderem auch Künstler sind" (97).[28] The aesthetic ideal is part of Marx's "realm of freedom," beyond the necessity of material production, "jenseits der Privilegien" (97), in which the sole end of work is the development of man's own human capacity. Müller also speaks of the split between

"Realismus" and "Volkstümlichkeit" in the realm of necessity, which are joined in synthesis in the realm of freedom; here, with the quotation from Thomas Mann's *Doktor Faustus*, Müller's meaning becomes clear.

Adrian Leverkühn dreams of a new art that would resolve the split between the aesthetically advanced "high" art and the accessible "low" popular culture. Zeitblom relates: "Wir sprachen von der Vereinigung des Avancierten mit dem Volkstümlichen, von der Aufhebung der Kluft zwischen Kunst und Zugänglichkeit, Hoch und Niedrig ... dem Guten und dem Leichten, dem Würdigen und dem Unterhaltenden, dem Fortschrittlichen und dem allgemein Geniessbaren."[29] It is clear that Müller's own formulation "Realismus und Volkstümlichkeit" draws upon the basic dichotomy of "high" and "low" presented in Mann's novel, while interpreting and redefining it within the specific problematic of East German culture: the split for Müller occurs also between the official socialist aesthetic and its audience.[30] Despite Müller's particular focus, however, the task at hand is the same. To paraphrase Leverkühn, art must find its way out of its isolation with an elite, and back to the broad base of the people; Leverkühn's great insight is that music,

> ... wie alle Kunst, der Erlösung bedarf, nämlich aus einer feierlichen Isolierung, die die Frucht der Kultur-Emanzipation, der Erhebung der Kultur zum Religionsersatz war, - aus dem Alleinsein mit einer Bildungselite, "Publikum" genannt, die es bald nicht mehr geben wird, die es schon nicht mehr gibt, so dass also die Kunst bald völlig allein, zum Absterben allein sein wird, es sei denn, sie fände den Weg zum "Volk", das heisst, um es unromantisch zuságen: zu den Menschen.[31]

This is the "Kunst ohne Leiden, seelisch gesund, unfeierlich, untraurig-zutraulich, eine Kunst mit der Menschheit auf du und du ..." of which Leverkühn dreams.³² For Müller such an art would be "ein sozialer Realismus," a realism not separated from the people, "der die Kluft zwischen Kunst und Wirklichkeit schliessen hilft, die *Kunst ohne Anstrengung, mit der Menschheit auf Du*" (96). Art and reality, realism and popular culture, beauty and truth are one in synthesis, the cultural elite is dissolved in the "realm of freedom," privilege gives way to "Chancengleichheit."

Within the contemporary German theater, this ideal is realized in terms of a restructuring or redefinition of the relationship between actors and audience, stage and auditorium, indeed, of the entire institution of theater. Such has been Müller's conscious project for at least the last fifteen years. In an interview discussing the 1969 Volksbühne production of *Horizonte* Müller stated:

> Thomas Mann lässt Leverkühn von einer freundlichen Kunst träumen, die kommen wird. Von einer Kunst ohne Anstrengung, mit der Menschheit auf Du. So etwas sehe ich eben bei den Figuren von "Horizonte". Ein Schritt auf dem Weg dieser Kunst ist für mich das Stück, möglich durch ein neues Verhältnis von Laien- und Berufstheater. Miteinander statt oben und unten. ... Die Aufführung ist nur ein Teil des Abends, Ausstellung und Nachspiel im Foyer und in den Salons der Volksbühne eine neue Qualität von "Foyergespräch" mit der Hoffnung auf ein neues Verhältnis zwischen Theater und Gesellschaft in der Einheit von Konsum und Produktion auch in diesem Bereich.³³

The synthesis in the theater of realism and popular culture, of art and reality, requires overcoming the separation between professional theater artists (privileged creators, the talented elite, specialized producers) and untrained, lay audience (consumers). The "Einheit von Konsum und Produktion auch in diesem Bereich" requires that privilege and private property be abolished in favor of collective production in art (the theater) as they have been in society; the restructuring of the theater in terms of "miteinander statt oben und unten" defines the specifically *socialist* theater. Müller speaks in the fourth section of his postmodernism essay of an "episches Theater, wie Brecht es konzipiert und nicht verwirklicht hat, mit einem Minimum an dramaturgischer Anstrengung und jenseits der Perversität, aus einem Luxus einen Beruf zu machen" (96-97).[34] The project of a truly socialist theater, of a proletarian revolution within art, is essentially a radical version of the Brechtian *Lehrstück*.

Müller makes this clear in a discussion with critics and fellow dramatists held under the auspices of the East German Academy of Arts and the Berliner Ensemble during a week-long commemoration of Brecht in 1973:

> Die Lehrstücke hat, wenn man etwas überspitzt formuliert, der Brecht doch offenbar verstanden als seinen Entwurf für ein Theater im Sozialismus. Also ein Theater, das letztlich überhaupt kein Publikum mehr braucht, wo aufgehoben ist der Widerspruch zwischen Bühne und Zuschauerraum. Es gibt nur noch Beteiligte. Und theoretisch sind wir uns ja darüber klar, dass es darauf hingeht.[35]

In the amusing exchange which follows with Ernst Schumacher, Müller adds that such a theater would have no need for either theater critics or dramatists;[36] all positions of privileged authority are dissolved, there is only participation on the basis of equality. Interestingly enough, the pioneers of this new "art without strain" are not the heirs of Brecht and of the Brechtian theater, but the authors of Latin America, and the anonymous graffiti-artists of the New York City subways.

## IV
## The Hope of the Third World

The importance of the Third World in Heiner Müller's work cannot be overstated. It is a rich and complex cipher for everything that is colonized and oppressed, subversive and violent in its efforts, revolutionary in its intent. As I hope to demonstrate in my subsequent chapters, thematically (in the figures of Sasportas and Ophelia) and formally (in terms of the "deconstructive" use of the structures of bourgeois and Brechtian drama), the Third World signals a release of revolutionary energy which seeks an alternative reality to that dictated by the institutions of oppression. In Müller's view the histories of Africa, Asia, and Latin America have been defined by persecution inflicted by the colonialists/capitalists of Europe,[37] and it is this experience of oppression that is the source of revolutionary force: "Die Revolution geht ja nicht von Europa aus. Ich schreibe nicht nur für Europa. Das eigentlich Revolutionäre in der Welt, das hat schon Büchner gesagt, ist der Hunger und der Gegensatz von arm und reich, und der wird nicht geringer, der wird grösser. Es wird Explosionen geben, die irgendwann Europa erreichen werden."[38] Not the privileged intellectuals Hamlet or Debuisson are the true revolutionary figures, but Ophelia and the slave Sasportas, whose bodies have experienced oppression and abuse. With the oppressed lies the unchannelled, unbroken force that can change history, or rather, that can make new history. "It's like a big waiting-room, waiting for history," Müller says. "And history now is history of the Third World with all the problems of hunger and population"; "I'm waiting for the Third World."[39]

Müller speaks of a new art and a new history and names the Latin American authors as representatives of this hope:

ROBERTO ARLT (1900-1942), an Argentinian, was the son of German immigrants. In his most significant work, a novel in two parts (*Los siete locos* [1929], *Los lanzallamas* [1931]), Arlt tells of a group of madmen who plot to destroy the corrupt city of Buenos Aires, and creates with fantastic figures and linguistic jokes and parodies a grotesque, pessimistic, savage portrait of capitalism.[40]

JULIO CORTÁZAR (b. 1914), convinced of the impossibility of life under Perón, left Argentinia in 1951 and established residence in Paris, where he remains today. His early short stories in *Bestiario* (1951), which present a world of human terror, phobias, and animal fantasies, reveal the influence of Verne, Cocteau, Jarry, Arlt, and Borges. The major work, *Rayuela* (1963), is replete with neologisms and Argentinian and pseudo-existentialist slang and is completely open in its structure; neither the place nor the order of events is of importance, and the novelist suggests an alternative sequence for reading the various chapters. A committed Marxist, Cortázar exposes in his works the stupidities and limitations of the well-ordered world of the Argentinian middle class.

Winner of the 1982 Nobel Prize for Literature, GABRIEL GARCÍA MÁRQUEZ (b. 1928) was born and raised in the small declining town of Aracataca in the tropical Atlantic region of Columbia that provides, as the fictional Macondo, the setting for most of his works. His masterpiece, *Cien años de soledad* (*Hundred Years of Solitude,* 1967), relates the history of a town which begins as "die Neubegründung einer geschichtlichen Existenz, einer kollektiven Existenz auf lateinamerikanischem Boden ... unter Zurücklassung der kolonialen Eroberungsgeschichte"[41] and which ends when foreigners and adventurers drift in for quick profit and then leave again during the banana boom of 1915-1918. (Historical fact is that the final abandonment of the plantation established by the United Fruit

Company led to a massive strike in which over a thousand Columbian workers were killed by soldiers.) Since 1955 García Márquez has lived abroad in Venezuela, Paris, Mexico, and Spain. In 1975 after the military overthrow in Chile he returned to political journalism to work for the liberation of the Chilean people, stating that he had nothing more to say in the form of the novel.

The Chilean poet and recipient of the Nobel Prize for Literature in 1971, PABLO NERUDA (1904-1973) like García Márquez grew up in an isolated frontier town, Temuco, in the far south of the country. The great change in his poetry occurred after his experiences during the Spanish Civil War and then in Paris working on behalf of the Spanish Republican refugees; Neruda joined the Communist Party of Chile in 1939 and, in the belief that excessive obscurity in poetry arises out of class prejudice and elitism, announced his concern for clarity in a new poetry of solidarity addressed to the "simple people." Forced to leave Chile in 1948 for his subversive activities, Neruda travelled in the USSR, China, and Eastern Europe before being allowed to return in 1952. In the presidential elections in 1970 Neruda stepped down in favor of Allende, who became the first Marxist president of Chile.

JUAN CARLOS ONETTI (b. 1909), born in Uruguay, moved as a young man to Buenos Aires, where he worked as a journalist from 1931-1934 and 1941-1955. His novels present a complex, often absurd fictional world defined by self-reflexivity and ambiguity. In 1974 Onetti was arrested, jailed, and committed for two months to a mental clinic for having awarded a literary prize to a short story considered subversive by the military regime. Since 1975 he has lived in Madrid.

The hope that these authors represent lies in the common features of their lives and work. All are politically committed, all have been in some sense exiles from or within their own countries (Arlt, for example, by nature of his German heritage); they are, like Kafka, voices from the desert, authors of a "small literature," writing subversively in a dominant language and within a dominating (oppressive) political climate. Yet the main issue is not one of revolutionary literature, but one of revolution. "Die Hoffnung garantiert für nichts: die Literatur der Arlt, Cortazar, Marquez, Neruda, Onetti ist kein Plädoyer für die Zustände auf ihrem Kontinent. Die guten Texte wachsen immer noch aus finsterm Grund, die bessre Welt wird ohne Blutvergiessen nicht zu haben sein" (96). To the bloodshed that brings about a better world corresponds a new literature, a new art, that is the *negation* of art.

Müller continues: "Das Duell zwischen Industrie und Zukunft wird nicht mit Gesängen ausgetragen, bei denen man sich niederlassen kann. Seine Musik ist der Schrei des Marsyas, der seinem göttlichen Schinder die Saiten von der Leier sprengt" (96). The satyr Marsyas, greatly skilled in playing the flute, dares to challenge the god Apollo to a contest with his lyre. The Muses award the victory to Apollo, who, being allowed to do as he pleases with the loser, ties Marsyas to a tree and flays him alive.[42] The scream that tears the strings from Apollo's lyre is Müller's invention. What Müller says, I believe, is that the duel, the revolution, ultimately is not fought with music played on a different instrument, with songs of revolution, but with the shedding of blood and with a death scream that silences *all* music: the revolutionary author cannot assert himself as a different kind of author, but achieves his revolution only in destroying all authorhood. In this respect the anonymous art of the New York City subways is closer to the ideal of "Kunst ohne Anstrengung, mit der Menschheit auf Du." The Third World, as Müller says, is found also in the great metropolises of the capitalist world: "In den Industriestaaten entstehen immer mehr Enklaven der Dritten Welt. Dass Westberlin die drittgrösste türkische Stadt ist, das finde ich ungeheuer wichtig. ... Die Dritte Welt ist ja nicht nur in Afrika und Lateinamerika, die entsteht in Zürich und in Berlin und in Hamburg, so wie zunächst in New York und in Italien ..."[43]

The seven characteristics of modernism or their postmodernist variations as formulated by Ihab Hassan apply equally well, according to Müller, to New York City as to Ovid's Orpheus myth or Beckett's prose (both of the latter are discussed in detail in Hassan's *The Dismemberment of Orpheus*).[44] Where Hassan's analysis is centered on the idea of the artist as gifted individual (the archetype: Orpheus), Müller takes as his own example of postmodernism an entire city. "Eine Stadt, die sich aus ihrem Zerfall konstituiert. Ein Gebilde, das aus seiner eignen Explosion besteht" (96): Müller's characterization of New York parallels his definition of the revolutionary author, whose function it is to work towards his own dissolution as a privileged being. New York as the metropolis of dilettantism: art is no longer the province of the talented (talent is, Müller says, already a privilege), but is open to all; "Kunst ist was man will, nicht was man kann" (96). Here, the outward impression of one's free choice, rather than privilege, is the first manifestation of freedom; the realm of freedom, as I understand Müller, is immanent and imminent in the city that constitutes itself out of its own decay.[45]

Art in New York has always been the art of the avant-garde. "Warhol in Basel, Rauschenberg in Köln sind Ereignisse, im Kontext von New York schrumpfen sie zu Symptomen" (96). The pop-art pioneers Andy Warhol, with his silk-screen photographic reproductions of soup cans, Marilyn Monroe and race riots, and Robert Rauschenberg, with his "combine paintings" composed of stuffed animals, electric appliances, photographs and brush work, represent a final, irreparable break with the high seriousness of art. The theater work of Robert Wilson, while still "elitär," "macht zwischen Laien und Schauspielern keinen Unterschied" (96); Wilson, who has used people off the street as "found objects" in his productions, tends in this one respect towards the abolition of the traditional separation between audience and stage: "Ausblick auf ein episches Theater, wie Brecht es konzipiert und nicht verwirklicht hat, mit einem Minimum an dramaturgischer Anstrengung und jenseits der Perversität, aus einem Luxus einen Beruf zu machen" (96-97). But potentially most revolutionary, the furthest stage in the development of a collective "art without strain," are the wall paintings of neighborhood ethnic groups and the anonymous graffiti covering the walls and cars of the New York City subway.

"Die Wandbilder der Minderheiten und die proletarische Kunst der Subway, anonym und mit gestohlener Farbe, besetzen ein Feld jenseits des Marktes. Vorgriff aus dem Elend der Unterprivilegierten in das *Reich der Freiheit*, das jenseits der Privilegien liegt" (97). The phenomena of the murals and, especially, of the subway graffiti are the subject of a brilliant political analysis by Jean Baudrillard, "Kool Killer oder Der Aufstand der Zeichen,"[46] which Müller has pointed to as being central to his dramaturgy.[47] The key to Baudrillard's analysis is the fundamental observation that the city is no longer primarily the location for the production of goods, the place of industrial concentration and exploitation, as it had been in the 19th century, but has become today a complex and oppressive network of signs: the city functions "nicht mehr als Ort der ökonomischen und politischen Macht, sondern als Zeit/Raum der terroristischen Macht der Medien, der Zeichen und der herrschenden Kultur."[48] Within this context of the change from industry to "semiocracy" defining the organization of the city, the subway graffiti, consisting largely of names taken from underground comics and, unlike graffiti elsewhere, devoid of political or pornographic content, exercise a powerful subversive effect:

> Denn SUPERBEE SPIX COLA 139 KOOL GUY CRAZY CROSS 136 - das bedeutet nichts, ist nicht einmal Eigenname, sondern symbolische Matrikel, gemacht, um das gewöhnliche Benennungssystem aus der Fassung zu bringen. Diese Terme haben keinerlei Originalität: sie stammen alle aus dem Comic-Strip, wo sie eingeschlossen waren in Fiktion, doch brechen sie explosiv aus ihr hervor, um in die Realität projiziert zu werden wie ein Schrei, als Einwurf, als Anti-Diskurs, als Absage an jede syntaktische, poetische und politische Elaboriertheit, als kleinstes, radikales, durch keinerlei organisierten Diskurs einnehmbares Element. Irreduzibel aufgrund ihrer Armut selbst, widerstehen sie jeder Interpretation, jeder Konnotation, und sie denotieren nichts und niemanden: weder Denotation noch Konnotation, derart entgehen sie dem Prinzip der Bezeichnung und brechen als *leere Signifikanten* ein in die Sphäre der erfüllten Zeichen der Stadt, die sie durch ihre blosse Präsenz auflösen.[49]

A wholly anonymous, collective art of radical rebellion: the subway graffiti, a "parody" of the Marxist vision of the overcoming of art in a society whose members are, among other things, also artists, yet a parody not as grotesque travesty, but as ironic realization. The new art arises not within a socialist society, but as an island of the "Third World" in the midst of a capitalist metropolis: "man muss diese Sioux-Litanei vernehmen, diese subversive Litanei der Anonymität, die symbolische Explosion dieser Kriegsnamen im Herzen der weissen Metropole."[50]

## V
## The Disappearance of the Author

What, once again, is the project of the author - specifically, of the socialist author - in the development of a true socialist, i.e. collective, participatory, unprivileged art? Müller returns to this question in the fifth section of his essay.

"Solange Freiheit auf Gewalt gegründet ist, die Ausübung von Kunst auf Privilegien, werden die Kunstwerke die Tendenz haben, Gefängnisse zu sein, die Meisterwerke Komplicen der Macht" (97). As long as there is no equality of opportunity ("Chancengleichheit"), as long as freedom is founded on the use of violence and the practice of art based on privilege - and here Müller addresses both capitalism and socialism in its present stage - works of art will tend to support the structures of oppression. This is the root of the failure of the intellectual, the necessity of his ultimate act of betrayal in *Leben Gundlings,* in *Hamletmaschine,* and in *Auftrag*: Friedrich II, Hamlet, and Debuisson, all privileged, abandon the revolution, becoming accomplices of an oppressive and colonial power. Masterpieces of art, the products of individual genius, of privilege, are works of betrayal. For the still-privileged revolutionary author there is only one possible route, one which has been travelled, in one way or another, by several before him. "Die grossen Texte des Jahrhunderts arbeiten an der Liquidation ihrer Autonomie, Produkt ihrer Unzucht mit dem Privateigentum, an der Enteignung, zuletzt am Verschwinden des Autors" (97). The great text and the great author must work towards their own dissolution; this is the definition of greatness. "Das Bleibende ist das Flüchtige. Was auf der Flucht ist bleibt" (97). Not the reterritorialization, to borrow from Deleuze and Guattari, the reestablishment or reentrenchment of oneself in traditional orders of "author" and "work," but the line of *flight* is the essential concern, the concern of emancipation. Müller lists the authors in flight who have defied established, oppressive structures of literature.

"Rimbaud und sein Ausbruch nach Afrika, aus der Literatur in die Wüste" (97). In 1873, ARTHUR RIMBAUD (1854-1891) completed *Une Saison en enfer,* which announced the collapse of his hope to create a new amoral society and with it an unconventional poetry. As Rimbaud was unable to pay the printing costs, only a few author's copies were distributed to friends and critics; the work was poorly received, and Rimbaud subsequently burned his books, manuscripts, and letters, abandoning literature at the age of nineteen for what appears to have been a solitary and adventurous life as trader, explorer and gun runner in Abyssinia (now Ethiopia), in the town of Harrar, accessible by a twenty-day ride on horseback through the Somali desert.

So little is known of the life of ISIDORE DUCASSE (LAUTRÉAMONT), that he is indeed the "anonyme Katastrophe" Müller calls him (97). Ducasse was born in 1846 in Montevideo, Uruguay; his father was a clerk at the French Consulate, his mother died the next year, possibly having committed suicide. At the age of thirteen he travelled to France, where he studied for the next six years in Tarbes and Pau; in 1867 he moved to Paris. Chant 1 of *Maldoror* was published in 1868, all six cantos in a complete edition in 1869, and both books of *Poésies* a year later. On 24 November 1870, Ducasse was found dead in his hotel room and buried the next day; the cause of death is unknown, as is the grave site. More significant than the lack of biographical detail, however, is Ducasse's own contribution to his "anonymity": the use of the pseudonym.[51] One critic sees in the author's refusal to sign his name a programmatic rejection of the romantic aesthetic of the art work as a self-expression of individual genius.[52] Ducasse himself provides strong evidence for this interpretation; "La poésie doit être faite par tous. Non par un," the most famous line from *Poésies*, later taken up as a slogan by the Surrealists, expresses a view strikingly similar to Müller's own.[53]

Central to Müller's authors in flight is their radical *abandonment* of a literature defined by the concept of "author" as authoritative creator. This revolt and flight, as is illustrated by the examples of Lautréamont and Rimbaud, takes various forms. FRANZ KAFKA (1883-1924), undeniably one of the world's greatest modern novelists, ordered that all of his papers and uncompleted manuscripts (of the three novels, *Amerika*, *Der Prozess*, and *Das Schloss*) be destroyed unread after his death.[54] His friend and editor Max Brod, who defied Kafka's instructions, revealed that almost everything Kafka had published during his lifetime "ist ihm von mir mit List und Überredungskunst abgenommen worden"; Kafka, in Brod's view, suffered from "gewissen traurigen Erlebnissen, die ihn zur Selbstsabotage, daher auch zum Nihilismus dem eignen Werk gegenüber führten."[55] What Brod and generations of Kafka critics have interpreted as the tragic inner conflict of a genius, Müller, following the perspective of Deleuze and Guattari, reinterprets as a political, revolutionary act: "Kafka, der fürs Feuer schrieb, weil er seine Seele nicht behalten wollte wie Marlows Faust: die Asche wurde ihm verweigert" (97). Where Marlowe's Faust offers to burn his books as a last desperate appeal to God before he is dragged down to hell,[56] Kafka orders his manuscripts destroyed as a final rebellion against divine author-ity, against his own immortality.

JAMES JOYCE (1882-1941) seems, paradoxically, to embody the idea of the author as gifted individual creator that Rimbaud, Lautréamont and Kafka - themselves hailed as literary geniuses - reject in word and deed. One possible - and admittedly impressionistic - interpretation of Müller's

epithet "Stimme jenseits der Literatur" (97) is
that Joyce, with tremendous technical and linguistic virtuosity, rendered an absolutely precise
portrait of individual lives, of Dublin, finally,
of Western civilization, in a literary "recording"
that in effect transcends the traditional realm of
literature. The "author" himself disappears behind
an intricately designed fabric of the everyday
idioms of language and of life; the authorial
voice dissolves into the stream of Irish, human,
mass consciousness.

With the example of VLADIMIR MAYAKOVSKY (1893-1930),
the dissolution of the author into the voice of the
masses is programmatic. "Majakowski und sein Sturzflug *aus den Himmeln der Dichtung* in die Arena der
Klassenkämpfe, sein Poem *150 Millionen* trägt den
Namen des Autors: *150 Millionen*. Der Selbstmord
war seine Antwort auf das Ausbleiben der Signatur" (97). One of the great revolutionary figures
of 20th-century poetry, Mayakovsky believed in
and wrote before the October Revolution an art
free of any utilitarian function; several shorter
poems were purely formal exercises. But in 1917,
Mayakovsky was one of few Russian artists who
unhesitatingly supported the Bolsheviks from the
beginning. He turned - in a move similar to Pablo
Neruda's in 1939 - to a simpler, more popular poetry
addressed no longer to the artistic avant-garde,
but to the masses, devising propaganda posters,
slogans and rhymes, and travelling throughout the
new Soviet state reciting his verse. "Proletarians /
come to communism / from down under," one poem
reads from 1925, "I - / from my poetic skies
above."[57]

Mayakovsky dreamt of creating a new, collectivist
poetry which would correspond to the new order of
society. The importance of this effort for Müller's
own aesthetic is two-fold. First, like Joyce,
Mayakovsky drew from the popular idiom of the
streets. He explains in *How Are Verses Made?* (1926):

> The Revolution ... has thrown up on to the streets
> the unpolished speech of the masses, the slang of
> the suburbs has flowed along the downtown boulevards;
> the enfeebled sub-language of the intelligentsia,
> with its emasculated words "ideal", "principles of
> justice", "the transcendental visage of Christ and
> Antichrist" - all these expressions, pronounced in
> little whispers in restaurants, have been trampled
> underfoot. There is a new linguistic element. How
> can one make it poetic? The old rules about "love
> and dove", "moon and June" and alexandrines are no
> use. How can we introduce the spoken language into
> poetry, and extract poetry from this spoken language? [58]

For Müller, Mayakovsky represents the first great attempt to bring the language of the streets and the jargon of industry into poetry;[59] the project is essentially one of breaking down the barriers between "high" art and "low" popular culture. Secondly, Mayakovsky represents an author's attempt, accomplished finally in suicide, to overthrow the institution of the author as sole and absolute creator of an art work. The long poem *150,000,000* (1919-20), one of the classics of Revolutionary literature, in which the decadent, capitalistic West and the young Soviet state are personified in the gigantic figures of Woodrow Wilson and Ivan who battle for supremacy, bears the name of its author as its title: the poem begins, "Einhundertfünfzig Millionen: / Das ist der Name des Dichters dieses Gedichts."[60]

ANTONIN ARTAUD (1896-1948), one of the seminal theoreticians of the modern avant-garde stage, envisioned a ritualistic, magical theater that would break through the artificiality of culture and bring human beings back to their primal, uncorrupted, instinctual nature. In essence Artaud broke with the Western logocentric theater (the theater whose core is rational dialogue) in favor of a concrete language of the senses, incorporating gesture, movement, color, light, sound, and words spoken for their sonority rather than for their meaning, expressing thoughts beyond the reach of discursive, logical speech. "Artaud, die Sprache der Qual unter der Sonne der Folter, der einzigen, die alle Kontinente dieses Planeten gleichzeitig bescheint" (97); Müller quotes from Sartre's preface to Frantz Fanon's *The Wretched of the Earth*, a work which provides the theoretical underpinnings of Sasportas' revolution in *Der Auftrag*. "Today, the blinding sun of torture is at its zenith; it lights up the whole country. Under that merciless glare, there is not a laugh that does not ring false, not a face that is not painted to hide fear or anger, not a single action that does not betray our disgust, and our complicity."[61] For Müller, Artaud's non-rational "language of suffering" represents a rejection of the values and tyrannical (colonial) culture of the European Enlightenment; Artaud in Europe speaks with the voice of the oppressed and colonized Third World, speaking, also, against himself:

> Artaud, die Sprache der Qual. Schreiben aus der Erfahrung, dass die Meisterwerke Komplicen der Macht sind. Denken am Ende der Aufklärung, das mit dem Tod Gottes begonnen hat, sie der Sarg, in dem er begraben wurde, faulend mit dem Leichnam. Leben, eingesperrt in diesem Sarg. DAS DENKEN GEHÖRT ZU DEN GRÖSSTEN VERGNÜGUNGEN DER MENSCHLICHEN RASSE lässt Brecht Galilei sagen, bevor man ihm die Instrumente zeigt. Der Blitz, der das Bewusstsein Artauds gespalten hat, war Nietzsches Erfahrung, es könnte die letzte sein. Artaud ist der Ernstfall. Er hat die Literatur der Polizei entrissen, das Theater der Medizin. Unter der Sonne der Folter, die alle Kontinente dieses Planeten gleichzeitig bescheint, blühen seine Texte. Auf den Trümmern Europas gelesen, werden sie klassisch sein.[62]

Reason gives way to betrayal under the pain of torture; the hypocrisy of Enlightenment/European values is demonstrated in the real experience of the peoples of the Third World (Fanon). Artaud, turning literature in a subversive way against the institutions of a controlling, dominating, conservative order, creates a theater that will achieve its purpose and exhaust its revolutionary energy when the cultural-colonialist hegemony of enlightened European reason is finally broken.

Müller's list concludes with Brecht and Beckett: "Brecht der das Neue Tier gesehn hat, das den Menschen ablösen wird. Beckett, ein lebenslanger Versuch, die eigene Stimme zum Schweigen zu bringen" (97-98). Indeed, the works of SAMUEL BECKETT (b. 1906) can be seen as increasingly radical experiments in silence, moving towards the sparest prose, or towards plays without words.[63] Beckett gives perhaps the best statement of his poetic project in the three dialogues with Georges Duthuit from 1949:

> B. - The only thing disturbed by the revolutionaries Matisse and Tal Coat is a certain order on the plane of the feasible.
> D. - What other plane can there be for the maker?
> B. - Logically none. Yet I speak of an art turning from it in disgust, weary of its puny exploits, weary of pretending to be able, of being able, of doing a little better the same old thing, of going a little further along a dreary road.
> D. - And preferring what?
> B. - The expression that there is nothing to express, nothing with which to express, nothing from which to express, no power to express, no desire to express, together with the obligation to express.[64]

For Beckett, whose silence speaks of the impossibility of being an author, nothing remains of the author's role but the sheer "obligation to express."

The Brecht reference is to a - to my knowledge - unpublished section of the *Fatzer* material.[65] The issues presented in the Brecht fragment appear to have been a constant preoccupation in Müller's work from the late 1960's through the 1970's.[66]

> Der Fabelansatz von Brecht: vier Leute desertieren aus dem Ersten Weltkrieg, weil sie glauben, die Revolution kommt bald, verstecken sich in der Wohnung des einen, warten auf die Revolution, und die kommt nicht. Und nun sind sie ausgestiegen aus der Gesellschaft. Da es keine besseren, keine expansiven Möglichkeiten gibt für ihre angestauten revolutionären Bedürfnisse, radikalisieren sie sich gegeneinander und negieren sich gegenseitig. Das ist eine grosse Formulierung einer Situation, die sich in der deutschen Geschichte immer wieder ergeben, immer wiederholt hat. Also die Isolierung der Linken seit den Bauernkriegen.[67]

With the "isolation of the leftists" Müller means, also, the isolation of the intellectuals from the revolutionary movement. In a discussion of *Fatzer* in the Berliner Ensemble in 1967, Alexander Stillmark, Guy de Chambure, and Müller spoke of the play as a depiction of "das Warten auf den grossen Umsturz, das Inaktiv-sein, was das Gesellschaftliche angeht. ... das Beharren in der Isolation, das auf-Nummer-sicher-gehen, das Wissen, das nicht in die historische Tat umgesetzt wird."[68] As a play about knowledge that does not give forth to action, it is another treatment of the familiar Hamlet problematic that Müller explores in *Hamletmaschine* and in *Auftrag*: the intellectual cannot turn his revolutionary insight into a revolutionary act. Yet Brecht's *Fatzer* is not simply the story of the "Untergang des Egoisten" who threatens to betray the collective, but the collective (as the new type of the "Massenmensch") is itself brought into question, in a struggle which is Brecht's attempt to overcome his own privileged, intellectual, egoist status. Müller writes:

> Ein inkommensurables Produkt, geschrieben zur Selbstverständigung.
> Der Text ist präideologisch, die Sprache formuliert nicht Denkresultate, sondern skandiert den Denkprozess. Er hat die Authentizität des ersten Blicks auf ein Unbekanntes, den Schrecken der ersten Erscheinung des Neuen. Mit den Topoi des Egoisten, des Massenmenschen, des Neuen Tiers kommen, unter dem dialektischen Muster der marxistischen Terminologie, Bewegungsgesetze in Sicht, die in der jüngsten Geschichte dieses Muster perforiert haben.[69]

Fatzer is the egoist; Keuner, in Walter Benjamin's view "der alle Betreffende, allen Gehörende" and in Müller's, "der Schatten der Leninschen Parteidisziplin ... der Kleinbürger im Mao-Look, die Rechenmaschine der Revolution," is the man of the masses - the capitalistic, individualistic egoist and the socialistic follower, two sides of Brecht.[70] "'Fatzer' als Materialschlacht Brecht gegen Brecht (= Nietzsche gegen Marx, Marx gegen Nietzsche). Brecht überlebt sie, indem er sich herausschiesst. Brecht gegen Brecht mit dem schweren Geschütz des Marxismus/Leninismus."[71] The first view of something new and unknown, of something beyond Brecht, beyond the struggle of capitalism and socialism, of the "new animal" that comes to replace man: is this the wild, untamed, irrepressible energy of the Third World?

Rimbaud who burned his manuscripts and fled to Africa, never to write again, and Kafka who wrote prodigiously but ordered his manuscripts destroyed; Beckett who seeks to express the impossibility of writing, Ducasse who wrote under a fictional name, the fiction of the "author" giving way to a literature written by "all"; Joyce, Mayakovsky, Artaud and Brecht, who began to move towards this new literature of the people, Joyce and Mayakovsky disappearing behind the street jargon of the masses, Artaud reaching for the non-verbal language of the primal human emotions, Brecht envisioning the "new" man that would replace the old outlived types that included himself: Müller places himself within a tradition of literature that has seen its own limitations and has actively sought its own end. The author working (writing) toward his own disappearance follows a new mythological model: "Zwei Figuren der Dichtung, in der Stunde der Weissglut verschmelzend zu einer Figur: Orpheus der unter den Pflügen singt, Dädalos im Flug durch die labyrinthischen Därme des Minotauros" (98). In the "Stunde der Weissglut," slaughtered buffaloes, alligators, swarms of sharks, earthquakes appear as projections on a screen in the play *Leben Gundlings*: violent, elemental, natural forces that will replace the junkyards of the capitalist West.[72] In this hour of revolution two figures merge: Orpheus, buried under the plows of the peasants who had had no place in his art, now singing among them, and Daedalus, the legendary craftsman and inventor who built for Pasiphäe, Queen of Crete, the disguise of a cow which enabled her to seduce Poseidon's bull and conceive the Minotauros, for Minos, King of Crete, the labyrinth in which the creature was kept, and for himself, in order to escape from Crete, artificial wings; Daedalus, fleeing in flight through the labyrinthian innards of the Minotauros, flies to freedom with, through, within the products of his own work. In the author who seeks his own disappearance, Orpheus and Daedalus, artist and worker, become one.

## VI

The Silence of Entropy or Universal Discourse

> Literatur nimmt an der Geschichte teil, indem sie an der Bewegung der Sprache teilnimmt; die sich zuerst in den Jargons vollzieht und nicht auf dem Papier.
> In diesem Sinn ist sie *eine Angelegenheit des Volkes,* sind die Analphabeten die Hoffnung der Literatur. (98)

In the final section of the statement on postmodernism Müller repeats remarks he made in an earlier essay, where the following comment is added to the passage quoted above: "Im andern Fall bleibt sie [die Literatur] geschichtslos elitär und wird als Kunstgewerbe in das System integriert, das mit der Kulturindustrie an der Betonierung des status quo arbeitet und so Geschichte verhindert."[73]

To return briefly to an earlier point, the socialist author in a developing socialist state finds himself, paradoxically, a still privileged being: there is a division between "high" art and the "low" culture of the masses; between the official aesthetic of "Realismus" and the everyday reality, the "Volkstümlichkeit" of the audience; between an artificial "Hochsprache" and the "Umgangssprache," the actual language of the streets, the jargons. It is, finally, a division between the talented elite and the established order it supports and represents, and the masses who are a powerful force of change and progress; between Orpheus and the peasants. The task of the revolutionary author is to dissolve this division. By dissolving his privileged authorial voice into the many voices and into the jargons of the streets, he participates in the "movement of language" that is the literary-linguistic parallel to the process of ongoing socialist history. To support the creation of art as the privilege of the talented is to create an art that is ahistorical and elitist ("geschichtslos elitär"), to lend "counter-revolutionary" support to the status quo of a culture industry that is a part of a gigantic system of oppression. To join with the jargon of the masses, on the other hand, is to renounce the oppression by a privileged elite in literature. Müller's revolutionary program is clear: it is no less than a workers' revolution in the realm of art. Privilege must give way to an equality of opportunity, the rule by an elite, even in art, to a rule by all. What is at stake is man himself: "Arbeit am Verschwinden des Autors ist Widerstand gegen das Verschwinden des Menschen" (98). "Aufgabe der Dichtung," Müller stated in 1957, "bleibt die Verteidigung des Menschen gegen seine Verwurstung und Verdinglichung."[74] In the final analysis, the true role of art is the revolt against oppression and the defense of humanity.

Müller concludes with a powerful and provocative formulation regarding the function of literary art in general and his own work in particular. There are two strategies for the author who seeks the preservation of humanity: one the willful dissolution of the privileged individual self, the other the creation of a collective subject in art. "Die Bewegung der Sprache ist alternativ: das Schweigen der Entropie oder der universale Diskurs, der nichts auslässt und niemanden ausschliesst" (98). To the tradition of the first might belong Rimbaud, Kafka, and Beckett who retreated into silence; to the second, Joyce, Mayakovsky, and Artaud who made the language of art commensurate to the language of life, and, more importantly perhaps, the unknown artists of the New York City subway who have made of art an anonymous, wholly collective act. The impulse of the first is the revolution of entropy, the spontaneous and increasing breakdown of established order;[75] the impulse of the second, the utopia of universality, total participation in a new order. In a theater that attempts not to reaffirm the order of the status quo but to move in the direction of the new, the audience experiences fear and horror. *"Die erste Gestalt der Hoffnung ist die Furcht, die erste Erscheinung des Neuen der Schrecken"* (98). Müller explains elsewhere, "Si l'on voulait risquer une formulation un peu générale sur ce qu'est le drame, je dirais que c'est la description, la représentation de la terreur et du plaisir de la transformation."[76] Müller's theater: not conservative affirmation, but subversion and continued revolution.

49

In my analysis thus far I have explored the issues of Müller's aesthetic project as he has outlined them in the essay on postmodernism. His formulations - "literature is an affair of the people," "art without strain," the "disappearance of the author," and finally, "entropy" and "universal discourse" - are programmatic, if not utopian slogans for a new, socialist art. The next three chapters present my studies of the three major plays written around the time of the postmodernism essay and attempt ultimately to show how Müller's poetic project is realized in terms of specific thematic and structural categories in these texts.

CHAPTER II

THE CRITIQUE OF THE ENLIGHTENMENT:

LEBEN GUNDLINGS FRIEDRICH VON PREUSSEN

LESSINGS SCHLAF TRAUM SCHREI  (1976)


*Leben Gundlings Friedrich von Preussen Lessings Schlaf Traum Schrei: Ein Greuelmärchen* (1976) is essentially a transitional work in Müller's oeuvre. On the one hand it follows in the line of *Germania Tod in Berlin* (1971) and *Die Schlacht* (1974) as a critical unearthing and questioning of the structural myths or models underlying modern German history, treating specifically the period and ideology of the German Enlightenment. On the other hand it begins the period of a new preoccupation: *Leben Gundlings*, *Die Hamletmaschine* (1977) and *Der Auftrag* (1979) examine the specific role of the intellectual in the process of revolution, while enacting in terms of their structure a revolutionary "deconstruction" of entrenched dramatic models. *Leben Gundlings* and *Hamletmaschine* treat respectively bourgeois ideology (as articulated during the Enlightenment) and bourgeois drama (as defined in theoretical writings by Lessing and Hegel), while *Auftrag* deals with the alternative socialist model of the Brechtian didactic play.

The synthetic title of the play reflects its organization into scenes focusing on three main figures of eighteenth-century Prussia and the Enlightenment: Jacob Paul Freiherr von Gundling (1673-1731), professor of history and law, Leibniz's successor as President of the Prussian Academy of Sciences, and member of Friedrich Wilhelm I's court (Scene 1); Friedrich II (1712-1786), King of Prussia from 1740-1786 (Scenes 1-7); and Gotthold Ephraim Lessing (1729-1781), the major intellectual and literary figure of the German

Enlightenment (Scene 9). To this list should be added the enigmatic literary genius Heinrich von Kleist (1777-1811) who, misunderstood and unrecognized in his time, took his own life at the age of thirty-four (Scene 8). Through the experiences of the academic (Gundling), the statesman and monarch (Friedrich), and the author (Lessing and Kleist), the main tenets of the Enlightenment are examined and retold in the form of "Greuelmärchen": reason as the essence of man and the world; the ineluctable progress of mankind towards a perfect, rational end; and the crucial function of education, *Erziehung,* in this process. Of central concern, both thematically and structurally, is the relationship of the individual to the Prussian Enlightenment state, developed in the main part of the play in Scenes 2 through 7 in terms of the relationship of Friedrich to his father, the Prussian king.

Jacob Paul Freiherr von Gundling: Scene 1

Scene 1, "Leben Gundlings," presents the Prussian monarch Friedrich Wilhelm with his officers, Gundling, and his young son Friedrich, gathered around a table for beer and tobacco. Gundling, for eight years professor at the Berlin Ritterakademie, now functions as Friedrich Wilhelm's official "Hofnarr";[1] his first speech reveals a trained intellect that now serves the state for its own use and amusement:

> ... und erhellt die Weisheit der von Majestät verfügten Massnahmen, das Verbot der ausländischen Zeitungen auf dem Territorium Ihrer Majestät betreffend, schon allein aus dem Umstand, dass die Welt, als von einem Gott geschaffen, nach Vernunftgründen nur einen Mittelpunkt haben kann, als welcher in Preussen befindlich, sozusagen mit Verlaub unter dem Königlichen

> Hintern Seiner Allergnädigsten Majestät, von Gottes
> Gnaden Friedrich Wilhelm. (Friedrich Wilhelm furzt.)[2]

The king appoints Gundling the new President of the Prussian Academy of Sciences, and as a congratulatory gift the officers bring in a bear which pursues, then hugs, the distraught academician. The incident, a parody of the anecdote related in Kleist's "Über das Marionettentheater," where the natural, unreflected grace of the bear promises a future grace of conscious man, "wenn die Erkenntnis gleichsam durch ein Unendliches gegangen ist,"[3] is used here to illustrate not the inherent and necessary perfectibility of man, but his perpetual "Unmündigkeit" in a despotic society. Friedrich Wilhelm explains to his young son: "Nehm Ers als ein Exempel, was von den Gelehrten zu halten. Und für die Regierungskunst, die Er lernen muss .... Dem Volk die Pfoten gekürzt, der Bestie, und die Zähne ausgebrochen. Die Intelligenz zum Narren gemacht, dass der Pöbel nicht auf Ideen kommt" (10). The intellectual, appropriated by the state, is made impotent in his role to inspire or initiate revolutionary change. The "castrated" Gundling quotes the woman Ophelia in Shakespeare's *Hamlet*, "O WHAT A NOBLE MIND IS HERE / O'ERTHROWN" (11),[4] and expresses nihilistic sentiments heavily reminiscent of Büchner's Danton:

> Betrachten Sie ... die Majestät des Firmaments. Und
> lassen Sie sich das ein Trost sein: es geht auch
> vorbei. Der Mensch ist ein Zufall, eine bösartige
> Wucherung. Und was wir Leben nennen ... ist so etwas
> wie die Masern, eine Kinderkrankheit des Universums, dessen wahre Existenz der Tod, das Nichts,
> die Leere. (11)

In doing so he signals his kinship with the later figures of Hamlet in *Hamletmaschine* and the Dantonesque Antoine/Debuisson of *Auftrag*, intellectuals who also ultimately fail to express their knowledge in revolutionary action.

Parallel to the specific problematic role of the intellectual within the despotic state is the fundamentally conflict-laden relationship of the rebellious son to the powerful father. The officers tease Gundling:

> Offizier 1: Gundling, wer hat Ihm das Horn aufgesetzt.
> Offizier 2: Hat Ihm sein Eheweib die Leviten gelesen, weil Er wieder besoffen war.
> Gundling: Das Los der Weisen, meine Herrn. Ich erinnere Sie nur an Sokrates, den Vater der Philosophie.
> Offizier 1: So hat Ihm sein Vater das Horn aufgesetzt.
> (Friedrich Wilhelm hält Friedrich die Ohren zu.)
> Offizier 2: Besser der Vater dem Sohn als der Sohn dem Vater.
> (Offiziere lachen.)
> Offizier 3: Wer den Vater nicht ehrt ist die Mutter nicht wert.
> (Offiziere lachen.) (9)

In the comparison Gundling makes to Socrates, the *tertium comparationis* is on an immediate level the shrewish wife, but also, more significantly, the persecution by the state. Socrates, condemned to death for impiety and for corrupting the youth of Athens, is the ancient model of the intellectual who educates the youth to adopt a critical stance toward the state. As such, he represents an alternative model for the relationship of the intellectual to the state, of knowledge to power. While Gundling allows himself to be used and supported by the king for the project of state domination, Socrates' knowledge, opposed to state power, has potentially a revolutionary function that makes it a victim of suppression.

Thus the deliberate ambiguity of the line "So hat Ihm sein Vater das Horn aufgesetzt": "Vater" is both Socrates, the "father of philosophy," and the paternalistic state, embodied in Friedrich Wilhelm (at this point the king covers the ears of his young son Friedrich); the intellectual must choose between two loyalties, one to the familial/civil father representing the state, the other to the "philosophical" father representing the claims of knowledge and truth. The Prussian officer's statement, "Besser der Vater dem Sohn als der Sohn dem Vater," reveals the state's view regarding the basic conflict between knowledge (the rebellious son) and power (the dominating father): the father must prevail. Further, acquiescence on the part of the son (Gundling's service to the king, for example) is tantamount to the son's becoming like his father, thereby preserving the established order: "Wer den Vater nicht ehrt ist die Mutter nicht wert"; the son identifies himself with the father and grows eventually to take his place in the family. The choice of the son, then, can be formulated as follows: the son aligns himself with the (familial) father and ultimately himself becomes the paternalistic figure of power, or he rebels, using his knowledge to question and to change the relationship of oppression, becoming a true son to the "father" of philosophy. Stated in other terms, the choice is between *Erziehung*, becoming what one is meant to or ought to be according to a "necessary" and organic development, and *Revolution*, breaking totally with that oppressive continuity. Gundling, it is clear, does not revolt.

## Friedrich II: Scenes 2-7

Scenes 2 through 7 present in detail the life of the exemplary Enlightenment son in his relationship to the powerful, authoritarian father-state. In Scene 2, the young Friedrich, his sister Wilhelmine, and his friend Katte are engaged in a game of Blind Man's Bluff. The structural relationship of father and son is evident even in this child's game. Wilhelmine, who bears the name and the mask of the father, acts in accordance with the demands of family and society in her feelings of affection towards the lieutenant Katte (she leans heavily against him as she unties his blindfold) and her policing of the affection between the two boys (she slaps their hands when they reach for one another). The revolt of the son is expressed through the role-playing of Act II, Scene 5 of Racine's *Phaedra,* in which Phaedra (played by Friedrich, in Wilhelmine's clothes) reveals her adulterous and incestuous love for her husband's son Hippolytus (Katte). The overlapping relationships are complex: the son Friedrich (as a woman/wife) betrays the father Friedrich Wilhelm (as the state and as husband) for the young soldier Katte (also a son of the state); the revolution of the son is complete when Friedrich and Katte tie Wilhelmine (wearing a Friedrich-Wilhelm mask) to a chair and proceed to execute her: "Stirb, mon cher Papa!" (14)

While the son betrays and kills the father in a game of playacting in the first part of Scene 2, the father in turn kills the rebellious son in proxy in the second part. "Sein oberster Kriegsherr, und königlicher Vater" Friedrich Wilhelm executes the soldier and "Hundesohn" Katte (15), intending thereby to make "einen Mann ... und einen König" out of Friedrich. "Sire, das war ich," Friedrich says following the execution of his friend (16). The change in the son is evident in the final part of the triptych: "Ich wollte, ich wäre mein Vater" (16), Friedrich remarks, as he beats the soldiers who flee from the ongoing battle. The son of the Enlightenment, now King of Prussia, becomes a butcherous military tyrant like his "Soldatenkönig" father;[5] the revolt of the refined and educated son against the despotic power of the father has been extinguished. Not Plutarch, whose *Lives* exemplified private virtue in the careers of

great men, is read aloud to the king while his
army is engaged in battle, but Racine's *Britannicus*, a drama of political intrigue and conspiracy
in which the young emperor Nero, through murder
and betrayal, is able to secure absolute power in
the state. Friedrich listens specifically to the
fourth act of the play; it is here that Nero's
mother Agrippina recounts the history of her son's
ascent to the throne (which is the history of her
crimes against her family and her husband) and
Nero decides to kill his half-brother Britannicus
against the wishes of his mother, establishing himself as the supreme ruler of Rome: it is the tyrant
emperor Nero, an extreme example of depraved state
power, who now provides the model for the young
Prussian king.

The third scene of the play places the military
exploits of the Prussian army under Friedrich II
in a broad international and historical context
(18). The title of the scene, taken from the fairy
tale "Rumpelstilzchen," points to the fundamental
exploitative, oppressive, acquisitive nature of
the monarch: the miller's daughter must weave straw
into gold for the king, or be executed.[6] In the
"patriotic puppet play" Friedrich plays war games
with his toy soldiers. The goose-stepping and the
uniforms of the "Wehrmacht" (the official name of
the German armed forces from 1935-1945) establish
a direct historical continuity between Prussia and
national-socialist Germany. Meanwhile, on the other
side of the stage, the "adults" John Bull (England)
and Marianne (France) divide the world between
themselves with knives torn out of the dead bodies
of Indians (North America) and Negroes (Africa, the
Caribbean).[7]

The scene makes historical reference to the bloody
Seven Years' War (1756-1763) fought between Prussia, joined by England, and the alliance of Austria, France, Russia, Sweden and Saxony, who hoped
to cripple the power of Friedrich II. For France

and England, engaged in a naval war, the conflict was primarily an extension of their colonial struggle in North America and India beginning before 1756. Prussia, although with tremendous losses, emerged from the war an undisputed, major European military power, while England overthrew French domination in Canada and India, securing the foundations of the British Empire: results with far-reaching consequences for the modern world. In the "Schule der Nation" (the subtitle of the scene), wars for military supremacy become, in more "mature" times, conflicts to establish the rights of colonial exploitation in other parts of the globe.

The scene dissolves into a film image of a ghost ship whose mutinous crew nails its captain to the mast. The film, running backwards and forwards through the centuries, presents the course of history as an endless series of uprisings: its continual progression and regression undermines the Enlightenment concept of historical process as an ineluctable movement towards a rational end and suggests in its place an "alternative" history, the unwritten ("ghost") history not of conquests and conquerors (Friedrich, John Bull, Marianne), but of the conquered, colonialized masses. Further, that this history of revolt is not supported, much less inspired, by the intellectuals of Europe but instead must occur without them, is suggested by the use of Johann Sebastian Bach's "Das musikalische Opfer" from 1747. Based on a theme composed by Friedrich II, the collection of canons and fugues was sent to the king as a token of "musical homage": the European intellectual of the Enlightenment, it appears, does not inspire rebellion against, but rather creates in honor of, the oppressive power.

Scene 4, "Herzkönig Schwarze Witwe," continues the story of the Enlightenment son Friedrich who becomes a military monarch like his father. Friedrich Wilhelm in Scene 1 accuses his young son of having no feeling of family ("Hat Er keinen Familiensinn" [7]), that is, of wishing to rebel against the necessary continuity of (family) history. In contrast, Friedrich, his adolescent rebellion ended by the execution of his friend Katte, states at the end of Scene 2: "Ich wollte, ich wäre mein Vater" (16). Finally, in Scene 4, the young ruler confirms his identity with his father: "Ich / Bin der König" (21). The "Erziehung" of the prince is complete; the scene is a complex critical examination of the pedagogical victory of the Enlightenment over itself.

A Saxon woman visits the king to plead for the life of her husband, a Saxon officer who had joined, then subsequently deserted, the Prussian army after having been taken prisoner. The husband is executed in full view of the woman after she refuses to allow Friedrich to compromise his sacred duty as king for her own personal happiness. The scene is based on Kleist's *Prinz Friedrich von Homburg* (1811). Both the Saxon officer and the prince follow the urges of their "Herz" and break the dictates of military law: the Saxon is "aus Liebe Deserteur ... weil / Nach Sachsen heim zog ihn sein volles Herz" (20-21); the Prince of Homburg, in the midst of battle, obeys the command he receives "vom Herzen" and rides to attack before he receives the official summons to do so.[8] Both are subsequently condemned to death by execution. The Saxon officer's wife and the prince's fiancée plead with Friedrich II, King of Prussia, and Friedrich Wilhelm, Kurfürst of Brandenburg, to exercise "Gnade ... vor dem Kriegsrecht" (21),[9] and both rulers allow the subject himself (in Kleist, the prince; in Müller's play the Saxon woman) to decide between the claims of the state and the claims of the individual:

> Friedrich: ... Und doch, was König, Preussen, was Geschichte, alles werf ich weg auf Ihr Wort.
> (Auf einem Knie.)

> Madame, ich schenke Ihnen meinen Nachruhm
> Wenn Sie es wollen, für Ihr kleines Glück. (24)

The Prince of Homburg recognizes the unconditional validity of the law and desires to die in accordance with its demands; the Saxon woman (here clearly parodying the Kleist play) sings from Johann Strauss's "Die Fledermaus": "GLÜCKLICH IST / WER VERGISST / WAS EINMAL NICHT ZU ÄNDERN IST" (24), ironic lines from a duet of a woman and her supposed lover who are awaiting the "necessary" arrest and imprisonment of her husband, a practical joke she plays on him. That the subject internalizes and unconditionally exercises upon himself the rigid demands of a supposedly higher external order (e.g. that of the state), is recognizably an Enlightenment ideal: reason, as the essence of man and of the universe, is that absolute law in accordance with which the individual must act. Yet what is presented (albeit problematically) as an ideal in Kleist's play is rendered as a cliché from a comic opera in *Leben Gundlings*.

The model of the Kleist play (where the subject assents to and executes upon himself the dictates of the king/law) is imbedded within the structure of another literary model: the myth of Leda, evoked by the backdrop of Rubens' "Leda and the Swan." Zeus in the shape of a swan approaches and seduces Leda; she bears his children Helen and Polydeuces, as well as Castor, who is conceived with her husband that same night: here a disguised king deceives and is able to rape his unsuspecting subject. Similarly, in the scene "Herzkönig Schwarze Witwe" Friedrich wears the disguise of inner torment in order to evoke sympathy and awe on the part of the Saxon woman for the king's difficult historical and political role. This effort to deceive is marked in moments by operatic and conspicuously melodramatic passages:

> Friedrich (singt):
>     Oh wenn Sie wüssten O Madame Meine
>     Einsamen Nächte.
> Sächsin (tritt auf ihn zu, Arme ausbreitend):
>                     Und meine, Majestät.
> Friedrich (tritt zurück, zieht seinen Degen): Ah
>     Wie diese Brust nach diesem Trost verlangt! -
>     Gekrönte Häupter! Faulendes Europa!
>     Euch dieses Beispiel, wie ein König stirbt!
>     (Will den Degen an die Brust setzen, die Arme
>     sind zu kurz, der Degen ist zu lang, er trifft
>     die Mitte.) (22)

The woman refuses to allow the king to sacrifice his "Nachruhm" for the sake of her own "kleines Glück" ("Wie könnt ich, Majestät! Mein grosser König!" [24]), even taking him in her arms to comfort him in the performance of his difficult duty: she is Leda, duped by the disguise of a king. The ruler reveals himself in the end as the ravager he is: as the woman's husband is executed, Friedrich springs onto her from behind and rapes her, all against the background of the painting of Leda and the swan. The simultaneity of the two images reveals that the woman, in assenting to the demands of the law over and against the claims of her own personal life, has assented to the ravaging of her self. Friedrich, wearing the mask of the eagle, symbol of Prussia and of Zeus, says the final words to her: "Meine Kanonen brauchen Futter, Weib. / Wozu sonst hat sie ein Geschlecht im Leib" (25). Zeus's rape of Leda, too, resulting in the birth of the beautiful Helen, is the origin of a long and bloody war.

Yet Friedrich, who in this scene executes the Saxon officer in full view of his own wife just as his father the king had executed Katte years ago, has suffered his own "rape" in becoming a king in his father's image. At the beginning of the scene Friedrich cradles and caresses, then tramples underfoot, a Prussian doll wearing the mask of

Friedrich Wilhelm. This is on the one hand a symbolic representation of the general action of the scene: the king seduces, then ravages his subjects; the seduction itself is an act of violence. On the other hand, the doll with its mask represents an authority in whose name the boy Friedrich has himself suffered violence; in this respect Friedrich too is a Leda figure who is seduced by (caresses) a power (here, the image of Prussia and a strong Prussian king) which he at the same time recognizes and seeks to reject (trample down) as oppressive. That Friedrich, like the Saxon woman who chooses to endure her husband's execution, is ultimately both subject and object of his own oppression, is poignantly expressed in a brief monologistic passage. While the Saxon woman weeps, Friedrich steps before a mirror:

> Welch wunderbares Bildwerk ist der Mensch.
> (Bedeckt die Augen mit den Händen, blickt durch die Finger, dreht sich vom Spiegel weg.)
> Wenn die Natur ihn nicht geschaffen hätte
> Ich
> (Kurzer Blick in den Spiegel.)
>    Und wie sieht er aus mit zwanzig Kugeln.
> Lassen wir das. (23) [10]

Friedrich, standing before the mirror, covering his eyes yet looking through his fingers at his own image, relives the execution of his other self, Katte. The external force of the authoritarian father has been internalized, as it is *Friedrich* who now forces *himself* to witness the destruction wrought by the twenty bullets. The rebellious son becomes the authoritarian father to others and to himself; Friedrich, like the Saxon woman, is made to exercise oppression upon himself in the name of the state. The Enlightenment ideal of harmony based on a unity of reason inherent in man and in society is revealed to be an exercise in self-execution.

Scene 5 presents the oppression of the individual in the name of enlightened reason as an established and organized institution of society. The distorted child's prayer, "Lieber Gott mach mich fromm / Weil ich aus der Hölle komm" (26) which provides the scene's title, is emblematic of the more general perversion of Enlightenment to "Irrenhaus" in its practical implementation of "Reason."[11]

A professor makes his rounds with his students through the Prussian mental asylum, visiting three patients, each a radical example of the failure of Enlightenment ideals. The first had been condemned to execution for adultery and for the murder of her husband. Unlike the Prince of Homburg who is pardoned when he recognizes the absolute necessity of the law/state that condemns him, the hapless woman is granted her life through an occurrence of pure comic happenstance, of sheer absurd chance in a supposedly rational world: her drunken executioner fails, after three attempts, to behead her. The woman who has committed her crimes of revolt against her husband is a forerunner of Ophelia in *Hamletmaschine* who destroys her home, her bed, and the photographs of her lovers, and takes to the streets. Like Ophelia, the woman tears off her clothes as a symbol of revolt and is finally subdued and forced into a strait jacket by men in white coats: the revolution is (temporarily) suppressed. In *Leben Gundlings* the strait jacket is presented as the physical manifestation of the dialectic which underlies the unconditional recognition of law:

> Ein Instrument der Dialektik. ... Eine Schule der Freiheit in der Tat. Sie brauchen nur hinzusehen, als Einsicht in die Notwendigkeit verstanden. Je mehr der Patient sich bewegt, desto enger schnürt er sich selbst, er sich selbst wohlgemerkt, in seine Bestimmung. Jeder ist sein eigner Preusse, populär gesprochen. Darin liegt der erzieherische

> Wert, das Humanum sozusagen, der Zwangsjacke, die
> ebensogut Freiheitsjacke genannt werden kann.
> (28-29)

The medical professor, whose intellect, like Gundling's, has become an instrument of the state, describes his vision of the enlightened society, its principles fully realized:

> Der Philosoph würde schliessen, dass die wahre
> Freiheit in der Katatonie beruht, als dem voll-
> endeten Ausdruck der Disziplin, die Preussen
> gross gemacht hat. Die Konsequenz ist reizvoll:
> der ideale Staat gegründet auf den Stupor seiner
> Bevölkerung, der ewige Frieden auf den globalen
> Darmverschluss. Der Mediziner weiss: die Staaten
> ruhn auf dem Schweiss ihrer Völker, auf Kotsäulen
> der Tempel der Vernunft. (29)

The physician presents what is only a trivial academic disagreement with the views of the philosopher: the stupefaction of the minds, and the sweat and excrement of the bodies, are essentially two complementary aspects of the massive oppression upon which the ideal Enlightenment state is founded. The final realization of the Enlightenment ideals of reason and autonomy is at once their self-destruction. The adulteress and murderer in *Leben Gundlings,* bound and brought to silence in a madhouse, is herself a victim of this movement; the more developed Ophelia of *Hamletmaschine* will overcome her victimization by screaming out for revolution from her "underground" of the Deep Sea.

The figure of the adolescent who is bound in a masturbation bandage provides another image of rebellion suppressed in the Enlightenment world. Here the play refers back to the incident in the first scene where the young boy Friedrich is reprimanded by his father for playing with himself under the table (" ... die Hände auf dem Tische. Spielt Er wieder am Beinkleid. Die Hände des Soldaten sind and der Hosennaht befindlich, bei Tafel

auf dem Tisch" [7-8]); once again, the central
issue is the revolt of son against father. The
bandage is purportedly the invention of the German physician and pedagogue Daniel Gottlob Moritz
Schreber (1808-1861), whose pedagogical regime
emphasizing obedience and physical discipline
produced mental illness in his own two sons.[12]
Praised in the scene as "ein Sieg der Vernunft
über den rohen Naturtrieb" (30), the bandage nevertheless fails to achieve its purpose: his arms
released, the adolescent grabs immediately for
his genitals. However, the revolt of the youth
against the authoritative "reason" of the "father,"
like Friedrich's own rebellion, is doomed to fail:
the bandage is tied even more tightly around the
body, now bent double, of the crying boy; historical fact is that Schreber's younger son died in an
insane asylum after thirteen years of confinement.

The third patient, an officer and pedagogue and as
such a typical institutional representative of
Prussian Enlightenment, is at once the radical executor and tragic victim of Enlightenment ideals.
His three names bring together in one the righteous
and vengeful Hebrew god, and the opposing Satanic
figure of darkness and ignorance: "Zebaoth," one of
the Biblical names for God, the "Lord of Hosts,"
emphasizes his military strength and the persecution of transgressors; "Baal," in the Old Testament, is the West-Semitic storm god whose cults
challenged the worship of Jahweh through Israelite
history; "Zebahl," derived from "Baal- or "Beelzebub," "Prince Baal," is the prince of demons in
the New Testament, identified with Satan. The
confusion of the "true" god and the "false" idol
captures the fundamental dialectic of the emancipatory Enlightenment that becomes, in practice,
institutionalized oppression.

The schoolmaster's story itself, in which established literary models are bizarrely distorted,
illustrates this fatal dialectic. The schoolmaster

allows his son and favorite pupil Jesus to take upon himself the punishment deserved by the other school children and, in order to double the pedagogical effect, appoints the children themselves to establish the nature of the punishment. As a result, the schoolmaster must suffer Jesus's death. The explicit parallels to the Christ story are deliberately perverted: God, who is here Baal/Satan, allows his only son Jesus to be sacrificed for the crimes of man, yet his death is not salvation, but simply senseless waste. And as in Kleist's *Prinz Friedrich von Homburg* (and in the earlier scene between Friedrich and the Saxon woman), the wrongdoers are required to examine and judge their own actions, yet here they do not willingly submit to the "rational" demands of the law, but instead willfully and irresponsibly execute their own punishment upon an innocent victim. The schoolmaster's story is that of all order run amok; the pedagogical enterprise of the Enlightenment becomes a nightmare of destruction.

Yet it is significant that Scene 5, the middle scene of the play, ends on a distinctly revolutionary note as Zebahl, alone, asserts his identity with a specifically non-rational (destructive, natural, untamed) reality: "Ich Kot meiner Schöpfung Erbrechen meiner Engel Eiterkorn in meinen Harmonien. Ich bin die Fleischbank. Ich bin das Erdbeben. Ich bin das Tier. Der Krieg. Ich bin die Wüste" (33). As the adulteress and murderer is a precursor of the revolutionary Ophelia figure of *Hamletmaschine,* so Zebahl reappears in a later play, as the ex-slave and revolutionary Sasportas of *Auftrag:* to the white European intellectual (an Enlightenment figure) who has betrayed the revolution Sasportas promises: "Der Aufstand der Toten wird der Krieg der Landschaften sein, unsre Waffen die Wälder, die Berge, die Meere, die Wüsten der Welt. Ich werde Wald sein, Berg, Meer, Wüste."[13] Zebahl's monologue of hate ends with a

scream (offstage) as black angels swarm silently
into the audience, a sign associated in the play
with the figure of Maldoror from the work by
Lautréamont. (In the Prologue written for the 1979
production in Frankfurt, a black angel recites from
the second of *Les Chants de Maldoror*.)[14] Lautréamont's work of hallucinatory vision and macabre
eroticism, a classic of the literary "underground,"
speaks of a man born good yet turning to embrace
evil in a revolt against the crimes of God and
mankind;[15] the passionately revolutionary thrust
of the work is discussed by Aimé Césaire in his
*Discourse on Colonialism,* where the *Songs of Maldoror* is interpreted as a fierce condemnation of
the European bourgeois/capitalist society.[16] In
this sense, the visual quote from Lautréamont
functions at the end of Scene 5 as a proclamation
of a revolutionary anti-Enlightenment, one which
finds its peculiar source in the colonized peoples
of the non-European Third World. Zebahl, confined
in a cage, prefigures also the caged Jamaican
slave of *Auftrag* who comes to signify for Sasportas the necessity of revolution wherever oppression is found; it is in an insane asylum that the
Enlightenment confines the seeds of its own overthrow.

Scene 6 returns to the central story of Friedrich
II. He is now totally the despotic ruler, as self-assured and deliberately demonstrative and arbitrary in the exercise of his power as his father
had been in Scene 1. The peasants, like well-trained
animals, obey the monarch's every command; their
turnips become Prussian oranges at his word; they
dance in the rows of their fields to the tune of
his flute. Johann Gottfried Schadow, court sculptor from 1788 and director of the Berlin Academy of
Arts from 1815, chisels at his slab of marble, his
talent, like that of the academic Gundling, placed
in service to his ruler: studying the peasant
woman when she stands to stretch her back, and

67

ignoring the beating she receives from her husband when she is too stiff to bend down again to her work, Schadow will render the peasant woman as "ein klassizistischer Akt" (36). Schiller in turn recites for Friedrich and his guest Voltaire the elegiac "Der Spaziergang" (1795); the poet presents an idyllic vision of a prosperous and aesthetic culture infused with the ideals of classical antiquity, which gives way to the destruction of culture and morality when - an allusion to the French Revolution - man, freeing himself from his bonds, tears also "den Zügel der Schaam" (1. 144).[17] The ensuing world of deceit and unrestrained desire is however only a dream from which the wanderer finally awakens; the poem ends with a strong affirmation of the proven traditions of the past, of *continuity* rather than radical, revolutionary change:

> Ewig wechselt der Wille den Zweck und die Regel, in ewig
>     Wiederhohlter Gestalt wälzen die Thaten sich um.
> Aber jugendlich immer, in immer veränderter Schöne
>     Ehrst du, fromme Natur, züchtig das alte Gesetz,
> Immer dieselbe, bewahrst du in treuen Händen dem Manne,
>     Was dir das gaukelnde Kind, was dir der Jüngling
>                                                 vertraut,
> Wiegest auf gleichem Mutterschoose die wechselnden Alter;
>     Unter demselben Blau, über dem nehmlichen Grün
> Wandeln die nahen und wandeln vereint die fernen Ge-
>                                                 schlechter,
>     Und die Sonne Homers, siehe! sie lächelt auch uns.
> (11. 207-16)

Schiller and Schadow, who display their artistic talent to honor and to ornament Friedrich's rule while the peasants, in full view, must suffer their degradation, once again illustrate the revolutionary impotence, indeed, the self-betrayal of the Enlightenment intellectuals. Friedrich demonstrates that he has learned well the lesson of his father: "Dem Volk die Pfoten gekürzt, der Bestie, und die Zähne ausgebrochen. Die Intelligenz zum Narren gemacht, dass der Pöbel nicht auf Ideen kommt" (10). "ET IN

ARCADIA EGO," he quotes, sweeping his arm towards the audience, "Sehn Sie das Rindvieh, friedlich grasend. Preussen, eine Heimat für Volk und Vieh" (36). The classic pastoral inscription claims that every man experiences at least a moment of true happiness in his life.[18] Friedrich's Prussia, as the homeland of a folk peacefully grazing as a herd of cattle, is a grotesque reversal of the idyllic tradition. The perfect state is one of despotic rule honored by the men of arts and letters, sanctioned by the veneer of Enlightenment ideals. Scene 7, "Friedrich der Grosse," which presents the death of the king, broadens the historical relevance of his life. As Friedrich dies, his ministers chase a flurry of paper across the stage: Prussia lives on in the modern bureaucratic state.

Heinrich von Kleist and Gotthold Ephraim Lessing: Scenes 8-9

The final two scenes of the play, "Heinrich von Kleist spielt Michael Kohlhaas" and the triptych "Lessings Schlaf Traum Schrei," move into the realm of literature and literary production to present also in these terms the destructive "dialectic of the Enlightenment." Traditional literary history includes the figure of Kleist (1777-1811) uneasily within German Romanticism: human understanding having been denied access to the ultimate truths of reason by the Kantian critical philosophy, the revolutionary ideas of Rousseau belied by the realities of post-1789 France, the young author sought to preserve his humanitarian Enlightenment ideals in the refuge of *feeling*. Failing to overcome the fundamental contradictions of his life, he kills himself at the age of thirty-four. In Scene 8 of *Leben Gundlings* Kleist rebels against the established order of society, yet with his violence channelled against his own literary creations, he achieves only his own self-destruction: Kleist plays Michael Kohlhaas.

Both the drama *Prinz Friedrich von Homburg,* evoked as a model in the earlier scene "Herzkönig Schwarze Witwe," and the short story "Michael Kohlhaas" present heroes whose feeling (of patriotism or of justice) lead them knowingly to break the law. Both are condemned to death and accept their fate without protest, as they believe that they would achieve true "justice" in dying; their executions are in fact affirmations of an authoritarian, paternalistic state system. The actions of the Kleist figure in "Heinrich von Kleist spielt Michael Kohlhaas" can be divided into three stages. (1) Kleist caresses the Kleist doll and the woman doll. As with Friedrich II and his Prussian doll in Scene 4, the caress can be understood as signifying the acceptance of a prescribed role: Friedrich, embracing the image of a strong Prussian monarch, cares for/seduces his people; Kleist, similarly, accepts the standard representation (doll) of himself, and of the woman as an object (doll) for man. (2) Just as Friedrich then beats and tramples his Prussian/Friedrich-Wilhelm doll in what is in part a childish rebellion against the figure of an authority that tyrannizes him, so too does Kleist enact his sudden revolt. He cuts off the head of the horse doll, a radical and symbolic reversal of the stance of Michael Kohlhaas, who does everything within his power to have his horses *restored* him in their original condition. The Kleist figure's rejection of this justice of the status quo is continued in the violence he commits upon the woman doll: he tears out its heart and eats it. Müller draws here, as he does again in *Hamletmaschine,* upon the climactic scenes of John Ford's *'Tis Pity She's a Whore* (1633), in which a brother cuts out the heart of his sister and lover on her wedding day and presents it upon his dagger to fiancé, father, cardinal, and other citizens at the marriage banquet.[19] The brother's act, reenacted by the Kleist figure of Müller's play, is a passionate revolt against the tyranny of society, which demands that the sister marry another man.[20] Yet the radical revolt Kleist stages against societal order, a revolt which ultimately does *not* occur in "Michael Kohlhaas" or in *Prinz Friedrich von Homburg* and the sole act of revolt among the play's Enlightenment intellectuals, leads to his own execution. (3) Wearing the horse's head, Kleist butchers the Kleist doll; laying the wig of the woman doll on the executioner's block, he carries out his own execution, slitting his wrists over the foot-long hair. With all the props of revolution, Kleist, like Michael Kohlhaas, succeeds only in self-destruction.

The failure of the literature of the Enlightenment to be a literature of revolution, and ultimately, the failure of the intellectual to be a revolutionary, is presented in clearest terms in the final scene of the play. While the later revolutionary figures of Ophelia and Sasportas are prefigured in the patients of the Prussian insane asylum, Gundling and the philosopher king Friedrich, both intellectuals, reveal in their quotes from the Shakespeare play their affinity to the counter-revolutionary Hamlet figure of *Hamletmaschine*. The play ends, as does its title, with the German Enlightenment's greatest spokesman and figurehead, Gotthold Ephraim Lessing, who shares certain basic features with the revolutionary turned traitor Debuisson of *Auftrag*.

Like Debuisson, the Lessing figure abandons his "Auftrag": "Ich habe ein/zwei Dutzend Puppen mit Sägemehl gestopft das mein Blut war, einen Traum vom Theater in Deutschland geträumt und öffentlich über Dinge nachgedacht, die mich nicht interessierten. Das ist nun vorbei" (40). His resignation is accompanied by a view of history not as a movement of positive change, but as the senseless continuum of death and suffering in which all efforts at revolution are slowly exhausted. "Ich habe ein neues Zeitalter nach dem andren heraufkommen sehn, aus allen Poren Blut Kot Schweiss triefend jedes. Die Geschichte reitet auf toten Gäulen ins Ziel" (40-41). The same image recurs in Debuisson's long speech announcing his abandonment of the mission of revolution:

> Dein Tod heisst Freiheit, Sasportas, dein Tod heisst Brüderlichkeit, Galloudec, mein Tod heisst Gleichheit. Es ritt sich gut auf ihnen, als sie noch unsre Gäule gewesen sind, der Wind von morgen um die Schläfe. Jetzt weht der Wind aus gestern. Die Gäule sind wir. Merkt ihr die Sporen im Fleisch. Unsre Reiter haben Gepäck: die Leichen des Terrors, Pyramiden von Tod.[21]

And as with the later Debuisson, Lessing's "betrayal" is accomplished as a *forgetting* of his revolutionary past. In the final scene of *Auftrag*, Debuisson, seduced by the beautiful angel of Betrayal, forgets "den Sturm auf die Bastille, den Hungermarsch der Achtzigtausend, das Ende der Gironde, ihr Abendmahl ... Danton ... Marat ... Robespierre ..."[22] Lessing, too, recognizing the impossibility of his efforts, begins to forget:

> 30 Jahre lang habe ich versucht, mit Worten mich aus dem Abgrund zu halten, brustkrank vom Staub der Archive und von der Asche, die aus den Büchern weht, gewürgt von meinem wachsenden Ekel an der Literatur, verbrannt von meiner immer heftigeren Sehnsucht nach Schweigen .... Ich fange an, meinen Text zu vergessen. Ich bin ein Sieb. Immer mehr Worte fallen hindurch. Bald werde ich keine andere Stimme mehr hören als meine Stimme, die nach vergessenen Worten fragt. (41)

Yet with all these striking similarities, important differences emerge. Unlike Debuisson, who abandons the revolution and goes on to live the happy life of the traitor, Lessing is slowly dying. His is not a genuine act of betrayal, of counterrevolution, but rather he is himself the victim of a fundamental philosophical weakness inherent to the literature and thought of the Enlightenment which Müller explores again and again through the various figures of his play: the ideal of *ratio* which defines real freedom as the *recognition* of the absolute *law* of reason can discredit from the outset the very idea of revolution. Thus the characters of Lessing's plays, who are traditionally understood to represent the rise of a new bourgeois morality, do not in *Leben Gundlings* proclaim new values, but rather are presented as the victims *and* the accomplices of the orthodox external paternalistic authority.

In the second part of the scene Emilia Galotti and Nathan der Weise meet in an American junkyard. The last president of the United States, a faceless robot, sits on an electric chair; among wrecked cars are scattered classical theater characters and film stars, all in a state of decrepitude. The striking image presents the failure of the Enlightenment as the source of the dehumanization, the mechanization, of man; Enlightenment Prussia in its final development: the end of the modern industrialized state. Emilia and Nathan, who will embrace and destroy each other and join the community of wrecked film and theater personages, recite the famous passages from their texts.

Emilia's "Gewalt! Gewalt! Wer kann der Gewalt nicht trotzen? ... Verführung ist die wahre Gewalt! ..." (42) inspires her father to kill her, saving her from the corrupt and licentious life at court that threatens to seduce her and separate their family. Lessing's play is based on Livius's account of the young Roman woman Virginia who is killed by her father in an effort to protect her from the advances of the decemvir Appius Claudius. Her death gives rise to a general civil uprising which -

significantly - is omitted in Lessing's adaptation. Müller's appropriation of the Lessing play criticizes, I believe, its omission of the open revolt against oppression in favor of an individual, familial morality to be preserved by total self-sacrifice. Emilia's death is the result of her denial of her instinctive, natural desires and her recognition (and thus, internalization) of the external paternal authority as true and necessary; like Kleist's Prince of Homburg, she desires the fulfillment and affirmation through her own death of a higher moral and political principle, embodied by the father. The internalization of the principle of authority and the execution upon oneself of the law - the pedagogical goal and ideal of the Enlightenment - result in their most complete form in the self-execution of the individual: stated in extreme terms, true freedom is achieved not by revolt, but by suicide. In the words of the professor explaining the use of the strait jacket in the Prussian mental asylum, "Sie brauchen nur hinzusehen, als Einsicht in die Notwendigkeit verstanden. ... Jeder ist sein eigner Preusse, populär gesprochen" (28); Emilia's "revolutionary" freedom lies in her recognition of the necessity of her death.[23]

The issue of the authority of the father and its internalization as the structure of morality underlies also the Parable of the Rings which Nathan recites. As *Emilia Galotti* ends without revolt, all conflicts in *Nathan der Weise* dissipate as its characters learn that they are all members of a single family, of which Nathan is made the spiritual father. The parable he tells presents a vision of mankind striving in its deeds to emulate the father whose ring "hatte die geheime Kraft, vor Gott / Und Menschen angenehm zu machen, wer / In dieser Zuversicht ihn trug."[24] The strife of the three brothers, who each claim to possess the original ring of the father, ends with the resolution that each son act in the spirit of their father, raising future generations of children who will demonstrate the effect of the ring:

> Es strebe von euch jeder um die Wette,
> Die Kraft des Steins in seinem Ring' an Tag
> Zu legen! komme dieser Kraft mit Sanftmut,
> Mit herzlicher Verträglichkeit, mit Wohltun,
> Mit innigster Ergebenheit in Gott,
> Zu Hülf'! Und wenn sich dann der Steine Kräfte
> Bei euren Kindes-Kindeskindern äussern:
> So lad' ich über tausend tausend Jahre,
> Sie wiederum vor diesen Stuhl.[25]

Once again, the dissolution of all conflict and possible injustice is achieved through the recognition and internalization of the authority of the father; the individual claims of the three sons are subsumed under a higher external, paternal principle. Emilia and Nathan, who then perform their symbolic double suicide in the last scene of the play, suggest the logical-absurd tendency of Enlightenment thought: the individual learns, in the name of an ideal, to deny the claims of his own individuality.

The stage darkens. What are left are projections into the future, not of more scrap metal in the junkyards of the American Midwest, but of violent, elemental forces: slaughtered buffaloes emerging from their canyons, swarms of sharks, alligators, earthquakes, fire and water. Müller stated in an interview from 1980:

> So ein Eindruck von der Mississippi-Mündung, wo Industrieanlagen verrotten in den Sümpfen. Da ist etwas ungeheuer Schönes in diesem Kapitalismus, der da bis an seine Grenze gelangt. Die Grenze ist die Landschaft. Dazu braucht es aber die Qualität von Landschaft. Die kann man eben nicht in den Supermarkt verpflanzen. Da bleibt immer noch ein Rest samt seinen Naturkatastrophen. Die sind dann ein Moment der Hoffnung. Sie sind belebend.[26]

The untamed forces of nature at the border of the industrialized world represent a revolutionary hope for mankind. The impulse for the preservation of humanity is perhaps not enlightened reason, but the distinctly "irrational" and catastrophic power of the natural world. The literature that carries the ideals of humanity, it is suggested, is not the product of the German Enlightenment, *Emilia Galotti, Nathan der Weise,* or *Prinz Friedrich von Homburg,* but the anti-literature of "LAUTREAMONT-MALDOROR" (43) and the unwritten "SPARTAKUS EIN FRAGMENT" (43), the play of the revolt of the Roman slaves which Lessing never completed.[27] The literature of open revolution remained unwritten: it is this that is Lessing's failure. His last desperate effort to uncover the "torso" of his unfinished revolutionary hero from the sand that threatens to smother its every trace is unsuccessful. The Lessing figure is immobilized in his own "strait jacket," the bronze of a Lessing bust. ("Je mehr der Patient sich bewegt, desto enger schnürt er sich selbst, er sich selbst wohlgemerkt, in seine Bestimmung" [28]). He becomes a "classic" to be placed on the shelf, deprived of any revolutionary relevance or impact; his final muffled scream is drowned by applause.

## The Enlightenment Dialectic

> Seit je hat Aufklärung im umfassendsten Sinn fortschreitenden Denkens das Ziel verfolgt, von den Menschen die Furcht zu nehmen und sie als Herren einzusetzen. Aber die vollends aufgeklärte Erde strahlt im Zeichen triumphalen Unheils.

So begins Chapter I of Horkheimer and Adorno's *Dialektik der Aufklärung.*[28] The project of the Enlightenment, to emancipate man from his dependence on and determination by the surrounding natural world, is accomplished by establishing scientific logical thought itself as a deterministic, authoritarian force; the Enlightenment, Horkheimer and Adorno argue, merely repeats the violence of nature upon the individual when it in turn subsumes all individuality under an abstract concept: "Die Abstraktion, das Werkzeug der Aufklärung, verhält sich zu ihren Objekten wie das Schicksal, dessen Begriff sie ausmerzt: als Liquidation."[29] The essentially totalitarian tendency of the Enlightenment is to create a society whose members are forced into conformity, as the bad totality of equality can only be secured by destroying what is different: "Es darf überhaupt nichts mehr draussen sein, weil die blosse Vorstellung des Draussen die eigentliche Quelle der Angst ist"; "[Der Mensch] schrumpft zum Knotenpunkt konventioneller Reaktionen und Funktionsweisen zusammen."[30] The enlightened society becomes in effect a huge machinery of domination in which the rational intellect plays the crucial role in the preservation of order and in the suppression of all individuality. "Damit ... wird notwendig das Ganze als Ganzes, die Betätigung der ihm immanenten Vernunft, zur Vollstreckung des Partikularen. Die Herrschaft tritt dem Einzelnen als das Allgemeine gegenüber, als die Vernunft in der Wirklichkeit."[31]

That reason, through which man is to achieve his complete autonomy and thus his humanity, becomes at the same time the very apparatus which destroys all individuality and enslaves man in total conformity and sameness, is also the thesis of *Leben Gundlings Friedrich von Preussen Lessings Schlaf Traum Schrei*. The criticism Müller launches is deeply rooted in the post-war experience of this Enlightenment heritage; the following statement by the author illuminates the direct political relevance of his text:

> Weil natürlich das preussische Erbe auch etwas ist, was die DDR zu tragen hat, in vieler Beziehung. Da

> war ein Beamtenstaat und ein Staat, wo die Leute zu
> Untertanen erzogen wurden. Und das bot sich an in
> der Situation nach 45. Damals war man froh über
> jeden, der sich wie ein Untertan verhielt und bereit
> war, die neue Richtung einzuschlagen. Und es hat
> einfach noch zu wenig Gelegenheit gegeben, den Leu-
> ten das abzugewöhnen. Die wenigsten Leute in der
> DDR kennen zum Beispiel die Verfassung, kennen alle
> ihre Rechte. Sie haben sehr viel mehr Rechte, als sie
> wahrnehmen. Es gibt einen ziemlich grossen Freiheits-
> raum, der von den meisten Leuten viel zu wenig ge-
> nutzt wird. Das kann man nicht der DDR anlasten. Das
> ist ein Erbe, das noch nicht bewältigt ist. [32]

Müller illustrates in his play the self-betrayal or "dialectic" of the Enlightenment specifically in terms of the failure of Enlightenment intellectuals: Gundling, Friedrich II, the professor in the asylum, Schadow, Schiller, Kleist, and Lessing all allow their potentially emancipatory intellect to be appropriated by the apparatus of the state; all sanction, directly or indirectly, the institutions of "enlightened" oppression. Yet these intellectuals, in supporting the paternalistic authority in one form or another, are also themselves victims of the Enlightenment reason they represent. Gundling, Friedrich, Kleist and Lessing must all suffer their own self-execution at the hands of the authoritarian ideal they embody and serve. The instrumentalization, the implementation of emancipatory reason leads to its destruction in tyranny, resignation, or suicide.

On a deeper level, the play reveals a certain ambivalence with regard to the relationship of the intellectual to the state, of knowledge to power. Basically knowledge is appropriated into the mechanism of state domination: Gundling is made a member of Friedrich's court, the figure of Friedrich himself embodies the fusion of enlightened reason and authoritarian state rule. But knowledge is appropriated only because it is a fundamentally revolutionary threat to state power ("Die Intelligenz zum Narren gemacht, dass der Pöbel nicht auf Ideen kommt" [10]). The invocation of the figure of Socrates, far from coincidental, points to the fundamental critical, emancipatory function of reason; because Socrates *refuses* to become an instrument of the power of the state, he becomes its victim. This un-appropriated, non-instrumentalized reason which sets itself *against* the paternalistic state authority is present also in the refined and intelligent young boy Friedrich, who rebels against his boorish father in part through his homosexual affair with his lieutenant and companion Katte. Sexuality forms also the basis of the "revolt" enacted by the adulteress and the chronic masturbator in the Prussian insane asylum; the third patient, a former pedagogue of the Enlightenment, identifies himself in his vision with the destructive forces of nature ("Ich bin das Erdbeben. Ich bin das Tier. Der Krieg. Ich bin die Wüste." [33]), which reappear in the final scene of the play as projections into a future beyond the "junkyard" of the industrialized, mechanized Enlightenment state. In essence Müller's play criticizes the Enlightenment ideal of a dominating, authoritarian reason and begins to suggest an alternative, linked with the irrepressible forces of youth, nature, and sexuality, and perhaps best embodied by the philosopher and supreme *lover* Socrates. The unknown "otherness" of nature, the domination of which has been from the first the Enlightenment project, begins to reassert itself. These issues are developed and given their most formulaic expression in Müller's next play, *Die Hamletmaschine*.

EXCURSUS: LESSING, HEGEL, AND THE MODEL OF
BOURGEOIS DRAMA


Since the time of the Enlightenment, with Gottsched's campaign for a theater based on the aesthetic and moral principles of reason and Lessing's efforts to establish a German national theater independent of the dominating French classical tradition, drama in Germany has been the privileged genre for national political and philosophical discussion.[1] Müller's criticism of the Prussian Enlightenment tradition in *Leben Gundlings Friedrich von Preussen Lessings Schlaf Traum Schrei* ends, significantly, with the figure of Gotthold Ephraim Lessing, the first and principal theoretician and playwright of German bourgeois drama.

Peter Szondi in *Theorie des modernen Dramas (1880-1950)* describes the form of drama which developed in Elizabethan England, seventeenth-century France, and German Classicism: dramatic figures express and objectify their inner motivation in the intersubjective realm of dialogue; in and through the interchange of dialogue, as words necessarily lead to deeds, the dramatic action develops as an absolute, causal sequence of events, a necessary continuity in which each event is the fulfillment or outcome of previous events and contains in itself the impetus for the future.[2] Szondi defines essentially what has come to be the normative model of drama within the German literary tradition: the bourgeois drama which reflects the bourgeois ideology of the Enlightenment. Through rational intersubjective discourse, the teleology of progress unfolds. In this brief excursus I draw from Lessing's *Hamburgische Dramaturgie* (1767-68) and from Hegel's *Vorlesungen über die Ästhetik* (1820-29) to delineate certain basic features of this definitive, dominant model - a model which, I will argue in Chapter 3, Müller's *Hamletmaschine* actively undermines.

A basic proposition of Lessing's dramaturgy is the centrality of *character:* "Die Facta betrachten wir als etwas zufälliges ... die Charaktere hingegen als etwas wesentliches und eigentümliches" (33. Stück).[3] Of dramatic characters two essential qualities are required: (1) They must be self-consistent, without inner contradiction; that is, their identities are constant and never undergo sudden change. This is the requirement of "Übereinstimmung": "Nichts muss sich in den Charakteren widersprechen; sie müssen immer einförmig, immer sich selbst ähnlich bleiben" (34. Stück). (2) Characters must exhibit intention or purpose ("Absicht"); their actions must all be guided by some overriding aim or will, some goal to be achieved, and, on another level, the characters themselves function within the author's intended project of moral edification (34. Stück).

Out of these absolutely defined, integral characters who act with express purpose in their interpersonal dramatic world unfolds the action of the play as an *inescapable chain of events,* "eine Reihe von Ursachen und Wirkungen." Events must develop in such a way "dass wir überall nichts als den natürlichsten, ordentlichsten Verlauf wahrnehmen ... dass uns nichts dabei befremdet, als die unmerkliche Annäherung eines Ziels" (32. Stück). Dramatic action moves ineluctably toward a logical (rational) and moral end reflecting the teleological order of the real universe:

> [Der Dichter] sollte ... ein Ganzes machen, das völlig sich rundet, wo eines aus dem andern sich völlig erkläret ... das Ganze dieses sterblichen Schöpfers sollte ein Schattenriss von dem Ganzen des ewigen Schöpfers sein; sollte uns an den Gedanken gewöhnen, wie sich in ihm alles zum Besten auflöse, werde es auch in jenem geschehen. (79. Stück)

These central aspects of the bourgeois drama as
defined by Lessing reappear in the discussion of
"Die dramatische Poesie" in Hegel's *Ästhetik* some
sixty years later. Drama for Hegel presents:

> ... die zu lebendigen Charakteren und konfliktreichen
> Situationen individualisierten Zwecke, in ihrem Sich-
> zeigen und -behaupten, Einwirken und Bestimmen ge-
> geneinander - alles in Augenblicklichkeit wechsel-
> seitiger Äusserung - sowie das in sich selbst be-
> gründete Endresultat dieses ganzen sich bewegt durch-
> kreuzenden und dennoch zur Ruhe lösenden menschlichen
> Getriebes in Wollen und Vollbringen.[4]

Dramatic characters in dramatic situations represent specific opposing ideas or positions ("Zwek-
ke"), which assert themselves and thereby incite
one another in dramatic conflict; drama is the
conflict of ideas presented or made objectively
manifest in the struggle of dramatic figures. The
dramatic action, as for Lessing, arises out of
these figures as they actively seek to realize
their conflicting goals: "Grund und Wirksamkeit"
of drama is, Hegel writes, "das selbstbewusste
und tätige Individuum .... Dadurch erscheint dann
das Geschehen nicht hervorragend aus den äusseren
Umständen, sondern aus dem inneren Wollen und Charakter" (477). Further, the action moves in dialectical fashion towards an end in which the conflict is consumed and sublated: "das in sich be-
gründete Endresultat" is the necessary outcome of
an unfolding process whose end is contained already in the dynamic of its beginning. As for
Lessing, dramatic action evinces a teleological
structure: drama presents "das lebendige Wirken
einer in sich selbst beruhenden, jeden Kampf und
Widerspruch lösenden Notwendigkeit" (480); in
what appears as confusion and the product of
chance the true dramatic poet is able to perceive
"das wirkliche Sichvollführen des an und für sich
Vernünftigen und Wirklichen" (481).

To Lessing's requirement of "Absicht" corresponds the inner "Wollen" of Hegel's dramatic characters, the "Zweck" which they embody and assert. The second demand of "Übereinstimmung" is also expressly stated in Hegel's aesthetic: "Das dramatische Individuum muss ... eine fertige Totalität sein, deren Gesinnung und Charakter mit ihrem Zweck und Handeln übereinstimmt." The self-consistency of a dramatic figure is defined as "die durchdringende Individualität, welche alles zu der Einheit, die sie selber ist, zusammenfasst und diese Individualität im Reden wie im Handeln als den einen und gleichen Quellpunkt dartut, aus welchem jedes besondere Wort, jeder einzelne Zug der Gesinnung, Tat und Weise des Benehmens entspringt" (500). These two fundamental requirements of dramatic character present an ideal of man as completely self-aware and wholly purposeful in his actions: the character must know and state what he wants/stands for, and he must act always to achieve this end. Intention or desire, word, and action are in complete harmony; one says what one thinks, one does what one says.

Hegel states explicitly in his *Ästhetik* what Lessing seems to assume throughout the *Hamburgische Dramaturgie*: the connection between the characters, on the one hand, and the teleology of action which develops out of their various purposes, on the other, is established in the medium of language, through *dialogue*. Hegel writes that it is not the actual actions of the dramatic figures ("das reale Tun") that are of essential importance to drama, but rather the exposition of the "inner spirit" of the action as a whole, "die Exposition des inneren Geistes der Handlung sowohl in betreff auf die handelnden Charaktere und deren Leidenschaft, Pathos, Entschluss, Gegeneinanderwirken und Vermitteln als auch in Rücksicht auf die allgemeine Natur der Handlung in ihrem Kampf und Schicksal" (490). This inner spirit of the action is specifically expressed through the speeches of the characters; indeed, the very essence of dramatic form lies in the self-expression and self-assertion in dialogue of the conflicting interests and goals of the dramatic figures:

> Die vollständig dramatische Form ... ist der *Dialog*. Denn in ihm allein können die handelnden Individuen ihren Charakter und Zweck ... *gegeneinander* aussprechen, in Kampf geraten und damit die Handlung in wirklicher Bewegung vorwärtsbringen. (493)

Dialogue, as Szondi points out, which is the linguistic medium of the interpersonal world represented in drama, comes to constitute in itself the form of the dramatic work of art.[5]

Both Lessing and Hegel discuss the nature of dialogue that is best suited to provide the medium of dramatic action. "Bei einer gesuchten, kostbaren, schwülstigen Sprache kann niemals Erfindung sein," Lessing writes; "Aber wohl verträgt sie sich mit den simpelsten, gemeinsten, plattesten Worten und Redensarten" (59. Stück). Only the simple, common, natural language, from which "Grobheit und Wust" are just as distant as "Schwulst und Bombast," is able adequately to express the thoughts and emotions of the dramatic figures. Hegel also steers between the extremes of "Höflichkeit" and "Grobheit":

> Zwischen dieser bloss formellen Allgemeinheit und jener natürlichen Äusserung ungehobelter Besonderheiten steht das wahrhaft Allgemeine, das weder formell noch individualitätslos bleibt, sondern seine doppelte Erfüllung an der Bestimmtheit des Charakters und der Objektivität der Gesinnungen und Zwecke findet. Das echt Poetische wird deshalb darin bestehen, das Charakteristische und Individuelle der unmittelbaren Realität in das

reinigende Element der Allgemeinheit zu erheben und beide Seiten sich miteinander vermitteln zu lassen. (492)

Lessing's and Hegel's remarks reveal the specific class character of their definition of drama. The true dramatic figure is neither coarse and vulgar (plebeian) nor pompous and artificial (aristocratic); the simultaneous opposition to "Grobheit" and "Höflichkeit" establishes the realm of the bourgeois individual, who poses as "das wahrhaft Allgemeine," as the realm of straightforward, genuinely human action and speech. The true language of drama as the expression of (bourgeois) man's universal nature is within the Enlightenment context the language of *reason*. Dramatic dialogue is essentially rational discourse.

To summarize, the model of the bourgeois drama of the Enlightenment is defined by:

(1) the independent, integral individual, the "hero" whose identity is bound to the particular end or idea he incorporates and whose actions are guided by this single purpose to be achieved;

(2) dramatic action which moves inescapably towards a logical, rational end, reflecting a teleological view of history;

(3) rational dialogue, which, as the medium in which dramatic individuals express, assert and finally resolve their particular conflicting purposes/identities, becomes the essential vehicle of dramatic action, and of historical progress.

The play *Leben Gundlings* examines the inherent flaw of this model; the Enlightenment individual achieves his purpose and *preserves* his identity only by internalizing the law of "reason" and choosing his own *death* in accordance with that law. In *Hamletmaschine* Lessing's Emilia Galotti gives way to an Ophelia who *refuses* to continue her project of suicide.

# CHAPTER III

## THE ENTROPY OF BOURGEOIS DRAMA:

## DIE HAMLETMASCHINE (1977)

> Sie können den Text der "Hamletmaschine" als fünfaktiges Stück lesen, ganz klassisch in der Dramaturgie.
> 
> Heiner Müller[1]

*Die Hamletmaschine* is perhaps Müller's most provocative and difficult play to date.[2] Its enigmatic "action" can be summarized only fragmentarily: Hamlet describes in Scene 1 the funeral of his father, during which he feeds the corpse to the hungry masses; the Ghost appears; Hamlet rapes his mother. Ophelia in Scene 2 destroys the home which has been her prison and takes to the streets, covered in blood. In the Scherzo of Scene 3, Hamlet tells Ophelia, who is dressed as a whore and now accompanies Claudius, that he wishes to be a woman. Dressed in Ophelia's clothes, he dances with the angel Horatio beneath the figure of a madonna with breast cancer. The Hamlet player in Scene 4 sheds his role which is, he describes, on both sides of a civil uprising, and heads home, retreating into his own flesh and excrement; suddenly he crawls into a suit of armor and splits the heads of the naked women Marx, Lenin, and Mao. Finally, Ophelia in Scene 5 sits wrapped in bandages in a wheelchair among the corpses and wreckage of the deep sea and smothers the world she has given birth to between her thighs.

Yet despite the apparently "anarchic" action of the play, a straightforward overall organization is distinguishable. The text is presented in five parts, divided between and dominated by two characters, Hamlet (Scenes 1 and 4) and Ophelia (Scenes 2 and 5), with the central third scene, in which both appear, functioning as an interlude. Basic differences in discourse between the Hamlet and the Ophelia scenes are immediately striking: the long scenes devoted to Hamlet display a variety of literary forms, ranging from narratives in the past and present tenses, to lyric in free verse, and contain a multitude of quotations from other works which continually disrupt the continuity of the text. The much shorter Ophelia scenes, in contrast, each consist of an integral, uninterrupted speech by a single voice. The third scene is unique in its employment of pantomime, long sequences of action without speech, and in the explicit presence and interaction of a number of dramatic figures; here, too, occurs the only instance of what might be considered "dialogue" in the entire text. Finally, the settings given for or evoked by the scenes reinforce the pattern of their division: Scenes 2 and 4 take place in an "Enormous Room," intact at the beginning of Scene 2, and in ruins in Scene 4; the "Tiefsee" filled with fish, corpses and "Trümmer" of Scene 5 recalls the initial setting of "Brandung" and "Ruinen" evoked by the first speech of Scene 1; again, Scene 3, set in the "Universität der Toten," stands alone.[3]

The overall chiasmic ordering of the five scenes suggests a particular strategy for reading and understanding the play. I first compare Scenes 1 and 5, and Scenes 2 and 4, linked by their settings, to uncover the nature of the contrast between the figures of Hamlet and Ophelia which structures the play as a whole. Subsequently, the Hamlet scenes (1 and 4) and the Ophelia scenes (2 and 5) will be examined more closely, to explore the individual, separate but related "dramas" of these figures. Finally, I discuss Scene 3 in terms of its central position in the play.

## Scenes 1 and 5:
## The Dramatic Hero and the Undramatic Victim

A comparison of the initial and final scenes of the play immediately highlights the sheer complexity of the Hamlet scene, in contrast with the singular starkness of the final Ophelia scene. While Hamlet is the sole organizing consciousness (but not necessarily the only actual speaker) of the many various passages of the first scene, a number of the characters of Shakespeare's *Hamlet* are also present or evoked: Claudius, Hamlet's mother the Queen, the Ghost, Horatio, Polonius, and Ophelia. Ophelia in Scene 5, on the other hand, remains totally alone on stage. The men in white coats who bind her in a strait jacket of bandages are not potential dramatic figures, but little more than props which complete the tableau of the scene, and Ophelia's speech, essentially unheard, does not interact with or imply the presence of any silent but active listener.

Further, while the texts of both scenes incorporate a number of quotes from other texts, the manner of their incorporation differs and helps to create the impression of complexity in the Hamlet scene and simplicity in the Ophelia scene. In Scene 1 Müller quotes most notably from Shakespeare's *Hamlet*:

> "ER WAR EIN MANN NAHM ALLES NUR VON ALLEN" (89)
> "He was a man, take him for all in all" (I.ii.187)

> "SOMETHING IS ROTTEN IN THIS AGE OF HOPE" (89)
> "Something is rotten in the state of Denmark"
> (I.iv.90)

> "LETS DELVE IN EARTH AND BLOW HER AT THE MOON" (90)
> "But I will delve one yard below their mines, / And
>     blow them at the moon" (III.iv.208-09)

> "WASCH DIR DEN MORD AUS DEM GESICHT MEIN PRINZ /
>     UND MACH DEM NEUEN DÄNEMARK SCHÖNE AUGEN" (91)

"Good Hamlet, cast thy nighted color off, / And let thine eye look like a friend on Denmark" (I.ii.68-69);

from T.S. Eliot's "Ash-Wednesday":

"OH MY PEOPLE WHAT HAVE I DONE UNTO THEE" (89)

If the lost word is lost, if the spent word is spent
If the unheard, unspoken
Word is unspoken, unheard;
Still is the unspoken word, the Word unheard,
The Word without a word, the Word within
The world and for the world;
And the light shone in darkness and
Against the Word the unstilled world still whirled
About the centre of the silent Word.

O my people, what have I done unto thee.[4]

and from the construction engineer Hasselbein in Müller's own play *Der Bau:*

WIE EINEN BUCKEL SCHLEPP ICH MEIN SCHWERES GEHIRN
ZWEITER CLOWN IM KOMMUNISTISCHEN FRÜHLING (89)

Hamlet in Leuna, Hans Wurst auf dem Bau, Zweiter Clown im kommunistischen Frühling. Mein Kopf ist mein Buckel.[5]

Quotes in Scene 1 disrupt the thematic, syntactic, and orthographic flow of speech within a single sentence:

... das Spalier der Bevölkerung, Werk seiner Staatskunst ER WAR EIN MANN NAHM ALLES NUR VON ALLEN. Ich stoppte den Leichenzug, stemmte den Sarg mit dem Schwert auf, dabei brach die Klinge, mit dem stumpfen Rest gelang es, und verteilte den toten Erzeuger FLEISCH UND FLEISCH GESELLT SICH GERN an die umstehenden Elendsgestalten (89);

or are simply presented in a disjointed series of apparently unrelated statements:

> OH MY PEOPLE WHAT HAVE I DONE UNTO THEE
> WIE EINEN BUCKEL SCHLEPP ICH MEIN SCHWERES GEHIRN
> ZWEITER CLOWN IM KOMMUNISTISCHEN FRÜHLING
> SOMETHING IS ROTTEN IN THIS AGE OF HOPE
> LETS DELVE IN EARTH AND BLOW HER AT THE MOON. (89-90)

Quotes in Scene 5, on the other hand, are virtually indistinguishable in theme or form from their immediate context:

> Hier spricht Elektra. Im Herzen der Finsternis. Unter der Sonne der Folter. An die Metropolen der Welt. Im Namen der Opfer. (97)

Joseph Conrad's *Heart of Darkness* is one obvious source of the line "Im Herzen der Finsternis."[6] "Unter der Sonne der Folter," as I have pointed out in my discussion of Müller's essay on postmodernism, quotes from Sartre's preface to Frantz Fanon's *The Wretched of the Earth* and appears in Müller's statements on Antonin Artaud.[7] In contrast to the disjointed series of quotations in Scene 1, the two quotations in sequence here *join* semantically to form part of a single statement. The final quotation and the last line of the play, "Wenn sie mit Fleischermessern durch eure Schlafzimmer geht, werdet ihr die Wahrheit wissen" (97), taken from the testimony of Susan Atkins, a member of the Charles Manson "family" responsible for the Tate-LaBianca murders in 1969, again does not function to disrupt the continuity of Ophelia's speech, but rather provides an eloquent and powerful conclusion to her call for revolution.

The simplicity and continuity of the final scene (a single figure with a single, integral speech) and the complexity and discontinuity of speech and cast of characters in the initial scene of the play are symptoms of the inherent - though problematic - *dramaticality* of Scene 1 and the programmatic *undramaticality* of Scene 5. "All that is left of Shakespeare's play went into this first scene," Müller stated in an interview on

*Hamletmaschine*.⁸ The dramatic action moves from the burial of the King, through the appearance of the Ghost and the meddlings of Polonius, and up to Hamlet's confrontation with his mother in her bedchamber (Act III, Scene 4 of the Shakespeare play). Dialogue is rendered as "BLABLA" (89), the unrelenting flow of seemingly unconnected words and speeches. While Scene 1 perverts the traditional form of dramatic action and dialogue, Scene 5 seems to present its complete *negation*. The tableau of immobility and Ophelia's revolutionary proclamation followed by deadly silence reject the very possibility of purposeful action and rational discourse as the vehicles for dramatic and historical progress.

Scene 1 essentially presents a "dramatic" development in two senses of the word: there is development of dramatic action (the Hamlet "plot" which the reader can recognize and follow) and, parallel to this, development of dramatic form, of the form traditionally expected of "drama." The scene can be divided into five parts, corresponding to a play in five acts, which articulate Hamlet's progression from distant observer of, to active participant in the history of his family:

(1) During the state funeral of the King, Hamlet's father, Hamlet expresses his disgust over the crimes of murder and adultery committed by his uncle and his mother, and over the hypocrisy of their grief.

(2) An interluding collage of quotations, a "monologue," calls for definitive action on the part of the dramatic hero: Hamlet, the would-be hero, needs "A CAUSE FOR GRIEF," "A REAL SORROW," a heroic task to accomplish (89); the too-meditative "CLOWN" with his heavy brain must become the "PRINCEKILLING KING," rather, the kingkilling prince (89).

(3) The Ghost appears, and Hamlet's task is made explicit.

(4) In a second "monologistic" interlude, Hamlet questions the wisdom and necessity of the duty to avenge murder by murder: "SOLL ICH / WEILS BRAUCH IST EIN STÜCK EISEN STECKEN IN / DAS NÄCHSTE FLEISCH ODER INS ÜBERNÄCHSTE" (90).

(5) Finally, Hamlet acts. After appearances by Horatio, Polonius, and Ophelia, Hamlet kills Polonius ("Sieh was aus der Wand wächst. Exit Polonius"), rapes his mother, and drags off Polonius' corpse: "Ich will die Leiche in den Abtritt stopfen, dass der Palast erstickt in königlicher Scheisse" (91).

The development from a passive, distant Hamlet to an active, engaged dramatic "hero" is mirrored in the discourse of the text. The speeches of Sections 1, 3, and 5, set off from one another by interluding meditations or quasi-monologues entirely in capital letters, differ significantly in narrative form. In Section 1, Hamlet relates the occasion of his father's funeral as an event in the past; he is distanced in time and space from the people and actions he describes. The story of the Hamlet who watches the funeral procession and suddenly tears open the coffin and distributes shreds of his father's corpse to the crowds presents *in nuce* the dramatic development of Scene 1: Hamlet, the distanced narrator in Section 1, becomes the hero actively engaged in the dramatic present of Section 5.

With the appearance of the first "other," the Ghost in Section 3, the discourse shifts from the imperfect to the present tense of drama. The Ghost, however, necessarily unable to act, is not a genuine dramatic figure but rather simply a vehicle for the exposition. While Hamlet addresses the Ghost in what is ostensibly "dialogue," we hear only Hamlet's private and introspective thoughts:

> Du kannst deinen Hut aufbehalten, ich weiss, dass
> du ein Loch zu viel hast. Ich wollte, meine Mutter
> hätte eines zu wenig gehabt, als du im Fleisch
> warst: ich wäre mir erspart geblieben. Man sollte
> die Weiber zunähn, eine Welt ohne Mütter. (90)

The speech of the hero is not tantamount to dramatic action, but rather Hamlet expressly states his undramatic *reluctance* to act in accordance with his role and duty as his father's son: "Was willst du von mir. ... Was geht mich deine Leiche an" (90). It is only in Section 5 that the "drama" is fully developed. Other, genuine characters appear, and the dramatic quality of the text is explicitly thematized: Hamlet speaks of "MEINEM TRAUERSPIEL," "Stichwort," "eine tragische Rolle" (90); HoratioPolonius is, he says, "ein Schauspieler," as Hamlet is himself, "Ich spiele Hamlet" (91). Most crucial of all, Hamlet engages in action in the immediate, dramatic present. The word "jetzt" becomes a litany as Hamlet describes his violent actions: "Jetzt binde ich dir die Hände .... Jetzt zerreisse ich das Brautkleid .... Jetzt beschmiere ich die Fetzen deines Brautkleids .... Jetzt nehme ich dich ..." (91).

While Hamlet's Scene 1 moves from the narrated past into the dramatic present, Ophelia's Scene 5 presents essentially the undramatic non-development of an immobile tableau. Like the action in Scene 1, immobility in Scene 5 is both a formal principle and the central thematic concern. Ophelia remains unmoving throughout, immobile in a wheelchair, wrapped and tied in bandages, finally left on stage, "reglos in der weissen Verpackung" (97). Further, her proclamation of hatred, contempt, rebellion and death, while a revolutionary act, does not carry the import of genuine dramatic action. Her own violent statements remain unaccompanied by concrete action; indeed, they are fundamentally unrealizable:

> Ich stosse allen Samen aus, den ich empfangen habe.
> Ich verwandle die Milch meiner Brüste in tödliches
> Gift. Ich nehme die Welt zurück, die ich geboren
> habe. Ich ersticke die Welt, die ich geboren habe,
> zwischen meinen Schenkeln. Ich begrabe sie in meiner Scham. (97)

Thus Ophelia's own litany expresses not the fulfillment of the long overdue deed, but the revolt of *non*-action, the renunciation of action and thereby also of traditional drama.

The programmatic rejection of conception, of birth, and consequently, of womanhood in general in the final scene establishes a strong thematic link to Hamlet in Scene 1. There, in response to the appearance of the Ghost and the act of revenge now explicitly required of himself, Hamlet rejects the event of his own birth and wishes for a new world without mothers. "Man sollte die Weiber zunähn, eine Welt ohne Mütter. Wir könnten einander in Ruhe abschlachten, und mit einiger Zuversicht, wenn uns das Leben zu lang wird oder der Hals zu eng für unsre Schreie" (90). Without the recreative, restorative process of birth which guarantees the continuity of life, the human history of continual murder and violence must necessarily come to an end. "Der Morgen findet nicht mehr statt" (90): Hamlet's dream is of the total disruption, the halting of historical "progress" which is nothing but an endless continuity of destruction. The vision of a radical break, of the breakdown of continuity, is Hamlet's moment of insight. "SOLL ICH / WEILS BRAUCH IST EIN STÜCK EISEN STECKEN IN / DAS NÄCHSTE FLEISCH ODER INS ÜBERNÄCHSTE / MICH DRAN ZU HALTEN WEIL DIE WELT SICH DREHT" (90): the revenge of murder by murder is a "necessity" sanctioned by custom, by the simple continuous revolution of the globe. The idiocy of preserving continuity for the sake of continuity, which Hamlet recognizes in Scene 1, is finally rejected by Ophelia in Scene 5.

The issue of continuity and discontinuity parallels the tension between the dramaticality and undramaticality of the two scenes. With the problematization of the traditional model of drama (the individual/hero, the purposeful action, the rational dialogue) comes also the problematization of the bourgeois model of history as teleological progression. Horatio's appearance as an angel with its head turned backwards in Scene 3 suggests a possible alternative view: the Angelus Novus of Walter Benjamin's "Geschichtsphilosophische Thesen," like Hamlet in Scene 1 who stands with his back to the ruins of Europe, is driven from the catastrophe of the past and towards the future by the inescapable stormy winds of progress.[9] Yet Benjamin's angel, unlike Hamlet, flies with its back to the future, staring at the ruins of the past which it desires to redeem. It is Ophelia, who sits among the wreckage of "Trümmer, Leichen und Leichenteile" (97) in Scene 5, who takes a revolutionary stance: Hamlet, facing forward, is an emblem of historical continuity and progress; Ophelia, immobile and surrounded by the destruction of the past, herself one of the victims of conquest, oppression, and violence, calls for radical *discontinuity*, the redemption of revolution.

The fundamental opposition of two views of history, one a "Hegelian" teleology occurring, as Benjamin says, in "homogeneous and empty space," the other, perhaps, the view of revolutionary classes in history who act, as Benjamin describes, with the consciousness of exploding the continuum of history, of starting a "new calendar,"[10] is reflected in the enigmatic titles of Scenes 1 and 5. The "FAMILIENALBUM" (89) of the first scene proclaims an organic historical continuity, the continuum of generations; "WILDHARREND / IN DER FURCHTBAREN RÜSTUNG / JAHRTAUSENDE" (97), on the other hand, a fragment from Hölderlin's late work and thus itself an emblem of literary "discontinuity," expresses the imminent release of a powerful, natural force.[11] The two scenes contrast also in the occurrence of specific historical and geographical references in Scene 1 (the state funeral of Stalin, the "Stechschritt" of the East German police, the "Räte" of the Soviet socialist government; the ruins of Europe, the Prague "Spring of Communism," Denmark), and their total lack in Scene 5. There time and place are not specifically historical, but mythical: "Jahrtausende," "Tiefsee"; Ophelia is now Elektra. Thus while Scene 1 presents the (uneasy) *adherence* to the traditional bourgeois understanding of drama and history as a rational continuum of events, Scene 5, in contrast, envisions a *revolutionary, renunciatory* theater which returns to the dimensions of myth as a rejection of the models of historicism and bourgeois drama, a theater of the non-event, of non-action, of immobility, and ultimately of silence.

Scenes 2 and 4: Two Attempts to Reject a Role

The second pair of corresponding Hamlet and Ophelia scenes share certain basic traits with Scenes 1 and 5. Scene 2, devoted to Ophelia, is again characterized by historically indeterminate, quasi-mythical time and space: "DAS EUROPA DER FRAU" (91). The text quotes from two previous works by Müller: "Die der Fluss nicht behalten hat" (91) from the vision of the dying worker Hilse in *Germania Tod in Berlin*, and "Die Frau am Strick Die Frau mit den aufgeschnittenen Pulsadern Die Frau mit der Überdosis AUF DEN LIPPEN SCHNEE Die Frau mit dem Kopf im Gasherd" (91) from Lessing's speech in the final scene of *Leben Gundlings* and from the short prose piece "Todesanzeige" on the suicide of Müller's first wife.[12] Ophelia's speech, nevertheless, maintains its integrity and unity as the speech of a single voice.

The second Hamlet scene, like Scene 1, defines its location with respect to specific historical events and places in - to coin a phrase - the "Europe of Man" divided by national boundaries: Budapest ("PEST IN BUDA") and Greenland, in the title of the scene (93), stand in sharp contrast to the historically and politically unspecific "EUROPA DER FRAU" of the second scene. The Russian Revolution is evoked in the mention of Boris Pasternak's "Doktor Schiwago" (93); the monument of a hated and honored man "geschleift drei Jahre nach dem Staatsbegräbnis des Gehassten und Verehrten von seinen Nachfolgern in der Macht" (93) refers to Stalin's death in 1953 and De-Stalinization in 1956; the October 1956 uprising in Hungary is alluded to in the scene title "PEST IN BUDA" and in the first line of the scene, "Der Ofen [earlier the official name of Buda, one-half of the city Ofen-Pest] blakt im friedlosen Oktober" (93). As in the first Hamlet scene, the discourse of the scene is composed of not one, but many voices, "Wortschleim absondernd" (95) paralleling the "BLABLA" of Scene 1: "A BAD COLD HE HAD OF IT JUST THE WORST / TIME / JUST THE WORST TIME OF THE YEAR FOR / A REVOLUTION" (93) quotes and distorts T.S. Eliot's "Journey of the Magi";[13] "IM WINTER MANCHMAL KAMEN SIE INS DORF / ZERFLEISCHTEN EINEN BAUERN" (93) is spoken in Müller's *Zement* by a Russian officer and rich landowner about to be executed;[14] "Ein Königreich / für einen Mörder" (95) is based on the famous line "My kingdom for a horse" from Shakespeare's *Richard III* (V.iv.7); the final passage "HAMLET DER DÄNE PRINZ UND WURMFRASS STOLPERND / ... / KRIECHT EIN BELEIBTER BLUTHUND IN DEN PANZER" (96-97) is a direct quote from Müller's "Lektionen. Zwei Briefe."[15] Yet despite their fundamental differences, Scenes 2 and 4 are strikingly similar in theme: both deal with the renunication of prescribed roles.

Enclosed in an "Enormous Room" (91) which evokes the French prison camp of E.E. Cummings' novel,

Ophelia rebels against the oppressive role of women as objects to be used by men.[16] Three stages in the process of her self-emancipation can be identified:

(1) The suicidal Ophelia attempts repeatedly to achieve her own destruction; like the exemplary figures of the Enlightenment in *Leben Gundlings*, she is both victim and accomplice in her own victimization.[17]

(2) Ophelia refuses to continue in the project of her own self-destruction; her body once again is her own: "Gestern habe ich aufgehört mich zu töten. Ich bin allein mit meinen Brüsten meinen Schenkeln meinem Schoss" (91).

(3) Finally, Ophelia destroys the instruments of her imprisonment and oppression, the chair, the table, the bed, her home. The same three stages (or their correlates) also occur in Hamlet's Scene 4, yet while Ophelia's rejection of her prescribed role is emancipatory, Hamlet serves as the opposite example of this rebellion: his is the "bad" dialectic which results in the failed revolution. Several conspicuous differences in the action of the two scenes suggest at the outset their fundamentally antithetical nature: Ophelia leaves her prison home and goes into the streets ("Ich gehe auf die Strasse" [92]); Hamlet leaves the popular uprising in the streets and heads home ("Ich gehe nach Hause" [95]). Ophelia destroys her home which is the site of her oppression, but Hamlet, the bloodhound who crawls into the panzer to perform his duty, finally chooses to accept his imprisonment. Finally, Ophelia tears the clock-heart from her body, combining in a single image the radical revolutionary break in the continuum of history signified by the spontaneous shattering of clocks, as Benjamin describes, during the first days of the French Revolution, and also the rejection of the mechanized, robotized industrial world

presented in the final scene of *Leben Gundlings* as the ultimate end of Enlightenment ideology.[18] Hamlet, in contrast, yearns to become a complete machine: "Ich will eine Maschine sein. Arme zu greifen Beine zu gehn kein Schmerz kein Gedanke" (96).

In the first lines of Scene 4 Hamlet addresses the problem of the individual caught between two historical epochs. It is the problem of Doctor Zhivago who cries for his wolves (in *Zement*, symbol of the Cossacks and pre-Revolutionary Russia),[19] of the Magi in T.S. Eliot's poem who must journey into a new age of mankind to which they cannot belong, and of the revolutionaries of the Hungarian uprising in 1956. Müller explains:

> *Hamlet* truly reflects the situation of the intellectual in German history, a situation which seemed to change after 1945, at least in East Germany. However, in 1956 - and for me even earlier in the fifties - it became evident that Hamlet was becoming a topical character again. Quite as Brecht once defined him: The man between the ages who knows that the old age is obsolete, yet the new age has barbarian features he simply cannot stomach.[20]

Set once again in the now destroyed "Enormous Room" of the second scene, Scene 4 occurs against the background of Ophelia's emancipatory rebellion. The "leere Rüstung, Beil im Helm" (93) which completes the set is the armor of the Ghost-Father of Scene 1, "das Gespenst das [Hamlet] gemacht hat, das Beil noch im Schädel" (90), and symbolizes the traditional role prescribed for Hamlet the son: in Scene 4 he must choose between avenging his father's murder and thereby upholding the paternal (paternalistic) principle of order, or, like Ophelia, rebelling against the oppressive tradition, between an obsolete old age and a new one with new barbarism.

The Hamlet player begins by refusing to play his role; it is at once a rejection of the established political order and of the traditional dramatic category of the hero. Set and action of the Hamlet drama are described, "wenn es noch stattfinden würde" (94). Against the backdrop of the toppled monument of a man (Stalin) who made history, the popular uprising occurs. "PEST IN BUDA," "Der Ofen blakt im friedlosen Oktober. ... JUST THE WORST TIME OF THE YEAR FOR / A REVOLUTION" (93): specific reference is made to the Hungarian revolt of October 1956. Hamlet's role would be, as he describes it, "auf beiden Seiten der Front, zwischen den Fronten, darüber" (94). Once again, the dialectic of the Enlightenment raises its Janus head: like the self-destructive, suicidal Ophelia who both inflicts and suffers violence upon herself, Hamlet is both revolutionary and ruler, executioner and executed, partisan fighter and fascist dictator (Mussolini) strung up by his heels: "Ich hänge mein uniformiertes Fleisch an den Füssen auf" (94).

Again following Ophelia who in Scene 2 refuses to continue in her self-destruction, the Hamlet player subsequently sheds his costume and leaves the theater in which he, too, has continually tried to kill himself. Ophelia sits at home "allein mit meinen Brüsten meinen Schenkeln meinem Schoss" (91); the Hamlet player heads home, "einig / Mit meinem ungeteilten Selbst" (95). But the Hamlet player, unlike Ophelia whose body has been the object of abuse and whose experience of exploitation has been personal and physical, enacts a purely intellectual rebellion. While Ophelia rejects her former life in which she has done actual physical violence to herself, Hamlet rejects only a drama of the stage in which he has played opposing roles. Ophelia sits alone with her body; the Hamlet player is alone with his thoughts.

Having renounced his ambiguous role as provocateur and police in the popular uprising (reflecting the ambivalent stance of the Enlightenment intellectuals with regard to societal injustices under the despotic rule of "reason"), the Hamlet player is beset by nausea in the face of the modern capitalist world: the "Kampf um die Posten Stimmen Bankkonten," the lies and hypocrisy and poverty without the dignity of resistance and rebellion, "Armut ohne die Würde / Des Messers des Schlagrings der Faust" (95). Simple withdrawal is not a viable political position. The Hamlet player recognizes the urgent need for violent change - "Ein Königreich / Für einen Mörder," he cries (95) - yet, still the romantic bourgeois intellectual, invokes false models for a revolution. Macbeth and Raskolnikow, who kill out of purely individual motives, might be powerful heroes of bourgeois literature, yet they cannot inspire real social change. The nausea of the intellectual is not a source of revolutionary energy, but a privilege itself defended by the repressive institutions of the state: "Ich bin / Ein Privilegierter Mein Ekel / Ist ein Privileg / Beschirmt mit Mauer / Stacheldraht Gefängnis" (96); the intellectual is by definition already compromised, Hamlet is inescapably the son of a king. In an attempt to shed this role the Hamlet player renounces all activity whatsoever: "Ich will nicht mehr essen trinken atmen eine Frau lieben einen Mann ein Kind ein Tier. Ich will nicht mehr sterben. Ich will nicht mehr töten" (96). A photograph of the author appears; it is torn to shreds.

The image is particularly laden. As a parallel to Ophelia's destruction of the photographs of her lovers, it is an emancipatory gesture. In the context of Müller's postmodernist aesthetics, it points to the privileged author's paradoxical endeavor to eliminate all privilege in art, to secure the expropriation of the talented elite and, thereby, his own disappearance. Yet here, the intellectual's symbolic rejection of privilege is criticized as a possibility itself open only to the privileged. "Irgendwo werden Leiber zerbrochen, damit ich wohnen kann in meiner Scheisse. Irgendwo werden Leiber geöffnet, damit ich allein sein kann mit meinem Blut" (96): Hamlet's attempt to reject his role as son and hero, his privileged status as scholar and as prince, is doomed to fail.

At the end of Scene 4, Hamlet betrays his own revolutionary insight into the oppressive nature of his role and privilege; it is a betrayal of his emancipatory resolution *not* to kill, a resolution which would reject the traditional understanding of the dramatic hero as well as an entire historical tradition. The Hamlet player dons again the mask and costume of Hamlet and, shortly before the third crowing of the cock, like Peter betraying Christ, becomes the fool who tears away the costume of the philosopher, becomes the fat bloodhound who crawls into the "panzer" of his father's armor. "Shakespeare hat *Hamlet* geschrieben," Müller writes, "ein Trauerspiel / Geschichte eines Mannes, der sein Wissen wegwarf / Sich beugend unter einen dummen Brauch."[21] The Hamlet player, having recognized the necessity not to kill one's fellow man ("Den Nächsten nicht zu töten"),[22] casts aside his wisdom as he resumes his role. While Ophelia in Scene 2 destroys the chair, the table, the bed, Hamlet takes his father's ax and splits the skulls of Marx, Lenin, and Mao; while Ophelia destroys the instruments of her oppression, changing or redefining the nature of her relationship to her lovers and oppressors, Hamlet like a bad dialectician destroys the very possibility of the "other" as alternatives to the established order of oppression. While Ophelia's acts of destruction signal her emancipation, Hamlet's acts of murder are a betrayal of humanity. " ... [Es] ZERREISST / EIN NARR DAS SCHELLENKLEID DES PHILOSOPHEN" (97): the image draws from the sheer nihilism of the "Prolog des Hanswurstes zu der Tragödie: der Mensch" in the *Nachtwachen* of Bonaventura:

> Der Totenkopf fehlt nie unter der liebäugelnden Larve, und das Leben ist nur das Schellenkleid das das Nichts umgehängt hat, um damit zu klingeln und es zuletzt grimmig zu zerreissen und von sich zu schleudern. Es ist alles Nichts und würgt sich selbst auf und schlingt sich gierig hinunter, und eben dieses Selbstverschlingen ist die tückische Spiegelfechterei als gäbe es Etwas, da doch wenn das Würgen einmal innehalten wollte eben das Nichts recht deutlich zur Erscheinung käme, dass sie davor erschrecken müssten; Toren verstehen unter diesem Innehalten die Ewigkeit, es ist aber das eigentliche Nichts und der absolute Tod, da das Leben im Gegenteile nur durch ein fortlaufendes Sterben entsteht.[23]

## The Hamlet Scenes:
## The Failure of the Intellectual

> Mich interessiert der Fall Althusser als Stoff, nicht das Phänomen. Althusser interessiert mich, wie mich Pasolini interessiert, der Fall Pasolini, oder ... der Fall Gründgens - das Versagen von Intellektuellen in bestimmten historischen Phasen, das vielleicht notwendige Versagen von Intellektuellen. ... ein stellvertretendes Versagen. Für mich ist das immer wieder Hamlet, die Figur, die mich seit langem am meisten interessiert hat. ... das was für mich als Stoff daran interessant ist, habe ich schon geschrieben: im "Hamlet".[24]

For Müller, the figure of Hamlet who casts aside his wisdom and kills according to his prescribed role represents the type of the failed intellectual in modern Western political history. Essentially Müller draws from Brecht, who wrote in the introduction to his "Zwischenszene" for Shakespeare's *Hamlet*:

> Die bürgerliche Hamlet-Kritik begreift für gewöhnlich das Zaudern Hamlets als das interessante neue Moment dieses Stückes, hält jedoch die Schlächterei des fünften Aktes, das heisst die Abstreifung der Reflexion und den Übergang zur "Tat" für eine positive Lösung. Die Schlächterei ist aber ein Rückfall, denn die Tat ist eine Untat.[25]

The "Schlussbericht" of Brecht's scene condemns Hamlet's act of violence with biting irony:

> Und so, sorgsam benutzend Schall zufälliger Trommeln
> Den Schlachtruf unbekannter Schlächter gierig aufnehmend
> Schlachtet er, durch solchen Zufall endlich ledig
> Seiner so menschlichen und vernünftigen Hemmung
> In einem einzigen, schrecklichen Amoklauf
> Den König, seine Mutter und sich selbst.
> Rechtfertigend seines Nachfolgers Behauptung
> Er hätte sich, wäre er hinaufgelangt, sicher
> Höchst königlich bewährt.[26]

Scenes 1 and 4 of Müller's *Hamletmaschine*, like Brecht's "Zwischenszene," depict Hamlet not as hero, but as traitor.

Both scenes begin with a narration by Hamlet of the failure and catastrophe of the past, symbolized by the state funeral. In Scene 1, Hamlet observes the sheer hypocrisy of his father's funeral ceremony: the mourning crowd which forgets its grief in a second when it is filling its stomachs, the adulterous mother and murdering uncle who consummate their crime on the King's coffin. For Hamlet the world is slowly rotting, he hears "die Welt ihre Runden drehn im Gleichschritt der Verwesung" (89); the continuous passage of time, the continuity of a family, of its history passed on from father to son, are deteriorating. The Hamlet player of Scene 4, too, describes the failure of

105

the past: the monument to a man who made history represents "die Versteinerung einer Hoffnung" (93). "Die Hoffnung hat sich nicht erfüllt. Das Denkmal liegt am Boden" (93). "SOMETHING IS ROTTEN IN THIS AGE OF HOPE," Hamlet cries in Scene 1 (89); the hope has failed, the monument has been toppled, in essence history has *not* been made. Müller explains:

> The *Hamletmachine* isn't anymore simply a description of people missing the occasions and chances of history, the characteristic feature of the "German misery" - as Brecht once called it. It is about the results of missed occasions, about history as a story of chances lost. That is more than plain disappointment, it is the description of the petrification of a hope ...[27]

Parallel to the failure of history, the failure of the past, is the failure of drama which provides in both scenes the background against which Hamlet must act. In Scene 1, a series of seemingly disconnected statements, for the most part quotations, presents images of this deterioration: the dramatic hero lacks a cause to champion ("I'M GOOD HAMLET GI'ME A CAUSE FOR GRIEF"); he becomes the intellectual incapable of action ("WIE EINEN BUCKEL SCHLEPP ICH MEIN SCHWERES GEHIRN"), the clown who is ordered about ("ZWEITER CLOWN");[28] words of revolution and redemption have remained unfulfilled ("OH MY PEOPLE ..."); the underlying assumption of a coherent, teleological world is questioned ("SOMETHING IS ROTTEN"); genuine dramatic action is reduced to a symbolic image: "LETS DELVE IN EARTH AND BLOW HER AT THE MOON" (89-90). In Scene 4, the Hamlet player, who refuses to continue his role, describes the drama of Hamlet as it would take place. It is not a familiar and orthodox drama which he narrates, but rather one in which traditional forms have been distorted or replaced: the protagonist-hero does not singlemindedly pursue his cause, but rather finds himself on both sides of the front, on both sides of the central conflict; further, he likens himself to a machine ("Ich bin die Schreibmaschine," "Ich bin die Datenbank" [94,95]), producing not dramatic speech as the clear and direct expression of his will, but "Wortschleim ... in meiner schalldichten Sprechblase über der Schlacht" (95). Drama here is a schizophrenic monologue in the subjunctive mode.

Within the context of this crisis of history and crisis of drama, both scenes share a particularly striking image: in Scene 1, the corpse of the great statesman and king, hacked to pieces by his son, is fed to the "Elendsgestalten" of the crowd (89); similarly, in Scene 4 the toppled and crumbling monument of the great leader houses the poor people of the cities: "In den geräumigen Nasen- und Ohrlöchern, Haut- und Uniformfalten des zertrümmerten Standbilds haust die ärmere Bevölkerung der Metropole" (93). The masses live upon and within the ruins of the past. In Scene 1, satiated and made happy by the flesh of their king, they are not yet a revolutionary force, and Hamlet, the individual, is left to be the maker of the revolution and the protagonist of the drama. In Scene 4, on the other hand, the masses of the metropolises are the hope of the future. They are the ones to stage the popular uprising which sweeps over Hamlet, and it is they whom Ophelia addresses in her call to revolt in Scene 5: "Hier spricht Elektra. ... An die Metropolen der Welt. Im Namen der Opfer" (97). In Scene 4, in contrast to Scene 1, the masses must make their own history and their own drama; for Hamlet is left only the task of examining his own relationship as an intellectual to the suffering, revolutionary masses.

Hamlet gains in Scene 1 the fundamental moment of insight into the possibility of breaking with the oppressive continuum of history: he is reluctant

to adhere to duty and custom, to kill to avenge
his father's murder; he wishes for a world without mothers, a world without tomorrows. "HERR
BRICH MIR DAS GENICK IM STURZ VON EINER / BIERBANK" (90): Hamlet affirms not the teleological
movement of history and drama in which each event
arises necessarily out of previous events, but
the sheer fact of absurd chance, the possibility
of disruption at any moment. In Scene 4, Hamlet
brings to light the dilemma of the privileged intellectual who is committed to the abolition of
privilege: here again, he refuses to kill, yet
realizes at the same time that his refusal and
subsequent withdrawal from conflict is itself a
privilege predicated on the suffering of others.
In both scenes, the insight is betrayed, the individual fails in his revolution which is the
renunciation of his prescribed identity. In
Scene 1, the morning Hamlet has sworn away arrives,
and Hamlet's thoughts are bloody: "Auftritt Horatio. Mitwisser meiner Gedanken, die voll Blut sind,
seit der Morgen verhängt ist mit dem leeren Himmel" (90). On this new day which maintains and
reaffirms the continuity of the passage of time,
of the revolution of the globe, Hamlet rapes his
mother: the dramatic act of violence is a perverse fulfillment of the order prescribed by the
title of the scene, "FAMILIENALBUM." The son Hamlet, like the young Friedrich of *Leben Gundlings,*
grows to become the butcherous father. In Scene 4
betrayal is not a private family drama but a political act against the revolutionary masses of
the world. "ES GILT ALLE VERHÄLTNISSE UMZUWERFEN IN DENEN DER MENSCH ..." (96): Marx, Lenin,
and Mao call for the overthrow of all conditions
under which men are enslaved; Hamlet, the "BELEIBTER BLUTHUND" (97), crawls into the empty
suit of armor and splits the heads of the three
revolutionaries. The Social Democrat Gustav Noske
saved the bourgeois republic by leading the Freikorps to put down the Spartacus uprising in Berlin

in January 1919, defending his actions with the statement, "Einer muss der Bluthund werden." The intellectual Hamlet becomes the counter-revolutionary who betrays the revolt of the masses; the ice age, metaphor for capitalism, returns.[29]

A crucial aspect of the two Hamlet scenes is the fact that Hamlet's act of betrayal is each time a man's act of violence against women. In Scene 1, Hamlet rapes his mother; in Scene 4, Marx, Lenin, and Mao are naked women. Further, the act of aggression represents in each case Hamlet's acceptance of the role of the father: in Scene 1, Hamlet literally becomes husband to his mother; and at the end of Scene 4, he puts on the armor which signifies both the memory of his father and the act of revenge he is required to accomplish in his father's place. The notion of fatherhood is closely associated with a particular understanding of history and of drama in which the continuity of teleology is the supreme value and organizing principle: Hamlet stumbles "VON LOCH ZU LOCH AUFS LETZTE LOCH ZU LUSTLOS / IM RÜCKEN DAS GESPENST DAS IHN GEMACHT HAT" (96), slowly, unwillingly driven by a historical, organic necessity represented by his father towards a final, logical end. The act of violence which is the climax and completion of the action of the Hamlet drama reestablishes and reaffirms the traditional political, familial, and moral order; continuity is preserved, Hamlet fulfills his role, the rebellion is suppressed. Hamlet emerges as the reactionary defender of the old, oppressive, paternal order, the bourgeois intellectual hero turned counterrevolutionary.

The Ophelia Scenes:
The Revolutionary Gone Underground

While Hamlet is essentially the champion of the dominant, ruling tradition, Ophelia represents all the aspects of life which are necessarily and systematically suppressed to allow the imposition and maintenance of that order; she is the force held captive in the asylums of the Enlightenment state. Ophelia's rejection of her role (as lover or object of lust in Scene 2, and as mother and woman in Scene 5), her destruction of the dramatic locus which defines her being (Scene 2), and her final, absolute silence and immobility (in Scene 5) entail a rejection of the traditional drama form. While the understanding of history and of drama associated with the figure of Hamlet and the notion of fatherhood is the traditional one of organic continuity and development, the opposing view of history and drama as discontinuous, associated with the figure of Ophelia who renounces all womanhood, is revolutionary. Scenes 1 and 4, devoted to the figure of Hamlet, present the failure of the intellectual, the intellectual turned counter-revolutionary; Scenes 2 and 5, devoted to Ophelia, present the violent breaking forth of a revolutionary force long held imprisoned.

While Hamlet embodies in his act of violence the bloodhound Gustav Noske, Ophelia, "die der Fluss nicht behalten hat" (91), is the literary archetype for the Socialist revolutionary Rosa Luxemburg. "Das Wasser hat dich nicht behalten, Rosa," recalls the dying Socialist Hilse in *Germania Tod in Berlin*.[30] Rosa Luxemburg, murdered by blows from a rifle butt to the head on January 15, 1919, in the counter-revolution led by Gustav Noske, was thrown into the Landwehr Canal where her body remained unrecovered until the end of May 1919: Ophelia in "Tiefsee." If Hamlet is the counter-revolutionary and traitor, Ophelia is the woman

revolutionary who stops at nothing to achieve her
goals. She is the Spartacist Rosa Luxemburg, and
in another historical period, the cultist and
anarchist Susan Atkins of the Manson group. Ophelia's emancipatory destruction of her home in
Scene 2, in addition, draws upon the biography of
the terrorist Ulrike Meinhoff; Müller explains:

> Une ... source est l'affaire Baader-Meinhoff. Ulrike
> Meinhoff, qui était pigiste dans une revue de
> gauche d'Allemagne de l'Ouest, écrivait des articles
> contre la ligne de la rédaction dirigée par son
> mari. Une partie du groupe a décidé un jour de s'en
> prendre au "Spiegel" et d'occuper les locaux. Comme
> il y avait un mouchard, les flics sont arrivés
> avant eux au journel. Le groupe a alors décidé de
> mener l'action dans l'appartement d'Ulrike où tout
> a été cassé, les meubles vidés par la fenêtre.
> Vraisemblablement, son mari a dû tout racheter
> le lendemain, mais c'était pour elle une façon de
> rompre, de quitter une situation établie.[31]

Together the Ophelia scenes present the increasing
radicalization of the oppressed, represented by the
figure of the woman: the victim Ophelia in Scene 2,
who breaks out of the bondage of her role, destroying the prison of the "Enormous Room" which
is her home, becomes the Electra of Scene 5, the
mythical figure of pure hatred and desire for
violent revenge.[32] The Ulrike Meinhoff in Scene 2
who is freed from an established life, from home,
husband, and employment, and who goes to the
streets for what will eventually become terrorist
activity, becomes the Rosa Luxemburg and Susan
Atkins of the final scene: the revolutionary and
the anarchist who have butchered and been butchered
for their beliefs, whose hatred lives on in the "underground" of "Tiefsee" (97). Ophelia in Scene 2 sits
alone with her breasts, thighs, womb; in Scene 5 these
have become the deadly weapons for revenge: "Ich
verwandle die Milch meiner Brüste in tödliches
Gift. ... Ich ersticke die Welt, die ich geboren

habe, zwischen meinen Schenkeln. Ich begrabe sie in meiner Scham" (97). While Scene 2 presents the emancipatory awakening of the oppressed from a long period of subordination and exploitation, Scene 5 presents their violent revolution; the victims have finally turned against their oppressors, promising their deaths. In Scene 2 Ophelia destroys her home and renounces her woman's role as object for sexual satisfaction; in Scene 5 the radicalized Ophelia repudiates all birth and all growth - womanhood in general. Finally, even time and place appear to exhibit an expansion and radicalization from Scene 2 (the destruction of spatial and temporal limitations, in the form of the home and the clock) to Scene 5 (the limitless time and space of "Jahrtausende" and "Tiefsee"). The concrete experience of Ophelia/Ulrike Meinhoff in Scene 2 and the everyday realism of the chair, table, and bed are magnified and transfigured to timeless, mythical proportions in Scene 5: here the woman is the embodiment of a violent, revolutionary force which has only been temporarily contained, not exhausted or defeated. It is an uneasy ending, full of promise for future revolutions staged by the victims of history.[33]

## Scherzo and the Play as a Whole

In the course of the foregoing analyses of various pairs of scenes, something very much like a "plot" has emerged. *Hamletmaschine* deals with the failure of an orthodox position based on notions of teleology and continuity, of necessary, ineluctable progress, which has been the philosophical and political stance of orthodox Marxism from the Social Democrats before and after World War I to the Russian and East German governments after World War II. The play also signals the awakening of a new revolution as a radical break with the old view of history as a continuum. Specifically, the action of the play presents the failure of the politically engaged intellectual who betrays his own historical insight and adheres to the orthodox, prescribed roles, suppressing the rise of the new order. The play is about the conflict between counter-revolutionary and revolutionary, between man and woman, oppressor and oppressed. Hamlet in Scene 1 takes on the role of his father and rapes his mother; in Scene 2 Ophelia, representing all women, makes an end to the constant rape she has been subjected to by the men she has loved, destroys her home and takes to the streets naked. In Scene 4, Hamlet no longer desires to continue in his assigned historical, political and dramatic role, yet his emancipatory resolution collapses at the last minute; he is the archetypal intellectual and would-be revolutionary, who in the final analysis serves loyally to maintain the ruling order. Marx, Lenin, and Mao are killed; as naked women they reveal the seeds of their revolution in the experience of Ophelia in Scene 2. Hamlet as the counter-revolutionary bloodhound Noske murders the Spartacist leader and revolutionary Rosa Luxemburg at the end of Scene 4, whose body, among other corpses, appears in the "Tiefsee" of Scene 5. Yet the revolution lives: "Es lebe der Hass, die Verachtung, der Aufstand, der Tod" (97).

The broad outlines of the action of the play are fairly clear and complete without the central Scene 3, and indeed, the meaning and function of the "SCHERZO" remain, I believe, deliberately obscure.[34] The third and middle of five scenes is foregrounded by the traditional five-act form as the climax of the play. Yet in a dramatic text which shatters the conventions of the bourgeois drama form and which deals with revolution against orthodoxy, the significance of the middle scene as dictated by convention becomes suspect.

The scene is entitled "Scherzo" (92); the musical term denoting the quick middle movement of the sonata places the third scene outside the "drama" of the other four. The scene as a whole is generically unique in a number of respects: it is for the most part built upon pantomime; is is the only scene in which both Hamlet and Ophelia appear, and the only scene in which two figures speak to each other. Further, the other four scenes present Hamlet and Ophelia solemnly concerned with the nature and the demands of their identities/ roles: "Ich war Hamlet" (89), "Ich bin Ophelia" (91), "Ich bin nicht Hamlet" (93), "Hier spricht Elektra" (97). Scene 3, in contrast, is a burlesque nightmare of multiple and exchanged identities: Claudius is also Hamlet's father, Ophelia is also Hamlet's mother, Hamlet wants to become Ophelia. "Wenn man die 'Hamletmaschine' nicht als Komödie begreift," Müller warns, "muss man mit dem Stück scheitern."[35] The "SCHERZO" is, perhaps, in a very basic way Müller's "joke" on the self-serious form of the bourgeois drama which demands that the dramatic figures confront each other in dialogue pregnant with philosophical significance.[36] Müller says regarding the "Scherzo":

> ... there was to be a scene in the graveyard where Horatio, having been killed by Hamlet, appears to him as an angel. They were having a long discussion on the situation of the world. But there wasn't enough historical substance for such a dialogue; this then became separate monologues for Hamlet and Ophelia.[37]

The scene which should build the climax of the play yet virtually defies interpretation is in effect the bizarre relic of an obsolete dramatic, historical, ideological order.

The scene opens in the "Universität der Toten" (92). Dead philosophers bombard Hamlet with their books; dead women ("Die Frau am Strick Die Frau mit den aufgeschnittenen Pulsadern usw." [92]) parade before Hamlet, who watches them with the distanced view of a museum- or theater-goer. The pantomime captures the central issue of the play: the intellectual Hamlet, like the Enlightenment intellectuals in *Leben Gundlings*, has failed to adhere in his actions to the revolutionary claims of his own knowledge; the results of his failure are an endless parade of victims, like Emilia Galotti and an earlier Ophelia, honored in artistic and literary works as heroines: a system of oppression, sanctioned and defended by intellectuals. Yet here *Hamletmaschine* moves beyond the earlier *Leben Gundlings*: the dead women suddenly turn against Hamlet, tearing the clothes from his body, as Hamlet had done to his mother in Scene 1. The victims, united, revolt.

Claudius appears with the whore Ophelia out of the coffin of Hamlet the father. The merging of the usurper-uncle and the kingly father, the suicidal, virginal lover and the whoring mother, reveals the essence of the tension between the sexes played out in this scene: the male, the father, is the tyrant; the female, the mother, is the victim. In this context the temptation of Ophelia's striptease represents an attempt to lure Hamlet the son to join the oppressive, paternal tradition. At the same time, Ophelia, who now belongs to the king Claudius/Hamlet-the-father, reveals the inherent *threat* of the dominant order to the desires and integrity of the individual. Her flirtatious line "Willst du mein Herz essen, Hamlet" (92) is an actual challenge to Hamlet to reenact the brother's defiant murder of his sister and lover in John Ford's *'Tis Pity She's a Whore*, to defy the threat of the established societal order that awards the sister to another man, or the lover to a tyrannical, lecherous king.[38] It is, in essence, a call to revolt.

In Scene 1, Hamlet, reluctant to fulfill the Ghost-father's demand for revenge, yearns for a world without mothers, in which the endless chain of murder passing from fathers to sons would come to an end. Ophelia in Scene 5, renouncing all birth and turning her woman's body into a weapon of death, enacts the revolt Hamlet is incapable of. Hamlet's response to Ophelia in Scene 3, "Ich will eine Frau sein" (92), is an admission of his own inadequacy and a recognition of the woman, the victim of oppression, as the true revolutionary force. Dressed in Ophelia's clothes and wearing the mask of a whore, Hamlet must watch as Ophelia and Claudius return into the coffin; Hamlet's response to the challenge of revolution is, once again, the ineffectual response of the intellectual who merely dons the trappings of the revolutionary. Hamlet dances wildly with Horatio as Angelus Novus, the angel of history staring helplessly at the catastrophic destruction of the past, driven unwillingly but inescapably into the future; the past oppression remains unredeemed by revolution. "Was du getötet hast sollst du auch lieben" (92): the voices from the coffin allude once again to the murder of revolt in Ford's play, the revolutionary act Hamlet cannot perform; the ensuing laughter reveals the unseen flirtation between king and young woman and emphasizes Hamlet's impotence.

The scene ends with the apocalyptic image of the Madonna on a swing, her breast cancer/crab shining like a sun over Hamlet and Horatio, who stand frozen under an umbrella. The play as a whole contains a number of important Christological references: the journey of the magi to the Christ child, the ghostly (spiritual) father sending the corporeal son to complete a mission of·redemption in the world, finally, the third crowing of the cock signalling the betrayal of Christ before his crucifixion. The Christ story as that of the son fulfilling the plan of the father, and the Judeo-Christian view of history as an ineluctable, incomprehensible, divine teleology, are reflected in the Hamlet story of Müller's play. Within this context the holy mother figure of the Madonna with breast cancer, occurring in the central scene of the play, represents a radical renunciation of the divine plan of the father. Like Ophelia in Scene 5 who turns the milk of her breasts to poison, the cancerous Madonna halts the sacred teleological progression of history. Hamlet's (the son's) dance with the angel of history stops; the two figures lock in a frozen embrace.

The striking image of the rotting demise of motherhood and procreation which is, in terms of the play, the banner of revolution, quotes from the conclusion of Antonin Artaud's one-act play, "Le Jet de Sang" (1925). The mother, breastless, raises her skirts to reveal a bed of scorpions in her vagina, which swells and shines like a sun:

  LE CHEVALIER, (d'un voix terrible.)

Où les as-tu mis? Donne-moi mon gruyère.

  LA NOURRICE, (gaillardement.)

Voilà.

(Elle lève ses robes. Le jeune homme veut courir, mail il se fige comme une marionette pétrifiée.)

  LE JEUNE HOMME, (comme suspendu en l'air
    et d'une voix de ventriloque.)

Ne fais pas de mal à maman.

  LE CHEVALIER

Maudite.

(Il se voile la face d'horreur. Alors une multitude de scorpions sortent de dessous

les robes de la nourrice et se mettent à
pulluler dans son sexe qui enfle et se fend,
devient vitreux, et miroite comme un soleil.
...)[39]

The scorpions become, in Müller's play, the crab on the Madonna's breast.

The use of Artaud is highly significant. If the Hamlet figure is associated with a particular understanding of both history and drama as teleological, reflecting the ideology of the bourgeois Enlightenment, so also Ophelia. The notion of history associated with her revolt borrows clearly from Walter Benjamin's "Geschichtsphilosophische Thesen," which presents an alternative understanding of history as discontinuous, of the past as redeemable at any moment in the present. The view of drama associated with the Ophelia figure is inspired by the theater of Antonin Artaud, which rejects the logocentrism of the Western theater in favor of a ritualistic, magical language of the senses that would express the primal nature of man lying beyond the reach of discursive reason. In his "Manifeste pour un théâtre avorté" (1926-27), Artaud envisions a theater that would not produce plays as such, but would instead aim at the expression or manifestation of "tout ce qu'il y a d'obscur dans l'esprit, d'enfoui, d'irrévélé": "Tout ce qui dans la vie a un sens augural, divinatoire, correspond à un pressentiment, provient d'une erreur féconde de l'esprit, on le trouvera à un moment donné sur notre scène."[40] The theater of Ophelia, too, expressly rejects the staging of usual plays (*Hamlet*) to present instead the dark, hitherto undisclosed and uncovered side of the spirit, the prophetic meanings and insights arising out of a kind of productive madness: Ophelia, immobilized in a strait jacket of white bandages by men in white uniforms, speaks from the "heart of darkness."

"Im Rücken die Ruinen von Europa"

"The first preoccupation I have when I write drama is to destroy things," Müller stated in an interview from 1981. "For thirty years Hamlet was a real obsession for me, so I tried to destroy him by writing a short text, *Hamlet-Machine*."[41] In my analysis of the play, Hamlet emerges as the type of the revolutionary intellectual who knows what he must do (namely, not kill according to the dictates of tradition and, in not doing so, break with the established order of an historically obsolete age), yet who ultimate *fails* to act in keeping with his insight. The bloody deed required by tradition affirms the established institutions of oppression: the Hamlet player accepts the role of Hamlet, reaffirming the Shakespearean model. In raping his mother he becomes Hamlet the father, preserving the continuity of the family. Finally, the violent act makes of Hamlet the traditional dramatic hero who, in destroying others and himself, reestablishes the status quo and reaffirms the order of the world.

The figure of Ophelia, unlike Hamlet, expressly *rejects* the role required of her, as the lovelorn, suicidal Shakespearean character, and as lover or wife or woman to the dominant, violent male. A number of opposing categories emerge which delineate the central contrast between Hamlet and Ophelia: male vs. female, the intellectual (the Enlightenment) vs. the tortured body (nature), the counter-revolutionary vs. the revolutionary. The failure of Hamlet is the disintegration of the bourgeois intellectual hero; the revolution of Ophelia signifies the irrepressible emergence of a new type. One aspect underlying Hamlet's failure is the changed role of the intellectual in the modern world. Müller explained once his position regarding various alternative, "revolutionary" movements:

119

> Ich kann nicht für die Homosexuellen sprechen, das
> müssen die selber machen. Ich kann nicht für die
> Hausbesetzer sprechen oder die Arbeiter. Das müs-
> sen die auch selber machen. Ich würde durch meine
> Stellungnahme nur verzögern, dass die selbst aktiv
> werden. Die Intelligenz hier wie drüben krankt an
> dieser falschen Selbstüberschätzung. Die Rolle,
> die sie spielen möchte, spielt sie gesellschaftlich
> gesehen längst nicht mehr. [42]

Essentially the intellectual hero is no longer the representative or carrier of universal values and cannot subsume such alternative ("Ophelian") movements under the overriding, paternalistic authority of "reason."[43]

Underlying the dichotomy between Hamlet and Ophelia (and, one might suggest, between the modern revolutionary intellectual and spontaneous, alternative revolutionary movements) are two sets of ideologies: the figure Hamlet belongs to a drama based upon rational discourse which unfolds as an inescapable and undeviating movement towards a logical end; Ophelia, on the other hand, representing the hitherto suppressed, dark forces of the heart, is associated with an Artaudian theater of myth which appeals directly to the senses. Parallel to this is the opposition of two views of history: one the essentially Hegelian model of continuity and ineluctable progress; the other, the Benjaminian understanding of a radically discontinuous time in which the present can be charged with, and can avenge and redeem at any moment, the catastrophic suffering of the past. The opposing models of drama and of history present the authoritarian structure (Hamlet) on the one hand, and the possibility of an alternative reality (Ophelia) on the other, which frees itself from its long oppression. In the failure of Hamlet and in the revolt of Ophelia, *Hamletmaschine* points to the beginning disintegration of the dominant, rational, European view of the world, to the "entropy" of Europe. "The European concept of history is over," Müller states. "European politics or history is based on a Father principle, a paternal principle. I see Asia as the rising of the maternal principle."[44]

Ophelia's speech in the last scene calls for continued revolution and suggests a final pair of contrasting categories which will be of central importance in *Der Auftrag*. She speaks "im Herzen der Finsternis" (Joseph Conrad's famous novel tells of a voyage into the heart of the Congo brutally exploited by ivory companies) and "unter der Sonne der Folter" (from Sartre's preface to Frantz Fanon's powerful psychological analysis of colonialism, *The Wretched of the Earth*); Ophelia's call to revolution is addressed to the giant metropolises of the world in the name of its victims (97). It is a cry arising out of the experience of colonized peoples in the Belgian Congo and French Algeria, announcing the uprising of the Third World against the White European.

CHAPTER IV

THE EMERGENCE OF AN ALTERNATIVE DISCOURSE:

DER AUFTRAG: ERINNERUNG AN EINE REVOLUTION (1979)

> Brecht gebrauchen, ohne ihn zu kritisieren, ist Verrat.
>
> Heiner Müller[1]

*Der Auftrag* at first glance appears to return to the dramatic structures abandoned in *Hamletmaschine*: there is a cast of characters; there is dramatic dialogue, through which the conflict between the characters (their differing stances towards their project of revolution) is developed and debated; there is dramatic action, as the characters are engaged in the fulfillment of an end (or ends) central to their very identities.[2] Yet paradoxically, this apparent reappearance of familiar ordering structures is paired with inherent *ambiguity* on the thematic level. The fronts clearly and irreconcilably drawn in *Hamletmaschine* are blurred in *Auftrag*. Müller explains:

> Für mich war es nach *Hamletmaschine,* wo der Monolog sofort als Fetisch genommen werden kann und man sich selbst auch wieder dingfest und verfügbar macht, entscheidend, davon wegzukommen vielleicht auch durch eine diffuse Bewegung, die nicht an einer klaren Perspektive oder Intention festgemacht werden kann. Eine Bewegung, in einen Raum mit Fragen, für die ich keine Antworten parat habe.[3]

A diffuse movement that cannot be bound to a clear perspective or intention, a movement into a realm of questions for which there are no authorial, authoritative answers - this is all the more perplexing given the fact that Müller adopts as the overall structural model of the play the Brechtian

*Lehrstück*, just as the bourgeois drama provided the organizational foil for *Hamletmaschine*.

The theater critic Andrzej Wirth makes the valuable suggestion in his review of Müller's production of the play: "kein Lehrstück, obwohl vielleicht als Verinnerlichung und Subjektivierung eines Lehrstücks begreifbar."[4] The positions delineated in *Hamletmaschine* reappear in *Auftrag*, but are internalized and subjectivized *within a single consciousness*: Hamlet and Ophelia are conflicting poles of the woman figure of *Auftrag* (represented by Antoine's wife, the angel of despair, and ErsteLiebe) as well as of the man (again, represented by three connected characters: Antoine, Debuisson, and the man in the elevator). Thus the internalization of the didactic play: Antoine, the chorus who directs the present reenactment of a past event while interpreting, judging that event, becomes in this reenacted, remembered action one with Debuisson, the comrade who has endangered/betrayed the revolution. The didactic play becomes the self-examination of a proclaimed revolutionary who must deal with his own desire and readiness for counterrevolution. The sado-masochism which Wirth's article points to is thus not merely a psychological, but also a *political* category involving an immanent dynamic of the self-betrayal of the revolutionary intellectual.

Specifically, the play treats the failure of the *white* revolution, the revolution of the European man of reason and Enlightenment, of Danton and Robespierre. For there are two "protagonists" in the play: the demise of the traditional hero, the Debuisson-Hamlet figure who has betrayed the Ophelia, the mission of revolution, within himself, is accompanied by the rise of a new hero, the Sasportas-Ophelia who rejects all there is of the Hamlet, the white European, in himself. Here *Auftrag* develops certain issues suggested by the quotations in the last scene of *Hamletmaschine*:

Ophelia, speaking with the words of Joseph Conrad and Frantz Fanon, calls for the uprising of the Third World against the domination of the White European; in *Auftrag*, the ex-slave Sasportas continues his mission without the white man Debuisson. "It is," to quote Fanon, "a question of the Third World starting a new history of Man."[5]

## The Overall Structure of the Text

The text of *Auftrag* is a collage of dramatic scenes (the delivery of the letter to Antoine, the three revolutionaries before the caged Negro in the Jamaican harbor town, their final separation when their mission is rendered void by new events in France), burlesque numbers ("the return of the prodigal son," the "theater of white revolution"), monologues (the man in the elevator), prose narratives (the arrival of the three men in Jamaica, Debuisson's final dance and betrayal), and documents (Galloudec's letter, and the placard "DIE REVOLUTION IST DIE MASKE DES TODES DER TOD IST DIE MASKE DER REVOLUTION ..."). These various "scenes" are not marked by numbers and titles as in the *Lehrstücke* of Brecht, but may be identified and ordered as follows:

1 Galloudec's letter to Antoine

2 The sailor delivers the letter to Antoine

3 The Angel of Despair appears

4 (Narration:) The arrival of Debuisson, Galloudec, and Sasportas in Jamaica

    5 Debuisson, Galloudec, Sasportas put on their masks

        6 Curtain: "DIE REVOLUTION IST DIE MASKE DES TODES DER TOD IST DIE MASKE DER REVOLUTION"

The Theater of Revolution:

7 "Heimkehr des Verlorenen Sohnes": ErsteLiebe tortures Debuisson

8 "Theater der Revolution": Danton and Robespierre

9 Sasportas sentences Debuisson to death: the end of the theater of white revolution

10 Curtain: The elevator-monoloque

11 Debuisson releases the three revolutionaries from their mission; shedding of masks

12 (Narration:) Debuisson's dance and betrayal

Thematically and structurally, *Auftrag* is based on the model of Brecht's *Die Massnahme*. Scenes 1-3 correspond to the beginning of Brecht's play: the four revolutionary agitators have returned from their mission and report their execution of their comrade; the control chorus orders them to depict what has happened in order that the action can be examined and judged. "Stellt dar, wie es geschah und warum, und ihr werdet unser Urteil hören."[6] In *Auftrag* Galloudec's letter and the sailor who delivers it report the outcome of the revolutionary mission: the deaths of Galloudec and Sasportas, Debuisson's betrayal. Antoine, visited by these "ghosts," functions as the *Kontrollchor* which must mediate and judge the reenactment of the past events.

Scenes 4-12 are this re-membered reenactment. As a whole it corresponds to one central "episode" of the Brechtian *Lehrstück* as realized in *Massnahme* and follows the pattern:

(1) prose narration (past tense), Scene 4;

(2) dramatic presentation/recreation of the past events, Scenes 5-11;

(3) narrated conclusion (past tense), Scene 12;
(4) discussion and judgment of the control chorus.[7]

The narrated sections in *Auftrag* are the arrival of the three revolutionaries in Jamaica (in Scene 4) and Debuisson's betrayal (Scene 12), which frame a "drama" that is symmetrically structured: Debuisson, Galloudec and Sasportas put on their masks in Scene 5 (the beginning of their work in Jamaica), and remove them in Scene 11 (its official end); Scenes 6 and 10, which frame the central action of the play, are essentially commentaries on the task of revolution; Scenes 7-9 form the "play" which is performed in Jamaica by the masked revolutionaries; Scene 8, explicitly called "Theater der Revolution," travesties the great *Kampfgespräch* in the crucial middle act of the classical play. The judgment on the part of the control chorus (the fourth component of the *Lehrstück* model) is significantly *absent* in Müller's play, for both dramaturgical (the audience is called upon to judge for themselves) and thematic reasons: the control chorus Antoine is fundamentally identical to the comrade to be executed, Debuisson. Scenes 11 and 12 essentially *repeat* Scenes 2 and 3 (this is evident in the multitude of shared motifs); Debuisson's final betrayal of the revolution is thus also finally Antoine's.

Scenes 1-3: The "Auftrag" of Remembering

*Die Massnahme* begins with the call of the control chorus to the four agitators:"Tretet vor!"[8] The two dead revolutionaries in *Auftrag* return to their *Kontrollchor* and *Auftraggeber* Antoine only via the letter written by one of them on his deathbed (Scene 1). As in the Brechtian model, the exact nature of the mission remains unspecified until the first scene of the actual dramatic

127

reenactment of events; the reader of *Auftrag*, however, waits for this information for a significantly longer period of time than does the reader of *Massnahme*.

Galloudec's letter supplies only the following information: the mission has not been accomplished, Galloudec is dying, Sasportas has been hanged, Debuisson is a traitor. A number of markers establish the time period of the French Revolution: "Bürger" Sasportas, "Konvent," "republikanischem Gruss" (7); "Port Royal" is located at the mouth of Kingston Harbor in Jamaica. The mission itself has something to do with a revolution, "wenn die Völker in Blut gehn" (7). In Scene 2 the letter, delivered to Antoine by the sailor, becomes part of - a "prop" in - the dramatic action. Yet here again, essential information concerning the nature of the mission is deliberately withheld. The sailor begins, "Es ist nicht meine Schuld, wenn der Brief schon alt ist und vielleicht hat sich die Angelegenheit erledigt," then goes on to give not a statement of this "Angelegenheit," but rather a long account of the trials experienced in reaching Antoine: "Die Spanier haben uns festgehalten auf Kuba, dann der Engländer in Trinidad, bis euer Konsul Bonaparte den Frieden gemacht hat mit England" and so forth (7). And again: "Ich weiss nicht, was [Galloudec] an dem Brief so wichtig war. Etwas mit einem Auftrag. Den er zurückgeben muss, damit andre seine Arbeit weiter machen. Was immer das für eine Arbeit war" (8). The text explicitly refuses to provide the crucial information which motivates it. The central problematic of the play is reflected here in the smallest details of its discourse: one is faced with an *unspecified mission*.

What the sailor does tell, and at great langth, are the facts elaborating the deaths of Galloudec and Sasportas: Galloudec in a hospital-prison in Cuba, burning with fever, the pain coming in waves, his left leg amputated first at the knee, then at the hip; Sasportas at the gallows on a cliff, his body dropped into the sea to be devoured by sharks. But there are no details concerning the fate of Debuisson. The silence is structurally significant: it is filled by an Antoine withholding the facts of his own identity. The first speech of the scene begins with the sailor's question, "Sind Sie der Bürger Antoine" (7), and stubbornly maintains this focus: "... wenn Sie dieser Antoine sind," "... wenn das Ihr Name ist, Antoine," "... wenn Sie der sind" (7-8). Antoine is equally insistent in his denials: his first words are, in response to the sailor's long opening speech, "Ich kenne keinen Galloudec" (8); to the sailor's second speech, "Ich weiss von keinem Auftrag. Ich vergebe keine Aufträge, ich bin kein Herr" (8). Müller draws upon the Biblical motif of the thrice-made betrayal, yet the third time Antoine, unlike Peter, confesses his complicity: "Ich bin der Antoine den du gesucht hast" (9). The incomplete realization of the essentially structural Biblical motif is left ambiguous: is Antoine definitely *not* a traitor, or is he yet to become one?

The ambiguity is deliberate and is fundamental to the figure of Antoine. In his denials of his identity and his knowledge of the mission in Jamaica he is indeed on the one hand a traitor, yet also, equally, the revolutionary grown weary and cynical in the wake of events following the initial revolt and seizure of power. In this he is a figure in the mold of Büchner's Danton.[9] "Die Freiheit führt das Volk auf die Barrikaden, und wenn die Toten erwachen trägt sie Uniform. Ich werde dir jetzt ein Geheimnis verraten: sie ist auch nur eine Hure" (9). The metaphor is borrowed from Büchner: "Die Freiheit und eine Hure sind die kosmopolitischsten Dinge unter der Sonne."[10] Antoine has taken part in putting down the Vendée uprising of the peasants, he has betrayed the truly revolutionary

129

movement of the people, he is another counter-revolutionary Hamlet figure, crawling into the panzer to still the revolts in East Berlin, Budapest, Prague. Yet Antoine proudly remembers the French Revolution in a play in which it is *forgetting* that imports betrayal: "Ich war dabei, als das Volk die Bastille gestürmt hat. Ich war dabei, als der Kopf des letzten Bourbonen in den Korb fiel. Wir haben die Köpfe der Aristokraten geerntet. Wir haben die Köpfe der Verräter geerntet" (9). Upon the ruins of the failed revolution Antoine looks forward towards a future day of new reckoning: "Sieh sie dir an, mein Frankreich. Die Brüste ausgelaugt. Zwischen den Schenkeln die Wüste. Ein totes Schiff in der Brandung des neuen Jahrhunderts. Siehst du, wie sie schlingt. Frankreich braucht ein Blutbad, und der Tag wird kommen" (9). Paradoxically, Antoine remains a revolutionary while his actions label him traitor and counter-revolutionary. His difficult situation arises out of the conflict between the intellectual's moral commitment and his obligation to the reigning institutions, once again, between knowledge and power. It is the conflict central to Müller's Hamlet type who realizes the senselessness of avenging murder by murder "WEILS BRAUCH IST,"[11] yet who lacks the strength to defy the authority of the ruling traditions of the patriarchal monarchy.

With the figure of Antoine Müller reexamines the problematic of the intellectual who finally betrays his own insight. Here Brecht's "Zwischenszene" for *Hamlet* provides an important key to understanding Antoine's position.[12] Brecht's Hamlet is faced with the duty of murdering the new king Claudius, who has signed a mutually beneficial peace agreement with the Norwegian enemy. The ferryman explains to Hamlet, "Da ist kein Krieg mehr. Wir haben nachgegeben und auf den Küstenstrich verzichtet, und sie haben sich verpflichtet, unsere Fische abzunehmen. Seitdem haben wir dort mehr zu sagen als früher, wirklich, Herr."[13] War has been replaced by diplomacy as a means for resolving conflict between nations; Claudius, ushering in a new age in world politics, is clearly a progressive figure in Brecht's presentation. His people enjoy a new prosperity unknown to them in times of war:

>Hamlet: Dann sind wohl die Fischer sehr für den neuen König?
>Fährmann: Sie sagen: der Kriegslärm macht die Mägen nicht voll, Herr. Sie sind für den König.[14]

Hamlet's "menschliche[n] und vernünftige[n] Hemmung"[15] is expressed in a monologue:

>Der Handel blüht, das üppige Grab zerfällt.
>Oh, wieviel mehr anklagend, wenn zerfallend!
>Ein Handel ist nicht abgeschlossen, doch
>Den Schlussstrich ziehend, streichst du einen neuen
>Voreilig durch, vielleicht gibt's auch nacheilig?
>Jedoch ein Schurke atmet auf? Und wird
>Fast schon ein guter Mann, scheint's nicht nur, ist's!
>Und du reiss ein, was aufgebaut wird, weil's
>Auf Trümmern steht (und wächst und Früchte bringt!)[16]

The situation is strikingly similar to that faced by Antoine: business is booming in the Napoleonic regime, while the freed slaves of Haiti starve. Antoine quotes from Hamlet's monologue in the Brecht scene: "Der Handel blüht. Denen auf Haiti geben wir jetzt ihre Erde zu fressen. Das war die Negerrepublik" (9). The revolution has not been (is not) able to feed its people; what is then the duty of the revolutionary in times of a prosperous restoration, what is the duty of the revolutionary whose concern is the well-being of the masses? Along with the debauchery and philosophical bankruptcy of the revolutionaries in *Dantons Tod* Büchner depicts also the poverty and desperation of the people.[17] GalloudecDanton of *Auftrag* cries out in the "Theater der Revolution," the central scene of the action on Jamaica, "Die Guillotine ist keine

Brotfabrik" (19). Therein lies the source of betrayal: (the quote from *Hamlet* I.ii.180 is not coincidental) "Wirtschaft, Horatio, Wirtschaft" (19); the revolutionary accomodates himself to the restorative order of prosperity. "FLEISCHBERG DANTON KANN DER STRASSE KEIN FLEISCH GEBEN": the problem is a central one for Müller even in his earliest poems.[18]

Scene 2 of *Auftrag* ends with the visit of the ghosts of Galloudec and Sasportas, whose appearance signifies the delivery of an unspoken "mission." Antoine responds, "Was wollt ihr von mir" (10), repeating the words of the reluctant Hamlet in *Hamletmaschine* to the ghost of his father: "Was willst du von mir."[19] Like Hamlet, Antoine must face the choice between revolution and its betrayal. The "Auftrag" will be accomplished within Antoine's memory, as a remembering and reliving of the revolutionary past, as Antoine's private reevaluation, accomplished through the mediation of the "angel of despair," of the betrayal he lives in a time of restoration.

The angel which appears to Antoine in Scene 3 recalls the "hapless angel" of an earlier text (1975) by Müller:

> DER GLÜCKLOSE ENGEL. Hinter ihm schwemmt Vergangenheit an, schüttet Geröll auf Flügel und Schultern, mit Lärm wie von begrabnen Trommeln, während vor ihm sich die Zukunft staut, seine Augen eindrückt, die Augäpfel sprengt wie ein Stern, das Wort umdreht zum tönenden Knebel, ihn würgt mit seinem Atem. Eine Zeit lang sieht man noch sein Flügelschlagen, hört in das Rauschen die Steinschläge vor über hinter ihm niedergehn, lauter je heftiger die vergebliche Bewegung, vereinzelt, wenn sie langsamer wird. Dann schliesst sich über ihm der Augenblick: auf dem schnell verschütteten Stehplatz kommt der glücklose Engel zur Ruhe, wartend auf Geschichte in der Versteinerung von Flug Blick

Atem. Bis das erneute Rauschen mächtiger Flügelschläge sich in Wellen durch den Stein fortpflanzt und seinen Flug anzeigt.[20]

Müller's image builds once again on Walter Benjamin's Angelus Novus. Unlike Benjamin's angel, however, who is driven from the ruins of the past into a future which appears as paradise, Müller's figure is threatened, oppressed, suffocated by both past and future. The image presents the situation of the intellectuals caught between an obsolete past and a future with new barbarian features: the Magi, Doctor Zhivago, Hamlet.[21] Müller's angel in this situation of despair intermittently ceases its flight and stands buried in the wreckage of the past; time stands still, the angel waits for history: the revolutionary consciousness Benjamin describes explodes the continuum of history, redeems the past in the moment of the present. Yet the hapless angel each time recommences its flight through the rubble into the future which tortures him. Hamlet, the exemplary intellectual, reaffirms also in his actions the continuity of a history of oppression. As Müller stated in an interview: "... quand des intellectuels se résignent, c'est pire que lorsqu'ils désespèrent, dans la mesure où le désespoir est une forme active qui se traduit par le suicide ou par la découverte de quelque chose."[22] The "active form" of despair, essentially ambivalent, has two possible expressions: suicide, which, as I have argued with respect to Ophelia and the victims of the Enlightenment, in effect maintains the status quo of oppression, and the discovery of something, the revolutionary moment of new insight. In *Auftrag*, despair shows the same two faces: it is a self-dissolution, a total forgetting which essentially leaves the continuity of oppression unbroken, and, alternatively, it is the explosive promise of revolution.

The angel appears while Antoine is engaged in sexual intercourse with his wife (for Danton too, the comfort of the marriage bed provides a respite from the visions of the past which haunt him).[23] She speaks with the voice of the wife: "Ich bin der Engel der Verzweiflung. Mit meinen Händen teile ich den Rausch aus, die Betäubung, das Vergessen, Lust und Qual der Leiber" (10). With the appearance of the angel Antoine begins to "remember," the drama on Jamaica begins. The encounter with the angel of despair in Scene 3 is the playing out in Antoine's mind of the attempt to organize the Caribbean revolution (Scenes 4-11), ending finally with Debuisson's betrayal (Scene 12). Yet the angel is not only a vision of Antoine's ultimate abandonment of the revolution:

> Meine Rede ist das Schweigen, mein Gesang der Schrei. Im Schatten meiner Flügel wohnt der Schrecken. Meine Hoffnung ist der letzte Atem. Meine Hoffnung ist die erste Schlacht. Ich bin das Messer mit dem der Tote seinen Sarg aufsprengt. Ich bin der sein wird. Mein Flug ist der Aufstand, mein Himmel der Abgrund von morgen. (10-11)

Speech which is silence, a song which screams; horror which dwells in the shadow of protective wings (compare "Keep me as the apple of thy eye, hide me under the shadow of thy wings," *Psalms* 17:18); hope which lies in the last breath of life, the moment of hope which lies in the onset of battle: the speech of the angel of despair belongs equally to the revolutionary Ophelia of the last scene in *Hamletmaschine*.

"Hoffnung" and "Schrecken" have special significance for Müller as the threshhold of the new: his dictim from a note to *Mauser*, "DAMIT ETWAS KOMMT MUSS ETWAS GEHEN DIE ERSTE GESTALT DER·HOFFNUNG IST DIE FURCHT DIE ERSTE ERSCHEINUNG DES NEUEN DER SCHRECKEN,"[24] repeated in his essay on postmodernism,[25] is echoed in the speech of the angel of despair. "Messer" also is a signal word for the outbreak of a new order: "Ich bin das Messer mit dem der Tote seinen Sarg aufsprengt. Ich bin der sein wird. Mein Flug ist der Aufstand, mein Himmel der Abgrund von morgen." Sasportas will take a knife to cut a new banner into his black skin, an act of liberation from the European order. The image of the dead man who springs open his coffin draws from the earlier note on Artaud: "Artaud, die Sprache der Qual. Schreiben aus der Erfahrung, dass die Meisterwerke Komplicen der Macht sind. Denken am Ende der Aufklärung, das mit dem Tod Gottes begonnen hat, sie der Sarg, in dem er begraben wurde, faulend mit dem Leichnam. Leben, eingesperrt in diesem Sarg."[26] The Enlightenment with its ideals of rationality and reason is the coffin; the knife liberates those buried alive in this White European order, those for whom the heaven of light is a dark "Abgrund." Ophelia, too, who speaks from the heart of darkness in the name of the victims of the world, warns: "Wenn sie mit Fleischermessern durch eure Schlafzimmer geht, werdet ihr die Wahrheit wissen";[27] truth comes armed with knives. Revolution, and its betrayal: Antoine, the revolutionary and also counter-revolutionary, is visited by an angel signifying both. In this realm where there are no clear answers, he must remember, and relive, the events on Jamaica.

Scenes 4-6: The Donning of the Masks

"Wir waren auf Jamaika angekommen, drei Emissäre des französischen Konvents, unsre Namen Debuisson Galloudec Sasportas, unser Auftrag ein Sklavenaufstand gegen die Herrschaft der britischen Krone im Namen der Republik Frankreich" (11). Scene 4 presents the play's first clear statement of the "Auftrag," patterned after the four agitators' dramatic presentation of the events of their mission in Brecht's *Die Massnahme:* "Wir kamen als Agitatoren aus Moskau, wir sollten in die Stadt Mukden fahren, um Propaganda zu machen und in den Betrieben die chinesische Partei zu unterstützen."[28] The speech in Scene 4 of *Auftrag,* however, unlike its Brechtian model, is not attributed to any specific dramatic speaker(s) according to the conventions of a dramatic text: it does not follow the name of the dramatic figure who presumably would speak the text on stage. Rather, it is presented as a text of narrative prose, not spoken by one of the characters, but arising out of and unified in the single consciousness of the "narrator." In the reenacted drama of the three revolutionaries on Jamaica, this consciousness is that of Antoine. The lack of commas separating the names and identities of the three figures ("unsre Namen Debuisson Galloudec Sasportas") creates a single name of three. The three roles do not represent independent characters who interact within a dramatic world, but serve only to articulate the changing constellations within the contradictory consciousness of their *Auftraggeber* Antoine.

Thus it is not any (or all) of the three revolutionaries who describes the French Republic with such cynicism: "Die das Mutterland der Revolution ist, der Schrecken der Throne, die Hoffnung der Armen. In der alle Menschen gleich sind unter dem Beil der Gerechtigkeit. Die kein Brot hat gegen den Hunger ihrer Vorstädte, aber Hände genug, die Brandfackel der Freiheit Gleichheit Brüderlichkeit in alle Länder zu tragen" (11). These are the sentiments of the disillusioned revolutionary Antoine. The phrase "gleich ... unter dem Beil der Gerechtigkeit" reoccurs in variations several times throughout the play, spoken by ErsteLiebe ("die Gleichheit [wohnt] unter dem Beil" [16]), Sasportasrobespierre ("unter dem Beil der Gerechtigkeit" [18]), and Galloudecdanton ("das Beil der Gerechtigkeit" [19]); it is the single consciousness of Antoine that directs, and expresses itself in the various figures of the reenacted drama.

The drama itself emerges in Scene 5, growing out of the narrated account in Scene 4. The reported speech of the newly arrived revolutionaries ("Wir sagten: Das ist Jamaika, Schande der Antillen, Sklavenschiff in der Karibischen See.") is continued without interruption as dramatic dialogue: SASPORTAS: "Bis wir mit unsrer Arbeit fertig sind" (11). Scene 5 corresponds to, yet at the same time exceeds the political and literary bounds of the second and third scenes of *Die Massnahme*: "Die Auslöschung," the erasure of the identities of the revolutionaries with masks of Chinese workers, and "Der Stein," in which the young comrade, succumbing to the spontaneous feeling of compassion at the sight of the suffering workers, forgets his revolutionary mission to provide immediate, temporary help.

The three revolutionaries stand before the cage of a runaway slave left to die in the sun; Sasportas wants to set him free. Müller uses the analyses of Frantz Fanon's *The Wretched of the Earth* and *Black Skin, White Masks* to rewrite Brecht's "Der Stein," focusing on the issues of race and culture. Sasportas, unlike Brecht's young comrade, is not moved by a universal, human compassion, but is a *black* man moved by the suffering of a fellow black man. His desire is not to liberate the oppressed, but to oppress his white oppressors: "Wenn ich von hier weggehe, werden andere in den Käfigen hängen, mit weisser Haut bis die Sonne sie schwarz brennt" (12); the whips of the slave-owners will write, he promises, "ein neues Alphabet ... auf andre Leiber in unsrer Hand" (13). His is the Manichean world view of colonialists and colonized that Fanon describes: "White and black represent the two poles of a world, two poles in perpetual conflict: a genuinely Manichean concept of the world; the word has been spoken, it must be remembered - white or black, that is the question."[29] In this world the desire of the colonized natives is simply to take the places of the whites; decolonization is in their view the replacing of one "species" of men by another, "a total, complete, and absolute substitution."[30]

Yet Fanon shows that the Manichean world view of Black vs. White inevitably breaks down in the experience of violent revolution. The conclusion of *The Wretched of the Earth* is a call for the black man to leave the European model of progress and civilization, to find something different, to create a new history of a new man.[31] The earlier work *Black Skin, White Masks* also ends with the abandoning of the Manichean structure at the base of the - here psycho-existential - black problem, and the uncovering and adoption of the universality of human experience: "I as a man of color do not have the right to seek ways of stamping down the pride of my former master"; "I recognize that I have one right alone: That of demanding human behavior from the other."[32] Sasportas too will come to learn that revolution is not a matter of blacks taking the places of and mimicking their white European masters, but of abolishing masters and slaves wherever they may exist.

Müller's adaptation of "Die Auslöschung" from Brecht's *Massnahme* borrows key themes from Büchner's *Dantons Tod*: that revolution is theater, and that revolutionaries play roles. Danton:

> Ob [die Leute] nun an der Guillotine oder am Fieber oder am Alter sterben? Es ist noch vorzuziehen, sie treten mit gelenken Gliedern hinter die Coulissen und können im Abgehen noch hübsch gesticuliren und die Zuschauer klatschen hören. Das ist ganz artig und passt für uns, wir stehen immer auf dem Theater, wenn wir auch zuletzt im Ernst erstochen werden.[33]

Shortly before their execution Danton and his friends, in the face of death, share a long philosophical monologue on the vanity of life as continuous disguise and role-playing:

> Das verlohnt sich auch der Mühe Mäulchen zu machen und Roth aufzulegen und mit einem guten Accent zu sprechen, wir sollten einmal die Masken abnehmen .... Schneidet nur keine so tugendhafte und so witzige und so heroische und so geniale Grimassen, wir kennen uns ja einander, spart euch die Mühe. ... Was sollen wir uns zerren? Ob wir uns nun Lorbeerblätter, Rosenkränze oder Weinlaub vor die Schaam binden, oder das hässliche Ding offen tragen und es uns von den Hunden lecken lassen?[34]

The monologue quickly becomes a questioning of the nature of the world and of the meaning of man's life in it, culminating in an uncompromising, unshakeable nihilism: "Die Welt ist das Chaos. Das Nichts ist der zu gebärende Weltgott."[35] Brecht's revolutionaries put on their physical masks (the disguises) of Chinese workers in order not to be recognized as foreigners; under their masks they continue to function in their roles as socialist revolutionaries. Their masks do not constitute actual roles, that is, the revolutionaries do not work in factories or pull barges of rice upriver, but merely look like Chinese workers. While the use of masks in *Die Massnahme* is purely instrumental, in *Dantons Tod*, the revolutionaries realize that there is a role or "mask" they put on and must act out in the "theater" of revolution; they are only the "puppets" in a history they once believed they created.[36] Here the significance of the mask is existential: without the masks, false or vain as they may be, one is faced with the unbearable vision of nothingness, a world of chaos. In Brecht's play one puts on a mask (a disguise) yet remains oneself beneath it. In Büchner one learns that one's self is inextricably bound in a mask (a role).[37] Finally in Müller's *Auftrag*, the privileged intellectual puts on a mask (a disguise which is a role), then learns that the mask is really himself.[38]

"Nehmen wir unsre Masken vor. Ich bin der ich war: Debuisson, Sohn von Sklavenhaltern auf Jamaika" (12): Debuisson's role is a former self, one he has renounced to join with the revolution in France. It is a role which will become his real self once again in his moment of betrayal; he cries to Galloudec and Sasportas at the end of Scene 11, "Lasst mich nicht allein mit meiner Maske, die mir schon ins Fleisch wächst und es schmerzt nicht mehr" (34). The situation is different for the two others. Galloudec, who plays "ein Bauer aus der Bretagne, der die Revolution hassen gelernt hat im Blutregen der Guillotine. Treuer Diener des gnädigen Herrn Debuisson" (13), is (or was) in fact a peasant and thus in one sense plays himself. Yet Galloudec, unlike Debuisson, never becomes his role of the peasant who has learned to hate the revolution, and who is a loyal servant to his master Debuisson. Indeed, his decision in Scene 11 to break with Debuisson and to continue working for revolution on Jamaica even without an official mission is clearly a rejection of the mask he dons in Scene 5.

The black man and ex-slave Sasportas, who plays the part of Debuisson's slave, will also shed his role. "Ich werde Wald sein, Berg, Meer, Wüste," he tells the white man Debuisson. "Ich, das ist Afrika. Ich, das ist Asien. Die beiden Amerikas sind ich" (33). Sasportas, who stands for the peoples colonized by the Europeans, for the wilderness threatened by the "Metropolen der Welt" (to quote Ophelia), ultimately rebels against the authority of the white civilization embodied by Debuisson, the slave-owner and counter-revolutionary leader of the mission. Of the three revolutionaries, only Debuisson, the doctor-son of rich slave-owners, becomes his role and thereby betrays the revolution. Debuisson, the educated White European, the privileged intellectual, never knowing the experience of oppression that is the source of all revolt, can only flirt with the *idea* of revolution. The related figure of the *Auftraggeber* Antoine also earns his living giving private lessons and is knowledgeable, he says, of human anatomy (is Antoine also a doctor?): both are Hamlet figures, both intellectuals who have betrayed the revolution.

The fundamental affinity between the two white intellectuals Antoine and Debuisson is also manifested in the structural organization of the play. It is Antoine's consciousness which directs the reenactment of the events on Jamaica, and Debuisson who directs the donning of the masks, correcting Galloudec and Sasportas when they fall out of their roles. Sasportas is told, for example: "Siegreiche Revolution ist nicht gut. So etwas sagt man nicht vor Herren. Schwarze Revolution ist auch nicht gut" (13). And when Sasportas wants to save the runaway slave left in a cage to die in the sun, again it is the intellectual Debuisson who takes charge of the action, preaching the lesson of the *Lehrstück*: "Einem können wir nicht helfen" (12). If the revolution is seen as a masked play, then it is Debuisson who is clearly its director: at the end of the scene the giant Negro slave from the Debuisson plantation spits at the runaway slave, kisses his master's shoes and carries him home on his back, all according to the "stage directions" specified by Debuisson to his fellow revolutionaries (14-15).

With Scene 6 the central motif of the play, the mask, is brought to the fore in its interconnectedness with the notions of death and revolution. "DIE REVOLUTION IST DIE MASKE DES TODES DER TOD IST DIE MASKE DER REVOLUTION ..." (15). "Revolution," "mask," and "death" weave black and forth to create a thick fabric of black print in block letters. As an image on the page, the passage appears as a dark wall; with a bit of imagination, as the stage curtain of the "theater of revolution," Scenes 7-9. Indeed in Müller's own production of the play in East Berlin, the text was not spoken, but printed on a large black cloth which dropped down before the playing area. Scene 10, the elevator-monologue, might also be viewed, in terms of its physical appearance as a printed text - a long block of print, unbroken by paragraph divisions - as the final "curtain" closing the masked performance: after ("behind") the "curtain" of Scene 10, the masks are removed (Scene 11). In the East Berlin production, the monologue was spoken from behind a plain black cloth again hung before the playing area; only with the transition to the street in Peru does a figure step out before the audience.

But more is presented in Scene 6 than simply the curtain signalling the beginning of a theatrical performance. Is the text, like a screen projection, a manifestation of the epic "narrator" which announces what one is about to see? Here the title or motto of the action is reminiscent of the "lesson" of Müller's learning play *Mauser,* in which the refrain is heard: "Das tägliche Brot der Revolution ... / Ist der Tod ihrer Feinde ... das Gras noch / Müssen wir ausreissen, damit es grün bleibt."[39] Revolution means/requires a constant death. "Revolution ist die Maske des Todes": revolution is the guise of death; as Danton realizes, it is a monster who eats its own children;[40] revolution is, in a greater sense, only death. Yet the text in *Auftrag* adds the reverse formula: "der Tod ist die Maske der Revolution"; the apparent "defeat" of death is itself revolutionary. While Danton yearns for death as a total forgetting, a self-dissolution and final release, Debuisson's act of "forgetting" in Scene 12 is a rejection of death and a passionate embrace of life and beauty; for both Debuisson and

Danton, however, revolution means death. For Sasportas, in contrast, death will itself be a revolution; indeed, it is the dead who will fight the decisive battles for freedom. Sasportas says, taking leave of the traitor Debuisson:

> Kann sein, mein Platz ist der Galgen .... Aber der Tod ist ohne Bedeutung, und am Galgen werde ich wissen, dass meine Komplicen die Neger aller Rassen sind, deren Zahl wächst mit jeder Minute .... Wenn die Lebenden nicht mehr kämpfen können, werden die Toten kämpfen. Mit jedem Herzschlag der Revolution wächst Fleisch zurück auf ihren Knochen, Blut in ihre Adern, Leben in ihren Tod. Der Aufstand der Toten wird der Krieg der Landschaften sein, unsre Waffen die Wälder, die Berge, die Meere, die Wüsten der Welt. (33)

The text of Scene 6 presents, in formulas which are mirror images of each other, the two main positions regarding revolution in Müller's *Auftrag*: that of the European intellectual who has essentially grown weary of a revolution that demands the total sacrifice of his individuality and his life; and that of the slave who has suffered oppression, whose life has been, as Sasportas says, "ein täglicher Tod" (28) and for whom revolt and emancipation are to be achieved through a fight unto and beyond death.

## Scenes 7-9: The Theater of Revolution

The "theater" that is the project of revolution on Jamaica is explicitly presented as such in Scenes 7-9; the metaphor of revolution as theater takes on, within the dramatic literary work, the reality of a play within a play. One striking and underlying characteristic of the three scenes is that their "protagonist" and central focus Debuisson remains totally silent and passive throughout: the

"theater of revolution," indeed, played before
and for his eyes, is the internal recollection
and reconstruction of Debuisson/Antoine's revolutionary past. Three scenes are enacted, which
present *in nuce* the action of the play as a whole:

(1) In the "Heimkehr des Verlorenen Sohnes" (Scene
7) Debuisson/Antoine returns to reexamine his privileged origins in the plantation home on Jamaica.

(2) The "Theater of Revolution" (Scene 8) is presented as the ineffectual and intellectual revolution of its privileged leaders.

(3) Finally, the privileged white revolution is
rejected by a new protagonist for a new age (Scene
9).

In Scene 7 the Prodigal Son Debuisson returns to
the slave plantation of his parents and is met by
ErsteLiebe, the woman abandoned for the "second
love" of Revolution who embodies the privileged
life Debuisson had first enjoyed. ErsteLiebe's
realm is above all the home, the slave plantation
on Jamaica; that of the revolution, "mit der [Debuisson sich] in der Gosse gewälzt [hat] zehn
Jahre lang" (16), the streets of Paris. "Home"
and "street," as the two poles of locality which
characterize Ophelia's enslavement and emancipation
in *Hamletmaschine,* identify Debuisson's two loves
as embodiments of the two essential - and opposite - aspects of Ophelia's experience. ErsteLiebe
is associated with the propertied life of the
slave-owner; Revolution is on the other hand "eine
Hure" (16), like freedom, as Büchner's Danton
says, the most cosmopolitan thing on earth. The
clearly defined female figures of *Auftrag,* however,
are actually fluid. Revolution is in the eyes
of her rival ErsteLiebe "die Schlange mit der
blutsaufenden Scham" (16). Yet ErsteLiebe, when
she reappears in the final scene of the play as
Betrayal, is herself a snake: "Galloudec und Sasportas ... liessen Debuisson allein mit dem Verrat,

der zu ihm getreten war wie die Schlange aus dem Stein" (34); and her own "blutsaufende[n] Scham" envelops Debuisson like the red sky of dawn: "der Verrat [warf] sich auf ihn wie ein Himmel, das Glück der Schamlippen ein Morgenrot" (35).
ErsteLiebe and Revolution appear to be fundamentally related, as the one contradictory woman figure loved by Debuisson, himself the contradictory revolutionary/counter-revolutionary. I would suggest that the Hamlet-Ophelia polarity of *Hamletmaschine* is a tension contained *within* each of the two figures, male and female, of *Auftrag*: revolution and counter-revolution, emancipation and oppression, each containing in itself its opposite, stand in an essentially dialectical relationship. ErsteLiebe for example is an "*anti*-Ophelian" figure when she, in a kind of masturbatory ritual, remembers the body of her young master Victor. It is a body that enslaves her still:

> Das sind die Lippen, die dich geküsst haben.
> ... Sie erinnern sich, Victor Debuisson, an deine Haut. Das sind die Brüste, die dich gewärmt haben, kleiner Victor. ... Sie haben deinen Mund und deine Hände nicht vergessen. Das ist die Haut, die deinen Schweiss getrunken hat. Das ist der Schoss, der deinen Samen empfangen hat der mein Herz verbrennt. (16-17)

The woman's body which has loved and been used by the man is exactly that which Ophelia reclaims for herself: "Ich bin allein mit meinen Brüsten meinen Schenkeln meinem Schoss."[41] Or rather, her body is exactly that which later becomes her weapon for *destroying* her male lovers: "Ich stosse allen Samen aus, den ich empfangen habe. Ich verwandle die Milch meiner Brüste in tödliches Gift."[42] Exactly *like* the revolutionary Ophelia, ErsteLiebe seeks her own revenge upon Debuisson:

> Mit den Zähnen meiner Hunde will ich aus deinem befleckten Fleisch beissen die Spur meiner Tränen,

meinen Schweiss, meine Schreie der Lust. Mit den
Messern ihrer Klauen aus deinem Fell mein Braut-
kleid schneiden. Deinen Atem, der nach den toten
Leibern der Könige schmeckt, übersetzen in die
Sprache der Qual, die den Sklaven gehört. (17)

Debuisson, Hamlet, the man, the master, is made the slave, the victim, the woman; ErsteLiebe seeks to destroy the very body she desperately loves. Ophelia's "Gestern habe ich aufgehört mich zu töten"[43] is externalized and radicalized by Erste-Liebe: "GESTERN HABE ICH ANGEFANGEN / DICH ZU TÖTEN MEIN HERZ," she says to Debuisson (17). Yet at the same time the externally directed hatred destroys also its source. "MEIN HERZ" is both the lover Debuisson and literally ErsteLiebe's own heart; killing the other is at the same time an act of love and merges with one's own death: "JETZT LIEBE ICH / DEINEN LEICHNAM / WENN ICH TOT BIN / WIRD MEIN STAUB NACH DIR SCHREIN" (17). Thus revolution (against the male oppressor) and betrayal of the revolution (in continued desire for him) are inextricably one in Debuisson's First-Love. The dialectical (contradictory) nature of the woman-lover illuminates the immanent dynamic of Debuisson's betrayal. His privileged origins in Jamaica are a fundamental part of, and unavoidably compromise, the revolution in which he participates. ErsteLiebe who tortures her runaway "slave" provides only a sadomasochistic sexual *fantasy* of "oppression" out of which grows the intellectual revolutionary passion of the rich white European.

The senile babblings of father and mother issue from their coffin.[44] The set is rearranged, and Galloudec and Sasportas are dressed as Danton and Robespierre. The theater continues with its second and central scene, "Das Theater der Revolution" (18), played before the throne of the white intellectual Debuisson. Scene 8, occurring exactly in the middle of the three scenes (7-9) of the masked revolutionary theater on Jamaica, and also in the middle of the scenes (4-12) constituting Antoine's remembering of the past mission, presents the great dramatic and philosophical debate, the crucial and central "Kampfgespräch" of the classical play. Like the middle Scene 3 of *Hamletmaschine,* Scene 8 of *Auftrag* is a travesty of the traditional form. Sasportasrobespierre and Galloudecdanton confront each other with long speeches rich in rhetoric, yet their debate is little more than an orgiastic bout of insults and namecalling, a cruel parody of the meeting of the two revolutionaries in Act I, Scene 6 of *Dantons Tod.*[45]

> SASPORTASROBESPIERRE: ... Seht den Schmarotzer, der das Brot der Hungrigen schlingt. Den Wüstling, der die Töchter des Volkes schändet. Den Verräter, der die Nase rümpft vor dem Geruch des Blutes, mit dem die Revolution den Leib der neuen Gesellschaft wäscht. ... Hast du Revolution gesagt. Der Griff nach dem Fleischtopf war deine Revolution. Der Freiplatz im Bordell. (18)
>
> GALLOUDECDANTON: ... Seht den Affen mit der zerbrochenen Kinnlade. Den Blutsäufer, der seinen Sabber nicht halten kann. Hast du das Maul zu voll genommen. Unbestechlicher, mit deiner Tugendpauke. ... Hast du Revolution gesagt. Das Beil der Gerechtigkeit, wie. Die Guillotine ist keine Brotfabrik. (19)

The scene ends with a final paroxysm of insults:

> SASPORTASROBESPIERRE: Parasit Syphilitiker Aristokratenknecht.
> GALLOUDECDANTON: Heuchler Eunuch Lakai der Wallstreet.
> SASPORTASROBESPIERRE: Schwein.
> GALLOUDECDANTON: Hyäne. (20)

What is presented here is the hopelessly rusted mechanism of a revolution which is not the violent struggle unto death of exploited and exploiter, but the impotent and childish bickering of intellectuals. Both Danton and Robespierre are beheaded; the great conflict of two revolutionaries ends pointlessly with their mutual annihilation. The revolution of privileged intellectuals is, in essence, little more than a comic debate.[46]

In Scene 9, the black revolutionary Sasportas condemns this theater of white revolution which, with its white thoughts, is itself an oppressive, colonialist force:

> Das Theater der weissen Revolution ist zu Ende. Wir verurteilen dich zum Tode, Victor Debuisson. Weil deine Haut weiss ist. Weil deine Gedanken weiss sind unter deiner weissen Haut. Weil deine Augen die Schönheit unserer Schwestern gesehen haben. Weil deine Hände die Nacktheit unserer Schwestern berührt haben. Weil deine Gedanken ihre Brüste gegessen haben ihren Leib ihre Scham. Weil du ein Besitzer bist, ein Herr. Darum verurteilen wir dich zum Tode, Victor Debuisson. (20)

Debuisson, the former slave-owner and educated white man of Europe, is rejected as a carrier of revolution. The white revolution, a contradiction in terms, is a revolution of "tote[n] Ordnungen, in denen der Rausch keinen Platz hat"; it is a "Revolution ohne Geschlecht" (20-21), a stale intellectual experiment which neither grows out of nor redeems the real experience of oppression, indeed, which itself suppresses the powerful natural forces of life.

The sentencing and final execution of Debuisson are carried out as a process of his dispossession; even the flesh and blood of his body, Sasportas claims, are the possessions of the privileged, based on the poverty of others:

> Liebst du diese Frau. Wir nehmen sie, damit du leichter stirbst. Wer nicht besitzt stirbt leichter.

> Was gehört dir noch. ... Deine Haut. Wem hast du
> sie abgezogen. Dein Fleisch unser Hunger. Dein Blut
> leert unsre Adern. Deine Gedanken, wie. Wer schwitzt
> für eure Philosophien. Noch dein Harn und deine
> Scheisse sind Ausbeutung und Sklaverei. Von deinem
> Samen nicht zu reden: Destillat aus toten Leibern.
> Jetzt gehört dir nichts mehr. Jetzt bist du nichts.
> Jetzt kannst du sterben. Grabt ihn ein. (21)

The scene is based on Brecht's *Das Badener Lehrstück vom Einverständnis,* in which a downed pilot and his crew, who have forgotten their mission for humanity in their race to fly ever higher and faster, are taught to accept the necessity of their deaths. "Wir haben nicht viel Zeit. / Wir können nicht mehr viel lernen," the fallen fliers object. The "Gelernte Chor" answers: "Habt ihr wenig Zeit / Habt ihr Zeit genug / Denn das Richtige ist leicht."[47] The fliers listen to a number of commentaries teaching the proper attitude towards death: the philosopher ("der Denkende") overcomes the great storm by giving up his plane and his coat and lying on the ground "in seiner kleinsten Grösse"; the fliers are told they can overcome death "wenn ihr das Sterben kennt und einverstanden seid mit dem Sterben. Wer aber den Wunsch hat, einverstanden zu sein, der hält bei der Armut. An die Dinge hält er sich nicht! ... Auch an das Leben hält er sich nicht. ... Auch an die Gedanken hält er sich nicht ..."[48] While his crew members are able to attain the "kleinste Grösse," the young flier alone continues to insist on his individuality and his individual greatness:

> Aber ich habe mit meinem Fliegen
> Meine grösste Grösse erreicht.
> Wie hoch immer ich flog, höher flog
> Niemand.
> Ich wurde nicht genug gerühmt, ich
> Kann nicht genug gerühmt werden
> Ich bin für nichts und niemand geflogen.
> Ich bin für das Fliegen geflogen.

> Niemand wartet auf mich, ich
> Fliege nicht zu euch hin, ich
> Fliege von euch weg, ich
> Werde nie sterben.[49]

The young flier is forced to give up his plane, and is exiled "in das Nichts," while the crew members who have accepted their death are asked to continue their work for mankind: "Richtet euch also sterbend / Nicht nach dem Tod / Sondern übernehmt von uns den Auftrag / Wieder aufzubauen unser Flugzeug."[50]

The parallels with Scene 9 of *Auftrag* are clear. The unique and privileged individuals Debuisson and the young flier are unable or unwilling to renounce their uniqueness and privilege in death. "Wer nicht besitzt stirbt leichter," Sasportas says (21); Debuisson and the flier, possessing much, must suffer their deaths as dispossession. Galloudec and Sasportas, on the other hand, like the crew members of Brecht's play, will continue their mission through their deaths. One important difference between the scenes by Brecht and Müller illuminates Müller's concern: while an outspoken didactic intent inspires Brecht's *Lehrstück*, what is instead of essence in Müller's Scene 9 is the pressing time of revolution: "... unsre Schule ist die Zeit, sie kommt nicht wieder und kein Atem für Didaktik, wer nicht lernt stirbt auch" (21). The ideology of the white revolutionary, beyond correction, is rejected completely by the black man. The task at hand is simply that of execution, not education. Where Brecht presents essentially a dialectical process of rational discourse in which the fliers, gaining insight into and thus overcoming their deaths, are allowed to continue their humanitarian mission, Scene 9 of *Auftrag* articulates an almost rigid opposition: on the one hand Debuisson, the white revolution, impotent reason, individuality, life; on the other, Sasportas, the black revolution, the sexuality of "Rausch" and "Geschlecht," the collective cause, death.


Scene 10: A "Walk into Oblivion"

The anachronistic tenth scene breaks the dramatic "continuity" of the text to restate in the single, unbroken monologue of a modern bureaucratic official the central problematic of the play: the ineffectuality, the failure of the white European in his attempts to complete a mission of great humanitarian importance. Like the young flier in the *Badener Lehrstück,* and like Debuisson in the last scene of the play, the official is left only to walk "weiter in die Landschaft, die keine andere Arbeit hat als auf das Verschwinden des Menschen zu warten" (26) - the exile "in das Nichts."

The Kafkaesque monologue begins in an elevator; the petty official is on his way to the head official's office to receive, he assumes, an important assignment. That this is, within the context of the play, a specifically European situation, is suggested by the fact that the thoughts expressed in the text of the monologue adhere (almost satirically) to the familiar formulas of deductive logic. The official constantly draws "rational" conclusions based on his observations: "Einige von [den Männern im Fahrstuhl] scheinen miteinander bekannt zu sein. Sie reden leise über etwas ..." (21); "Immerhin muss ihr Gespräch mich abgelenkt haben: beim nächsten Halt lese ich auf dem Etagenanzeiger ... die Zahl Acht" (21-22); "Es muss ein wichtiger Auftrag sein, warum sonst lässt [der Chef] ihn nicht durch einen Untergebenen erteilen" (22). His speech is steeped in the vocabulary of reason: "Ein schneller Blick auf die Uhr *klärt* mich *unwiderlegbar* über die *Tatsache auf* ..." (22, emphasis mine). A problematic situation is dealt with through a reasoned analysis of the consequences of all possible actions to be taken:

> Schnell überdenke ich meine Lage: ich kann beim nächsten möglichen Halt aussteigen und die Treppe hinunterlaufen, drei Stufen auf einmal, bis zur vierten Etage. Wenn es die falsche Etage ist, bedeutet das natürlich einen vielleicht uneinholbaren Zeitverlust. Ich kann bis zur zwanzigsten Etage weiterfahren und, wenn sich das Büro des Chefs dort nicht befindet, zurück in die vierte Etage, vorausgesetzt der Fahrstuhl fällt nicht aus, oder die Treppe hinunterlaufen (drei Stufen auf einmal), wobei ich mir die Beine brechen kann oder den Hals, gerade weil ich es eilig habe. (22)

It is only a small step further to the outright parodying of this appeal to science and reason in the face of absurdity:

> Mit einem Grauen, das in meine Haarwurzeln greift, sehe ich auf meiner Uhr, von der ich den Blick jetzt nicht mehr losreissen kann, die Zeiger mit zunehmender Geschwindigkeit das Zifferblatt umkreisen, so dass zwischen Lidschlag und Lidschlag immer mehr Stunden vergehn. Mir wird klar, dass schon lange etwas nicht gestimmt hat: mit meiner Uhr, mit diesem Fahrstuhl, mit der Zeit. Ich verfalle auf wilde Spekulationen: die Schwerkraft lässt nach, eine Störung, eine Art Stottern der Erdrotation, wie ein Wadenkrampf beim Fussball. Ich bedaure, dass ich von Physik zu wenig weiss, um den schreienden Widerspruch zwischen der Geschwindigkeit des Fahrstuhls und dem Zeitablauf, den meine Uhr anzeigt, in Wissenschaft auflösen zu können. Warum habe ich in der Schule nicht aufgepasst. Oder die falschen Bücher gelesen: Poesie statt Physik. (23)

Indeed, the official's perverse repetition of the fact that he privately refers to the head official as "Number One," and also the repeated punning on the "Fahrlässigkeit" of the young official travelling in an elevator run amok, indicate that we are dealing with a piece of comedy.

The humor, of course, is a profound effect. The world with which the official must deal is full of uncertainty. The unknown, unknowable facts begin with the very first sentence: "Ich stehe zwischen Männern, die mir unbekannt sind" (21). The official does not understand what they are talking about: "Sie reden leise über etwas, wovon ich nichts verstehe" (21). He has an appointment with the head official, but he does not know whether his office is on the fourth or on the twentieth floor. He believes, but he is not sure, that he is to be given some important assignment. His situation is made even more precarious by the apparent bracketing of the laws of nature which govern the world: the elevator travels more and more slowly while time, measured by the sweep of the hands of a wristwatch, passes with increasing speed. In such a world the official has no secure hold: reason and science fail to explain the anomalies of experience.

Furthermore, and here radically *differing* from the situation of the revolutionaries on Jamaica, the mission to save the world from destruction is never received. The official, the intellectual locked within the machinery of bureaucracy, who is also a Hamlet with a problematic task to fulfill, is faced with the added difficulty that no ghost appears to tell him of the task expected of him. The "Auftrag" remains buried with the father:

> Wie erfüllt man einen unbekannten Auftrag. Was kann mein Auftrag sein in dieser wüsten Gegend jenseits der Zivilisation. Wie soll der Angestellte wissen, was im Kopf des Chefs vorgeht. Keine Wissenschaft der Welt wird meinen verlorenen Auftrag aus den Hirnfasern des Verewigten zerrn. Mit ihm wird er begraben, das Staatsbegräbnis, das vielleicht jetzt schon seinen Gang nimmt, garantiert die Auferstehung nicht. (26)

The "Staatsbegräbnis" is a direct reference to *Hamletmaschine,* where the state funeral is that of the king Hamlet but also that of Stalin. The predicament of the official is in part that of the (Marxist) intellectual in a post-Stalinist era.[51] Leaving the elevator and finding himself suddenly, inexplicably, on a dusty street in Peru, he alone must define his mission, if there is to be one, in the unfamiliar Third World.

Two men approach; one is black, symbolizing the oppressed victims of the world who find their spokesperson in Ophelia, the other of silver, a machine symbolizing the final withdrawal from and betrayal of humanity (the Hamlet player: "Ich will eine Maschine sein").[52] The two men represent the two poles defining the experience of the white intellectual: on the one hand, the potential revolution of the Third World, on the other, the counter-revolution against humanity. The official feels fear at their approach, then is disappointed that they do not kill him: "Der Silberne geht hinter mir vorbei dem Schwarzen nach. Meine Angst verfliegt und macht einer Enttäuschung Platz: ich bin nicht einmal ein Messer wert oder den Würgegriff von Händen aus Metall" (25-26). Underlying the enigmatic encounter with the two men is once again the situation of the *Lehrstück:* in *Die Massnahme* by Brecht, and in Müller's *Mauser,* the young comrade who has betrayed the revolution comes to recognize the necessity of his own execution for the sake of the continuing revolution. In *Auftrag* the moment of "Einverständnis" is changed: the comrade (Debuisson) will ask to be killed *before* he betrays the revolution, to prevent himself from giving in to the temptation of counter-revolution which is the temptation of life, and his comrades will refuse to comply. The judgment of the collective is withheld; or rather, there is no longer an authoritative collective which defines the "correct" revolutionary position and passes judgment on the erring individual. In Scene 10 the official in Peru who is not killed by his strange "comrades" is left, like Debuisson at the end of Scene 11, to enact his betrayal.

"Etwas wie Heiterkeit breitet sich in mir aus, ich nehme die Jacke über den Arm und knöpfe das Hemd auf: mein Gang ist ein Spaziergang" (26). The walk "in die Landschaft, die keine andere Arbeit hat als auf das Verschwinden des Menschen zu warten" (26) is like the young flier's exile "in das Nichts" in the *Badener Lehrstück*; both the official and the young flier, unable to die, are no longer part of the process of revolution. Four situations, opportunities for action, four possible "Aufträge" arise. The dog with a human hand in its mouth, the young men with threatening mien, the woman with outstretched arms, the children building a steam locomotive: the enigmatic images suggest crime committed or to be committed, loneliness and desperation, ignorance and futility. The official each time does nothing. He does not accept the hidden task implied in each of the situations, but walks casually, happily on, unengaged.

The monologue ends with a difficult image: "Irgendwann wird DER ANDERE mir entgegenkommen, der Antipode, der Doppelgänger mit meinem Gesicht aus Schnee. Einer von uns wird überleben" (27). The walk into oblivion (obliviousness), the choice of life, is ultimately threatened by the rise of a vengeful, opposing force. Müller draws here, I believe, from Fanon's analysis of the particular psychology of the colonized: the black man recognizes himself as black (as having black skin), yet feels, according to the cultural code of the colonial situation in which he has grown up, that one is "black" to the extent that one is immoral, ugly, malicious. "If I order my life like that of a moral man, I simply am not a Negro. ... Color is nothing, I do not even notice it, I know only one thing, which is the purity of my conscience and the whiteness of my soul. 'Me white like snow,' the other said."[53] According to Fanon, the victimization of the black man by white civilization lies essentially in this betrayal: that the black man is made "white" by the colonial culture, yet the color of his skin remains black. The white European in Scene 10 of *Auftrag* walks towards the inevitable, final confrontation with "THE OTHER" made in his own image; it will be the final day of reckoning when the counter-revolutionary, the white intellectual who has betrayed his fellow man, must come to terms with the anger and violence of those he has betrayed.

### Scenes 11-12: "Das Schauspiel ist zu Ende": The Betrayal of Forgetting

Debuisson, who directed the donning of the masks and the beginning of the revolutionary work on Jamaica in Scene 5, announces in Scene 11 the end of the "Schauspiel" and the shedding of the masks:

> Die Regierung, die uns den Auftrag erteilt hat, hier auf Jamaika einen Sklavenaufstand zu organisieren, ist nicht mehr im Amt. Der General Bonaparte hat das Direktorium aufgelöst mit den Bayonetten seiner Grenadiere. Frankreich heisst Napoleon. Die Welt wird was sie war, eine Heimat für Herren und Sklaven. ...
> (Zerreisst das Papier.) Ich entlasse uns aus unserm Auftrag. Dich, Galloudec, den Bauern aus der Bretagne. Dich, Sasportas, den Sohn der Sklaverei. Mich, Debuisson
>
> SASPORTAS (leise): Den Sohn der Sklavenhalter
>
> DEBUISSON: Jeden in seine eigne Freiheit oder Sklaverei. Unser Schauspiel ist zu Ende ... (27)

The scene corresponds to Scene 6, "Der Verrat," from *Die Massnahme:* there the young comrade insists on calling the workless masses to rebellion, although his fellow agitators warn him of a trap. The misery of the masses is too much for the young comrade to bear:

> DER JUNGE GENOSSE: So frage ich: dulden die Klassiker, dass das Elend wartet?
>
> DIE DREI AGITATOREN: Sie sprechen von Methoden, welche das Elend in seiner Gänze erfassen.
>
> DER JUNGE GENOSSE: Dann sind die Klassiker also nicht dafür, dass jedem Elenden gleich und sofort und vor allem geholfen wird?
>
> DIE DREI AGITATOREN: Nein
>
> DER JUNGE GENOSSE: Dann sind die Klassiker Dreck, und ich zerreisse sie; denn der Mensch, der lebendige, brüllt, und sein Elend zerreisst alle Dämme der Lehre. Darum mache ich jetzt die Aktion, jetzt und sofort; denn ich brülle und ich zerreisse die Dämme der Lehre.
> (Er zerreisst die Schriften.) [54]

The young comrade will betray their revolutionary mission also by tearing the mask which was to protect his identity as a Russian agent:

> Warum jetzt noch schweigen?
> Wenn sie nicht wissen, dass sie Freunde haben
> Wie sollen sie da sich erheben?
> Darum trete ich vor sie hin
> Als der, der ich bin, und sage, was ist.
> (Er nimmt die Maske ab und schreit:)
> Wir sind gekommen, euch zu helfen.
> Wir kommen aus Moskau.
> (Er zerreisst die Maske.) [55]

It is interesting that, while in Brecht the traitor is the comrade who destroys the writings of the classical teachers (Marx and Lenin) and who breaks with the Party as embodied by the majority of three agitators, in Müller's *Auftrag* Debuisson's betrayal lies in his *adherence* to the supposed "Party" represented by the reigning forces in a distant France. While in *Massnahme* those comrades are loyal who urge restraint from action because of unfavorable political circumstances, in *Auftrag* this same restraint is exactly what makes Debuisson a counter-revolutionary. In *Massnahme* the young comrade who is moved by the plight of the masses and places this misery above all other considerations thereby betrays the revolutionary mission: in *Auftrag*, this same motivation makes of Galloudec and Sasportas the true revolutionaries. Underlying the distance between the two texts is the real experience and history of socialism in Germany, but also the crucial new factor of the Third World which cannot follow in its revolution the formulas of Europe.

Debuisson justifies his position with Dantonesque broodings on the inherently treacherous nature of revolution: "Vielleicht habe ich wirklich gewartet auf diesen General Bonaparte. So wie halb Frankreich auf ihn gewartet hat. Revolution macht müde, Galloudec. Im Schlaf der Völker stehn die Generäle auf und zerbrechen das Joch der Freiheit, das so schwer zu tragen ist" (28). Like Danton, Debuisson feels the powerlessness of the individual, the inefficacy of the human will in the process of history; man is no longer master of his own actions, but a plaything of historical forces: "Dein Tod heisst Freiheit, Sasportas, dein Tod heisst Brüderlichkeit, Galloudec, mein Tod heisst Gleichheit. Es ritt sich gut auf ihnen, als sie noch unsre Gäule gewesen sind, der Wind von morgen um die Schläfe. Jetzt weht der Wind aus gestern. Die Gäule sind wir" (31). Both revolutionaries succumb to a hopeless resignation: for Danton "die Welt ist das Chaos. Das Nichts ist der zu gebärende Weltgott."[56] Debuisson too looks toward the final end of the world and of the vain hopes of man:

> Vielleicht ist der Stern schon auf dem Weg aus den
> Kälten des Weltraums, ein Klumpen Eis oder Metall,
> der das endgültige Loch in den Boden der Tatsachen
> schlägt, auf dem wir immer neu unsre gebrechlichen
> Hoffnungen pflanzen. Oder die Kälte selber, die
> unsre Gestern und Morgen zum ewigen Heute friert.
> (31)

It is significant that both Galloudec and Sasportas *do not understand* the arguments of the intellectual Debuisson: GALLOUDEC: "Das geht mir zu schnell, Debuisson. Ich bin ein Bauer, ich kann so schnell nicht denken" (27); SASPORTAS: "Ich glaube, ich verstehe dich auch nicht, Debuisson. Nicht mehr" (28). The peasant and the ex-slave see only the fact of the work they have accomplished, the fact of the misery of the people of Jamaica who are ready for revolt: "Sie sind bereit zu töten und zu sterben für dein JOCH DER FREIHEIT, von dem sie geträumt haben ihr Leben lang, das ein täglicher Tod ist, wie von einer unbekannten Geliebten" (28). Philosophical reflections on the nature of revolution are irrelevant, "Sie fragen nicht nach der Beschaffenheit ihrer Brüste oder nach der Jungfräulichkeit ihrer Scham" (28). Galloudec and Sasportas, like the members of the flight crew in the *Badener Lehrstück*, will continue to carry out their mission, accepting the inevitability of their deaths. Debuisson and Antoine on the other hand, like the young flier, are condemned to the death of life without an "Auftrag." The flight crew says to the pilot:

> Du bist aus dem Fluss gefallen, Mensch.
> Du bist nicht im Fluss gewesen, Mensch.
> Du bist zu gross, du bist zu reich.
> Du bist zu eigentümlich.
> Darum kannst du nicht sterben.

The chorus adds: "Aber / Wer nicht sterben kann / Stirbt auch."[57] In Scene 11 of *Auftrag* Galloudec quotes from the Brecht passage to the lone traitor Debuisson: "Sterben müssen wir alle, Debuisson.

Und das ist alles, was wir noch gemeinsam haben. Nach dem Massaker in Guadeloupe haben sie in der Mitte von einem Leichenhaufen, alle schwarz, einen Weissen gefunden, der genauso tot war. Das kann dir jedenfalls nicht mehr passieren, Debuisson. Du bist heraus" (33-34). The white intellectual betrays his humanity by isolating himself from the "flow" of history. He is "zu gross ... zu reich ... zu eigentümlich," he is a privileged being, he has no mission, he does not die.

The difference between the one man who will not go on with the revolution and the two who will is for Brecht the difference between the individualist and those who can overcome the immediate claims of their individuality to act for a collective cause; for Müller, it is the difference between Europe and the Third World, between the oppressors and the oppressed, the conquerors of the world and their victims. "Solange es Herren und Sklaven gibt, sind wir aus unserm Auftrag nicht entlassen" (28); Sasportas attains the universal perspective of the oppressed regarding oppression which Fanon calls for at the end of *Black Skin, White Masks*:

> I as a man of color do not have the right to seek ways of stamping down the pride of my former master. I have neither the right nor the duty to claim reparation for the domestication of my ancestors.
>
> I find myself suddenly in the world and I recognize that I have one right alone: That of demanding human behavior from the other.
>
> I, the man of color, want only this: That the tool never possess the man. That the enslavement of man by man cease forever.[58]

The revolt of the slaves on Jamaica against their masters has its legitimacy not in the revolutionary mission authorized by a group of men in Paris, but in the universal human imperative that oppression be eliminated wherever it occurs. For the slaves on Jamaica, the revolt against enslavement means also breaking with the leadership and ideological rule of Europe. The ex-slave Sasportas will continue without the European Debuisson, the Jamaican revolt will occur without, or indeed *against,* the model of the French Revolution:

> Zehntausend Männer warten auf unsern Befehl. ... Was geht diese Männer Paris an, ein ferner Steinhaufen, der eine kurze Zeit lang die Metropole ihrer Hoffnung war, was Frankreich, ein Land, in dem die Sonne nicht töten kann, wo das Blut die Farbe des Morgenrots hatte eine kurze Zeit lang, auf einem bleichen Kontinent hinter dem Grab von Atlantis. (28-29)

Sasportas cuts a new banner into the palm of his black hand to replace that of the French Revolution: "Du hast mir eine Fahne zerrissen. Ich will mir eine neue schneiden aus meinem schwarzen Fell" (33). The banner carved into black flesh is the banner of the oppressed. "Ich gehe in den Kampf, bewaffnet mit den Demütigungen meines Lebens" (33). Sasportas' words echo those of Ophelia who destroys the home which was the scene of her own oppression: "Ich gehe auf die Strasse, gekleidet in mein Blut."[59] Sasportas' emancipation from the European Debuisson, like Ophelia's emancipation from the men who have used her body, both under the banner of their own blood, is the coming of age of the victims of the world. Fanon writes in the conclusion of *The Wretched of the Earth:*

> It is a question of the Third World starting a new history of Man, a history which will have regard to the sometimes prodigious theses which Europa has put forward, but which will also not forget Europe's crimes .... So, comrades, let us not pay tribute to Europe by creating states, institutions, and societies which draw their inspiration from her. Humanity is waiting for something from us other than such an imitation ....

... we must turn over a new leaf, we must work out new concepts, and try to set afoot a new man.[60]

The Third World finds itself and speaks to itself, Sartre says, through the voice of Frantz Fanon;[61] in the works of Heiner Müller the Third World finds itself for the first time in the figure of Sasportas, who speaks in the spirit of Fanon.

With Scene 11 the play comes full circle: Debuisson of Scene 11 and Antoine of Scene 2 merge into a single figure. Their identity is established through the large number of parallels in their speeches. Both speak, for example, of the end of the republic and the new military rule in France, and of the expansionist wars undertaken by Napoleon: "Die Revolution hat keine Heimat mehr" (30); "Frankreich ist keine Republik mehr" (9). The French economy prospers under the Restoration regime: "Der Handel blüht" (9,30), while the revolution of the slaves on Haiti has ended in failure. The two European intellectuals speak of the seductive treachery of revolution: "... aus der Bastille in die Conciergerie, der Befreier wird Gefängniswärter. TOD DEN BEFREIERN heisst die letzte Wahrheit der Revolution" (30); "Die Freiheit führt das Volk auf die Barrikaden, und wenn die Toten erwachen trägt sie Uniform" (9). And both, confronted by the men, Galloudec and Sasportas, who have known oppression and who are willing to die for their freedom, respond: "Was wollt ihr von mir" (10,32). Their total sacrifice is something which the intellectual cannot himself bring to bear; he distances himself from the revolutionaries and their death: "Sterbt euern eignen Tod" (32); "Willst du, dass ich mich danebenhänge" (10). The intellectual laughs at his former revolutionary idealism: freedom, after all, is only a whore (9,32). "Ich will mein Stück vom Kuchen der Welt. Ich werde mir mein Stück herausschneiden aus dem Hunger der Welt. Ihr, ihr habt kein Messer," Debuisson says (33). The intellectual retreats to his privileged status. Antoine: "Ihr denkt, mir geht es gut, wie. Habt ihr Hunger. Da. (Wirft Essen auf den Toten.)" (10).

Debuisson tells Galloudec and Sasportas of his dream from the previous night: like the official on a street in Peru, he walks through New York City in a rundown neighborhood uninhabited by whites. Before him on the sidewalk a golden snake raises its head; he crosses the street, and on the other sidewalk a shining blue snake appears. "Ich wusste im Traum: die goldene Schlange ist Asien, die blaue Schlange, das ist Afrika" (32). The dream presents in its imagery the rise of enclaves of the Third World *within* the centers themselves of Western civilization; "Peru" is also in the middle of a metropolis.[62] Debuisson continues:

> Und ich hörte eine Stimme sagen: SIEHE EIN GROSSES ERDBEBEN GESCHAH DENN DER ENGEL DES HERRN KAM VOM HIMMEL HERAB TRAT HINZU UND WÄLZTE DEN STEIN VON DER TÜR UND SETZTE SICH DRAUF UND SEINE GESTALT WAR WIE DER BLITZ UND SEIN KLEID WEISS WIE DER SCHNEE. (32)

The passage is a quote from the Book of Matthew: "Suddenly there was a violent earthquake; an angel of the Lord descended from Heaven; he came to the stone and rolled it away, and sat himself down on it. His countenance was like lightning, and his raiment white as snow" (Matthew 28:2-3). The tomb is empty; the followers of Jesus of Nazareth will discover that he has risen from the dead. The resurrection recalls the passage from the official's monologue in Scene 10: "Wie soll der Angestellte wissen, was im Kopf des Chefs vorgeht. Keine Wissenschaft der Welt wird meinen verlorenen Auftrag aus den Hirnfasern des Verewigten zerrn. Mit ihm wird er begraben, das Staatsbegräbnis, das vielleicht jetzt schon seinen Gang nimmt, garantiert die Auferstehung nicht" (26). In Scene 11, the impossible occurs in a dream: the dead "Chef" rises, the great task at hand will finally be revealed. Yet like the official in Peru who walks away from situations which call for action, Debuisson no longer wants any part of an "Auftrag" on behalf of humanity: "Ich will das alles nicht mehr wissen" (32). Antoine, too, confronted with the ghosts of Galloudec and Sasportas, wants to forget: "Geht. Geht weg. Verschwindet. Sag du es ihnen, Frau. Sag ihnen, sie sollen weggehn, ich will sie nicht mehr sehn" (10). Their betrayal is clear, Hamlet once again withdraws from the revolution.

The fundamental affinity - indeed, the striking similarity - between Debuisson and Antoine suggests that it is Antoine who reenacts his *own* betrayal in and through the remembered figure of Debuisson; Debuisson's final embrace of Betrayal in Scene 12 is also simultaneously Antoine's. The Angel of Despair who appears to Antoine "während des Beischlafs" in Scene 3 brings him, she says, "den Rausch ... die Betäubung, das Vergessen, Lust und Qual der Leiber" (10). Her promise is finally fulfilled in the last scene of the play, in Debuisson's encounter with the angel of Betrayal. Debuisson's union with "seiner ersten Liebe ... die der Verrat war" (34) takes the form of a wild ecstatic dance ("Rausch") which his body cannot resist. Debuisson opens his eyes, the beauty of the woman banishes all memories of the revolution ("die Betäubung, das Vergessen"): he forgets the storming of the Bastille, the end of the Gironde, Marat's assassination, the execution of Robespierre. And as the last memory fades, the two bodies meet; the betrayal is accomplished in the "Lust und Qual der Leiber":

> Debuisson griff nach der letzten Erinnerung, die ihn noch nicht verlassen hatte: ein Sandsturm vor Las Palmas, Grillen kamen mit dem Sand aufs Schiff und begleitete die Fahrt über den Atlantik. Debuisson duckte sich gegen den Sandsturm, rieb sich den Sand aus den Augen, hielt sich die Ohren wegen den Gesang

der Grillen zu. Dann warf der Verrat sich auf ihn
wie ein Himmel, das Glück der Schamlippen ein Morgenrot. (35)

The "control chorus" Antoine, who directs the "Lehrstück" of remembered, reconstructed action within his own consciousness, merges with the "young comrade" Debuisson as he finally betrays the revolution. The theater on Jamaica presents not primarily Debuisson's betrayal, but Antoine's own betrayal through the imagined figure; the action of the play thus completes a full circle, as Debuisson in Scene 12 becomes the counter-revolutionary Antoine whom the sailor seeks in Scene 2. Further, with the betrayal of the *Auftraggeber* and the unifying consciousness of the play, the play in a way betrays itself: defined as "Der Auftrag: Erinnerung an eine Revolution," the play dissolves at the end into *forgetfulness*. The task of reconstruction and remembering which the learning play sets itself is finally abandoned, and no control chorus remains to pronounce its judgment and to present its lesson. Thus even on its most fundamental structural level, as the breakdown of the *Lehrstück* model, the play enacts the betrayal which is the fate of the European revolutionary intellectual.


The European Revolution(s) and the Third World

As *Hamletmaschine* worked toward the disintegration of the form and ideology of the classical bourgeois drama, *Auftrag* presents the "deconstruction" of the socialist aesthetic form, the Brechtian *Lehrstück*. The control chorus, represented by the privileged intellectual Antoine, no longer has the authority of a collective. Indeed, the objectivity which should characterize its role as mediator and judge is fundamentally compromised by

the fact that Antoine is called upon to reexamine
and judge his *own* betrayal of the revolution. The
subjectivization and internalization of the *Lehrstück* in turn gives rise to the basic ambiguity of
the dramatized action: almost reminiscent of the
Expressionist "Ich-Drama," the characters of the
revolution on Jamaica are creations (or recrea-
tions), and as such present contradictory aspects,
of a single, unifying consciousness. The learning
play of Müller's making is not the reasoned, objective examination of past events, but a "diffuse
movement without clear perspective,"[63] the semi-
conscious dream of a tortured revolutionary. The
result is not any explicit closure of a codified
or codifiable "teaching," but the final, apocalyptic, seductive and ambivalent embrace of betrayal.

Underlying the deconstruction or distortion of the
*Lehrstück* form is a fundamental thematic shift:
Heiner Müller presents in his learning play not
the Brechtian process of a young comrade gaining
insight into his betrayal of the revolution, but
the revolutionary's insight into the *process of
revolution* itself which leads to its own betrayal.
What is involved is in part the familiar issue of
the oppressive aspect of reason (the Enlightenment)
which Müller examined in depth in *Leben Gundlings*;
a related theme is that of the necessary failure
of the (privileged) intellectual in the staging of
revolution, exemplified by the Hamlet figure of
*Hamletmaschine*. But the position of *Auftrag* goes
further: the basic logic of the (bourgeois French)
revolution seems to be to promise emancipation and
then to establish in its guise a more insidious
oppression (prosperity and Napoleon). The "betrayal" both Antoine and Debuisson enact finds its
source in their insight into the essential dialectic of (bourgeois) revolution and betrayal: "Die
Freiheit führt das Volk auf die Barrikaden, und
wenn die Toten erwachen trägt sie Uniform" (9);
"TOD DEN BEFREIERN heisst die letzte Wahrheit der
Revolution" (30).[64]

With the figure of the ex-slave Sasportas who rejects the white slave-owner and French revolutionary Debuisson and continues the revolution in Jamaica under a new banner, the text intimates the possibility of an alternative, authentic revolution which would *not* be based on the "white thoughts" of "reason" and would not lead to betrayal. The drama of slave and slave-owner, Jamaica and France, and the explicit and extensive use of Fanon, point to an underlying criticism of bourgeois emancipation as inherently *colonialist* in the exportation of its "universal" values. However, the structural and thematic model of *Die Massnahme* which Müller adopts suggests that his criticism is more far-reaching: the use of Brecht's play, which deals with the export of the *socialist*, Russian Revolution, marks "Paris" as a metaphor also for "Moscow."

In this context the following extensive statement by Müller sheds crucial light on the ideological-political constellation of the three revolutionaries on Jamaica. Horst Laube makes the comment that Müller moves in his play "vom öffentlichen Aushandeln dramatischer Positionen zum in drei Figuren geteilten Monolog":

> LAUBE: Die drei Monologe geben drei Haltungen zur Revolution wieder: die proletarische, die des bürgerlichen Revolutionsliebhabers ...
>
> MÜLLER: Die dritte ist die mittlere. Kommunismus ist das Mittlere, wobei ich auch das nicht mehr glaube. Sicher ist das Mittlere eine Voraussetzung, aber man kann es nicht mehr zum Massstab für die Bewertung von Bewegung machen. Es ist eine Voraussetzung für die von uns aus gesehen völlig anarchischen oder absurden Befreiungsbewegungen. Khomeini oder was immer ... Die Erhaltung dieser mittleren Position in Osteuropa halte ich immer noch für wichtig als Voraussetzung für die Effektivität der anarchischen oder absurden Befreiungsbewegungen in anderen Erdteilen.[65]

Three positions regarding revolution are named: the proletarian, the bourgeois (clearly represented by Debuisson), and the communist. Müller distinguishes between the orthodox communist position of Eastern Europe and other, genuine revolutionary movements "in anderen Erdteilen" which, as "anarchic and absurd," lie beyond the (normal European) limits of rationality. This "proletarian" revolution, located in the Third World, is embodied by the figure of Sasportas who rejects the "toten Ordnungen" of Europe (20) and carves in his black flesh the banner of a new (non-white) revolution.

The designation of Communism as "das Mittlere" draws upon the poem of that name by Brecht, who writes:

> Der Kommunismus ist wirklich die geringste Forderung
> Das Allernächstliegende, Mittlere, Vernünftige.
> Wer sich gegen ihn stellt, ist nicht ein Andersdenkender
> Sondern ein Nichtdenkender oder ein nur Ansichdenkender
> Ein Feind des Menschengeschlechtes.[66]

For Müller the Communism of Eastern Europe is not the universal human imperative proclaimed by Brecht; it is "Voraussetzung" for indigenous revolutionary movements throughout the world, but not their "Massstab." While Debuisson is the "bürgerliche Revolutionsliebhaber" who returns to his former life as slave-owner after a brief flirtation with revolution, and Sasportas the proletarian revolutionary of the Third World, the ideal Communist position is represented by the peasant Galloudec who chooses to support, but does not dominate or lead, the revolutionary mission on Jamaica continued by the ex-slave Sasportas.

The crucial importance of Müller's statement lies in the recognition of *three* monologues, whereby the Third World is accorded its own undeniable integrity as a revolutionary force. In the figure of Sasportas and in the voice of Fanon, with their antecedents in Ophelia of *Hamletmaschine* and the inmates of the asylum in *Leben Gundlings,* emerges a new, emancipatory discourse of "anarchy" in Müller's plays, which asserts itself against the dominant European models of the bourgeois Enlightenment and the French Revolution, as well as of Marxist Communism. As a *dramatic* discourse, the theater of the Third World, which emancipates itself from the bourgeois model of Lessing (in *Hamletmaschine*) and from the Marxist model of the Brechtian *Lehrstück* (in *Auftrag*), finds its source in the revolutionary, anarchic vision of such artists as Lautréamont, Antonin Artaud, and Jean Genet.

CONCLUSION

> Das einzige, was ein Kunstwerk
> kann, ist Sehnsucht wecken nach
> einem anderen Zustand der Welt.
> Und diese Sehnsucht ist revolutionär.
>
> Heiner Müller [1]

In the four chapters comprising this study I have explored and formulated a clear statement of Müller's aesthetic project and, in close readings of three of his most recent texts, uncovered the essential structures and thematic categories through which this project is realized.

I began with a detailed analysis of the enigmatic essay on postmodernism. There Müller himself defines the literary tradition to which he belongs: the line of authors beginning with Rimbaud and Lautréamont and ending with Brecht and Beckett, who have worked, in various ways, towards their own dissolution. The truly revolutionary artist seeks his own "disappearance" as a privileged authority in favor of an anonymous, anarchic art of the masses. In his project of - what I have called - "revolutionary postmodernism," Müller develops basic views of certain major Marxist aestheticians. Walter Benjamin spoke in "Der Autor als Produzent" (1934) of the necessity of abolishing the privilege of the creative individual, of socializing the intellectual ("geistigen") means of production, and of organizing the workers into the production process of art.[2] Twenty years later Theodor Adorno in "Der Artist als Statthalter" (1953) redefined the artist not as individual genius, but as the medium through which the social intersubjective discourse of a "collective subject" occurs:

171

> Der Künstler, der das Kunstwerk trägt, ist nicht
> der je Einzelne, der es hervorbringt, sondern
> durch seine Arbeit, durch passive Aktivität wird
> er zum Statthalter des gesellschaftlichen Gesamt-
> subjekts. ... In solcher Stellvertretung des ge-
> samtgesellschaftlichen Subjekts aber ... ist zu-
> gleich ein Zustand mitgedacht, der das Schicksal
> der blinden Vereinzelung tilgt, in dem endlich
> das Gesamtsubjekt gesellschaftlich sich verwirk-
> licht.[3]

For Adorno, for Benjamin, and for Müller, the disappearance of the author as authoritative individual is connected to the establishment and preservation of a truly human society. The masterpieces of the privileged artist are accomplices of the system of oppression; the truly revolutionary art work, in contrast, works towards its own liquidation. The fundamental critical insight motivating Müller's revolutionary aesthetics is that an authored, authoritative discourse, even one which presents itself as (enlightened) reason and universality - "das wahre Allgemeine," to quote Hegel - is ideologically allied to, and thus easily allows itself to be appropriated by an oppressive political order.

Here Müller's Marxist aesthetics intersect another "revolutionary" line of thought: the later dramatic texts and theoretical statements of the East German Müller reveal also a shared concern, a fundamental affinity with certain of the French structuralists and poststructuralists.[4] The poetics of a "silence of entropy" and "universal discourse" for example express insights which parallel Roland Barthes' pronouncement of the "death of the author": "it is language which speaks, not the author," in the text which is not the carrier of a single authoritative message but "a multi-dimensional space in which a variety of writings, none of them original, blend and clash. ... a tissue of quotations drawn from the innumerable centres of culture."[5]

But perhaps more important than Barthes as an intellectual "sibling" is Gilles Deleuze, whose concept of the "small" literature provides the crucial key to Müller's statement on postmodernism. Here I establish a definite link between Deleuze and Müller; my strategy has not been to simply apply one set of ideas to Müller's plays as an academic exercise, but to explore an essential relation, Müller's recognition of himself in the thought of another. Deleuze's essay "Ein Manifest weniger" (1978) formulates a poetics of the theater strikingly similar to Müller's own: the vision of a "small" or "minor" theater is based on the elimination of "alles ... was Macht 'ausmacht', die Macht dessen, was das Theater repräsentiert (den König, die Fürsten, die Herren, das System), aber auch die Macht des Theaters selbst (den Text, den Dialog, den Schauspieler, den Regisseur, die Struktur)."[6] Deleuze's small theater specifically rejects the standard of the white, Christian, male American or European and presents instead the minority figure of the woman, the black, the Indian (the Third World) as a capacity within, a possibility for, all people.[7] Indeed, the three plays by Müller which I discuss seem almost to represent an attempt to realize Deleuze's radical vision.

Through close analysis of the dramatic "protagonists" Friedrich II, Lessing, Hamlet, and the Dantonesque Antoine/Debuisson, I have established as the thematic crux of *Leben Gundlings, Hamletmaschine,* and *Auftrag* the role of the white, European, male intellectual in the process of social upheaval (revolution). Whether the enlightened despot Friedrich, the bourgeois hero Hamlet, or the socialist revolutionary Debuisson, the pattern of their action is the same: the intellectual fails in his project of revolt. I have discussed this "betrayal" in terms of a "Foucaultian" criticism of a fundamentally counter-revolutionary aspect of reason: intellectuals, knowingly (Gundling) or unknowingly (Lessing), allow their knowledge to be appropriated and instrumentalized in the oppressive mechanism of state domination; and in terms of an extended "Marxist" analysis of privilege: in the case of Hamlet and Debuisson, reason as an emancipatory force is compromised by class, *but also* sex, race, and culture.

An inherently ambivalent stance with regard to the values of the Enlightenment underlies the failure of the intellectual: as I have shown, reason is essentially a revolutionary force in Müller's plays, yet, as the domain of the privileged intellectual, it is also fundamentally a counter-revolutionary instrument of continued domination. Hamlet's reflection on the custom of vengeance is an unambiguously *positive* moment, yet he ultimately upholds the tradition of violence, reenacting the counter-revolution of the Social Democrat Gustav Noske who rationalized, "Einer muss der Bluthund werden." Debuisson, attempting to bring the revolution of "liberté, égalité, fraternité" to the Third World, finally renounces these ideals and returns to his former life as slave-owner. The specific thrust of Müller's criticism is that the revolutionary intellectual, who is a member of a privileged, dominating class, engages in revolution simply as a matter of his privilege. The white revolution, as the central scene in *Auftrag* demonstrates, is only a theater of words. The emancipatory tradition of the Enlightenment, within the context of world-wide colonialization and oppression, is a privileged tradition.

I have shown that the structure of the action of the three plays is built around a complex "dialectic" of reason or knowledge as revolutionary/counter-revolutionary, of "rational" revolution and its betrayal or failure. The theme of revolution is closely tied to the theme of sexuality, which evinces the same paradigmatic structure;

within the complex gestural code of Müller's plays, revolutions are made and betrayed in sexual terms. The homosexuality of the young boy Friedrich, the adultery of the woman and the masturbation of the adolescent in the Prussian insane asylum, Ophelia's destruction of the bed and her ejection of sperm from her body, Hamlet's transvestitism and desire to be a woman in the middle scene of the play, are all acts of protest or revolt against a pervasive system of domination. On the other hand, the king Friedrich's rape of the Saxon woman, Hamlet's rape of his mother, Antoine's intercourse with his wife in an effort to forget the revolution, and Debuisson's final encounter with the seductress-angel of betrayal, carry the import of counter-revolution and betrayal; these acts demonstrate an acceptance and affirmation of the institutions of oppression.[8]

The betrayal enacted by the intellectual, expressed through rape and intercourse, essentially reaffirms and reasserts the power of the orthodox patriarchal order founded on the oppression of women: the act of betrayal, as I establish for each of the three plays, is primarily the act of the *son becoming the father,* participating in the reproduction and continuation of the system of oppression.[9] The young Friedrich becomes the tyrant king, Hamlet climbs into his father's armor, Debuisson becomes a slave-owner: the rebellious intellectual son finally abandons the revolution to assume the role of the father. The pattern is a pervasive one in Müller's thought and is of important interpretive value. Müller himself explains its political significance: the development in Brecht's *Fatzer* material of the figure of the functionary Keuner who supersedes the anarchist Fatzer is seen as a paradigmatic turn to paternalism which betrays genuine revolutionary forces. Müller writes in "Fatzer ± Keuner":

> Hier, aus der revolutionären Ungeduld gegen unreife Verhältnisse, kommt der Trend zur Substitution des Proletariats auf, die in den Paternalismus mündet, die Krankheit der kommunistischen Parteien. Es beginnt, in der Abwehr des anarchisch-natürlichen Matriarchats, der Umbau des rebellischen Sohns in die Vaterfigur, der Brechts Erfolg ausmacht und seine Wirkung behindert.[10]

Brecht as the sanctioned "father figure" of East German literature functions himself as a modern, socialist Hamlet. The critique of paternalism in art and politics is the critique of authoritative leadership which ignores or replaces the particularity of the actual revolutionary situation; Müller opposes, in a word, the dictatorship of ideas or forms of thought over the manifoldness of life.

If the paternalistic, patriarchal betrayal is manifested in Müller's plays in the act of intercourse, the "anarchic-natural matriarchy" of revolt is approached through alternative, explicitly non-reproductive modes of sexual behavior: masturbation and homosexuality, which are, notably, the acts of the rebellious young male, and also the programmatic anti-sexuality of the woman (Ophelia). The woman, by virtue of gender, represents at the outset a potential revolutionary force within the patriarchal system; thus the male intellectual often expresses his own desire for emancipation in various acts of transsexuality: Gundling quotes from Ophelia ("O WHAT A NOBLE MIND IS HERE / O'ERTHROWN"), the young boy Friedrich reveals his feelings for Katte while wearing the dress of his sister and with the words of Racine's Phaedra, Hamlet also dons Ophelia's clothes and answers her challenge to revolt: "Ich will eine Frau sein."

However the revolutionary potential of the woman lies not in her sex per se, but in the experience of oppression which has defined her. Thus it is with the male figure of Sasportas that the revolutionary principle of sexuality emerges in its full significance. The ex-Haitian slave who does not understand the counter-revolutionary, nihilistic rationalizations of the European intellectual but hears instead the drums of the uprising through the pores of his black skin, represents a specifically non-white sexuality of revolt; identifying himself with forest, mountain, ocean, desert, Sasportas calls for a revolt of *nature*. If patriarchy is the order of the privileged whites of Europe, the anarchic matriarchy is the revolutionary alternative of the oppressed peoples of the Third World. My study of the complex thematic "architecture" of Müller's plays thus establishes a second complex of ciphers which signify authentic revolution: the Third World, the female, the physical or natural, are the banners of the oppressed who are beginning to rise in revolt against the counter-revolutionary categories of white, European, male, and intellectual. While Friedrich, Hamlet, and Debuisson are carriers of the "rational" patriarchal order that dominates and colonizes, the victim Ophelia and the slave Sasportas represent, in contrast, the forces of anarchism and natural revolt which arise out of the experience of oppression.

In my initial discussion of Müller's statement on postmodernism, I described the impulse of "entropy" in the privileged author's project of self-dissolution (Rimbaud, Kafka, Beckett, and others provided models of this author "in flight"), and the alternative "universal discourse," the creation of a collective subject in art, a utopia of universality and total participation which begins to emerge in the depths of the New York City subways. Essentially the enigmatic categories of Müller's statement on postmodernism define a revolutionary poetics which is realized in the specific discursive strategies of Müller's later plays; the two thematic and characterological complexes I have identified, counterrevolutionary rationality and revolutionary Third-World "anarchy," articulate the "entropy" and "universal discourse" of the revolutionary postmodernist project.

The basic and pervasive structural strategy of the three plays is that of deconstruction: "die erste Funktion von Dramatik," Müller stated, "ist Zerstörung."[11] Most importantly, I describe how bourgeois (Lessing) and socialist (Brecht) models of drama are adopted and thematically and structurally undermined. But the deconstructive strategy operates on many levels of the text. For example, historical, literary, mythological figures are alluded to, quoted, reincarnated on stage in order to de-heroicize, de-mythologize, *de-mystify* - Müller's deconstruction of Enlightenment ideology is notably itself an Enlightenment project of emancipation. I have shown that Zeus, Jesus, Friedrich II, Kleist, Lessing, the Prince of Homburg, Emilia Galotti, Hamlet, Ophelia, Gustav Noske, Rosa Luxemburg, Danton, Robespierre, and others all provide the material "stuff" which is reshaped and *redefined* within Müller's plays. In addition, quotations from other texts - from T.S. Eliot's "Ash-Wednesday," Shakespeare's *Hamlet,* Brecht's *Badener Lehrstück* and *Massnahme,* from Grimms' fairy tales and Strauss's *Fledermaus,* to name only a few - are presented in deliberately *distorted* form. On a number of levels, Müller practices the "entropy" which is the breakdown of established order. The deconstructive strategy against dominant, authoritative structures of various kinds is the formal parallel to the thematic issue of the failure of the white intellectual: in the three plays the reigning (formal) models of European revolution, I demonstrate, are potentially oppressive institutions.

The ideological and revolutionary motivation for the project of "entropy" is the necessity of dissolving the elite and oppressive, privileged authorial voice. Müller has consistently denied the role of the author as authoritative and privileged creator of the art work. Recently he stated bluntly: "Ich hab ja gar keine Ideen. Ich hab nie Ideen gehabt. ... Ich schreibe so viel ab, dass kein einzelner es merken kann."[12] The author engages in a project of deliberate and extensive, "anarchic" disordering in which, tendentially, any authoritative stance dissolves in the pure function of transcription ("abschreiben"); the authorial position dissolves into a complex, intersubjective, multisubjective discourse.

Thus the anonymous "universal discourse" of a multiplicity of voices is the complementary result of the "disappearance" of the privileged author: the breakdown or distortion of models/orders (defined as forms of drama, literary works, literary and historical characters, or quotations) essential to the author's project of "entropy" is not purely deconstructive, but creates a *new* ordering. The montage or collage of the three plays I have discussed takes specific meaningful elements (quotes, figures, images, etc.) from established literary works or historical events, thereby destroying the original contexts ("entropy"), and juxtaposes these selected elements in a disharmonious way (as the "universal discourse") within a new framework. The entropic deconstruction of established models is at the same time the universal discourse of montage, claiming a total openness to other texts and other voices. Thematically: the failure of the dominant models of white revolution is accompanied by the recognition of alternatives hitherto oppressed or ignored, voices of particularity the Enlightenment has or would have subordinated; the discourse of revolution is opened to - no longer imposed upon - the non-rational, the non-white, the non-European, the non-male.

I began my study with an analysis of Müller's "revolutionary postmodernist" aesthetics. I might conclude now with the suggestion that Müller's real aesthetic project is the articulation of the "postmodern revolution." The renunciation of the privileged authorial stance and the programmatic openness of a discourse "der nichts auslässt und niemanden ausschliesst"[13] formulate the basic poetic principles of a genuinely socialist text, a text that overthrows the "paternalism" of both bourgeois and orthodox (official) socialist aesthetics. The project is "postmodern" in its anarchistic openness to non-rational (non-European) elements. It signifies a genuine "revolution" for the Communist Müller in that *all* voices are engaged in the process of production. The implicit criticism of orthodox Socialism lies in its ("counterrevolutionary") adherence to the dictates of a model - to the idea that the revolutionary process can (should) be guided by an intellectual elite, to the belief that emancipation can be exported or imposed. Müller's aesthetic and political revolution lies in his inclusion of the "minority" voices of Artaud, Lautréamont, Fanon, Ophelia, Sasportas in the discourse of revolution.

It is at this point of a new beginning, "die erste Erscheinung des Neuen,"[14] that Müller's texts arrive, and suddenly fall silent. Zebahl's whispered proclamation of impending natural catastrophe at the end of the scene in the Prussian asylum is accompanied by black angels swarming silently into the audience; one is left with a powerful vision of Maldororian revolt, inexpressible in words. Ophelia's empassioned call for continued revolution in the last scene of *Hamletmaschine,* too, ends abruptly in silence and immobilization. And Sasportas proclaims a revolution in images of violent nature only to leave the stage. Unlike Beckett, whose silence is an attempt to express the fact that "there is nothing to express,"[15] Müller's silence marks the space of a new discourse of revolution, one which cannot be expressed in the traditional words and forms of rational European bourgeois or socialist drama. While Beckett's silence is empty, the silence of Müller's texts is laden, expectant, revolutionary. The revolutionary author struggles to express in a new language, in the image of a silent Ophelia wrapped in bandages, what has hitherto been suppressed, unexpressed, in Hamlet's "BLABLA." The intellectual Müller, writing in and against the tradition of a great literature, seeks his own third-world voice.

NOTES

## Introduction

[1] *Der Spiegel*, 9 May 1983, p.196.

[2] Ibid., p.5.

[3] See for example Marc Silberman, *Heiner Müller*, Forschungsberichte zur DDR-Literatur, Vol. 2 (Amsterdam: Rodopi, 1980), pp.14-21; and Helen Fehervary, "Enlightenment or Entanglement: History and Aesthetics in Bertolt Brecht and Heiner Müller," *New German Critique*, No. 8 (Spring 1976), pp.83-85.

[4] Honecker states, "Unsere DDR ist ein sauberer Staat. In ihr gibt es unverrückbare Massstäbe der Ethik und Moral, für Anstand und gute Sitte," and denounces works of art (including Müller's *Bau*) which exhibit "Tendenzen der Verabsolutierung der Widersprüche, der Missachtung der Dialektik der Entwicklung, konstruierte Konfliktsituationen," and "nihilistische, ausweglose und moralzersetzende Philosophien." "Die aktive Rolle der Kunst und Literatur," Honecker expressly states, "besteht gerade darin, die Überwindung der Widersprüche auf der Grundlage unserer sozialistischen Bedingungen im bewussten Handeln der Menschen durch die konstruktive Politik von Partei und Staat künstlerisch zu erfassen." "Bericht des Politbüros an das 11. Plenum des ZK der SED, vorgetragen von Erich Honecker," Dokumente 310, *Dokumente zur Kunst-, Literatur- und Kulturpolitik der SED*, ed. Elimar Schubbe (Stuttgart: Seewald, 1972), pp.1076-81. For a good overview of the "dialectic" of East German cultural politics and literary production, see Jost Hermand, "Das Gute-Neue und das Schlechte-Neue: Wandlungen der Modernismus-Debatte in der DDR seit 1956," in *Literatur und Literaturtheorie in der DDR*, ed. Peter Uwe Hohendahl and Patricia Herminghouse (Frankfurt am Main: Suhrkamp, 1976), pp.73-99; and Rémy Charbon, "'Denn das Schöne bedeutet das mögliche Ende der Schrecken': Versuch über Heiner Müller und das Theater der DDR in der Epoche des Neuen ökonomischen Systems," *Wirkendes Wort*, 30 (1980), 149-77.

[5] All dates are dates of completion. See Martin Laska, "Inszenierungstabelle der Stücke Heiner Müllers," *Text + Kritik,* No. 73 (January 1982), pp.82-87, for information on specific productions.

[6] Rüdiger Mangel and Georg Wieghaus, "Abgrenzung und Teilhabe: Thesen zu Heiner Müllers Position im Literaturprozess der DDR," *Text + Kritik,* No. 73 (January 1982), p.38.

[7] Silberman, p.22.

[8] See Silberman, pp.22-26.

[9] Georg Wieghaus, *Heiner Müller,* Autorenbücher, 25 (München: C.H. Beck; Verlag Edition Text + Kritik, 1981); Genia Schulz, *Heiner Müller,* Sammlung Metzler, 197 (Stuttgart: J.B. Metzler, 1980). A noteworthy attempt is made in the volume of essays, *Die Hamletmaschine: Heiner Müllers Endspiel,* ed. Theo Girshausen (Köln: Prometh, 1978), to present analyses of specific aspects of the play; individually or collectively, however, the essays fail to provide a detailed investigation of the play as a whole.

[10] Silberman, p.27.

[11] See the references given by Silberman, pp.26-27. More recent articles include, from *Text + Kritik,* No. 73 (January 1982): Florian Vassan, "Der Tod des Körpers in der Geschichte: Tod, Sexualität und Arbeit bei Heiner Müller," pp.45-57; Genia Schulz, "Abschied von Morgen: Zu den Frauengestalten im Werk Heiner Müllers," pp.58-70; and Hans-Thies Lehmann, "Raum-Zeit: Das Entgleiten der Geschichte in der Dramatik Heiner Müllers und im französischen Poststrukturalismus," pp.71-81. See also Helen Fehervary, "Autorschaft, Geschlechtsbewusstsein und Öffentlichkeit: Versuch über Heiner Müllers 'Die Hamletmaschine' und Christa Wolfs 'Kein Ort. Nirgends,'" in *Entwürfe von Frauen in der Literatur des 20. Jahrhunderts,* ed. Irmela von der Lühe, Literatur im historischen Prozess, Neue Folge 5 (Berlin: Argument, 1982), pp.132-53.

[12] Here the methodological strategy of Peter Szondi in his *Theorie des modernen Dramas (1880-1950)* (Frankfurt am Main: Suhrkamp, 1956) has been an irresistible influence and inspiration.

[13] "Der Schrecken die erste Erscheinung des Neuen," in Müller, *Rotwelsch* (Berlin: Merve, 1982), p.98.

## Chapter I: The Poetics of a Revolutionary Postmodernism

[1] *Rotwelsch*, pp.94-98. References to this text will be given in parentheses in the main body of the chapter. Müller's essay was originally published in *Theater heute*, 20 (March 1979), 1; the English translation by Jack Zipes and Betty Nance Weber appeared in *New German Critique*, No. 16 (Winter 1979), pp.55-57.

[2] For a survey of the literature on postmodernism, see the articles by Michael Köhler, "'Postmodernismus': Ein begriffsgeschichtlicher Überblick", pp.8-18; and Gerhard Hoffmann, Alfred Hornung, and Rüdiger Kunow, "'Modern,' 'Postmodern' and 'Contemporary' as Criteria for the Analysis of 20th Century Literature," pp.19-46, both in *Amerikastudien/ American Studies*, 22, No. 1 (1977).

[3] Ihab Hassan, *The Dismemberment of Orpheus: Toward a Postmodern Literature*, 2nd ed. (Madison, Wisconsin: Univ. of Wisconsin Press, 1982), first published by Oxford University Press in 1971. In my discussion I draw from the "Preface to the Second Edition" (xi-xv), "Tuning In" (xvii-xviii), and the first chapter, "PRELUDE: Lyre Without Strings" (pp.3-23). Hassan quotes the crucial passages from Ovid in the headnote (vii) to his book (I add the last line in parentheses, which Hassan omits):

> ... and then the women
> Rushed back to murder Orpheus, who stretched out
> His hands in supplication, and whose voice,
> For the first time, moved no one. They struck him down,
> And through those lips to which the rocks had listened,
> To which the hearts of savage beasts responded,
> His spirit found its way to winds and air.
> ... The poet's limbs lay scattered
> Where they were flung in cruelty or madness,
> But Hebrus River took the head and lyre

>     And as they floated down the gentle current
>     The lyre made mournful sounds, and the tongue murmured
>     In mournful harmony, (and the banks echoed
>     The strains of mourning.)

The full myth of Orpheus is given in *Metamorphoses* X.1-85 and XI.1-66; trans. Rolfe Humphries (Bloomington, Indiana: Indiana Univ. Press, 1955), pp.234-36, 259-61. Hassan quotes from Book XI.

[4] Hassan, xviii.

[5] Humphries, p.260.

[6] Franz Kafka, *Tagebücher 1910-1923,* ed. Max Brod (Frankfurt am Main: S. Fischer; Lizenzausgabe v. New York: Schocken Books, 1948-49), pp.147-150.

[7] Ibid., p.147.

[8] Ibid., p.149.

[9] Gilles Deleuze and Félix Guattari, *Kafka: Für eine kleine Literatur,* trans. Burkhart Kroeber (Frankfurt am Main: Suhrkamp, 1976); originally published in French, *Kafka: Pour une littérature mineure* (Paris: Les Editions de Minuit, 1975). I quote from the German translation, which Müller used.

[10] Personal interview, 18 July 1982.

[11] See Chapter III, "Was ist eine kleine Literatur?", pp.24-39.

[12] Ibid., pp.25-26.

[13] Ibid., p.26.

[14] Ibid., p.26.

[15] Ibid., p.27.

[16] Ibid., p.37.

[17] This striking formulation appears again in another essay the following year (1979): "Das Ende der Eliten ist Programm, die Lage fordert Privilegien. Privilegien müssen bezahlt werden: zu den Arbeiten der Intelligenz gehört ihre Selbstkritik. Schon Talent ist ein Privileg, der Eigenbeitrag zur

Enteignung gehört zu den Kriterien. Erst auf diesem Hintergrund kann Systemkritik produktiv werden, sind Optimismus und Pessimismus gleichermassen Zeitverlust." "'Und vieles wie auf den Schultern eine Last von Scheitern ist zu behalten ...' (Hölderlin)," in *Rotwelsch*, p.91. Originally published in French, in *Le Monde*, 5 Apr. 1979.

[18]"Der Dramatiker und die Geschichte seiner Zeit: Ein Gespräch zwischen Horst Laube und Heiner Müller," *Theater heute: Jahrbuch 1975*, p.123.

[19]Cf. also in this context Müller's statement in "Ein Brief" (1975), in *Theater-Arbeit* (Berlin: Rotbuch, 1975), p.126: "Talent ist ein Privileg, Privilegien müssen bezahlt werden. Mit der Enteignung im Sozialismus wird Weisheit borniert, der Aphorismus reaktionär; die Pose des Klassikers erfordert homerische Blindheit." With the overthrow of private property should come also the abandonment of certain literary forms - as well as of a certain understanding of the nature of the artist - which adhere to bourgeois-capitalist values of the individual, individual authority, and privilege. In a discussion that same year Müller stated: "Ich glaube nicht mehr an Werke als eine geschlossene Sache, die man der Nach- oder Mitwelt abliefert. Das ist für einige Zeit vorbei. Mit der Aufhebung von Privateigentum an Produktionsmitteln und mit dem Zweifel daran, der in anderen Gegenden entsteht, wird auch das Privateigentum an Kunst auf die Dauer in Frage gestellt." "Geschichte und Drama: Ein Gespräch mit Heiner Müller," *Basis: Jahrbuch für deutsche Gegenwartsliteratur*, 6 (1976), 49.

[20]Karl Marx and Friedrich Engels, *Die deutsche Ideologie*, in Karl Marx, *Werke. Schriften*, ed. Hans-Joachim Lieber, Vol. II: Frühe Schriften, II (Stuttgart: Cotta, 1971), 478.

[21]Consider also the following statement: "Ich sehe da [für die Kunst] eine Möglichkeit: das Theater für ganz kleine Gruppen (für Massen existiert es ja schon längst nicht mehr) zu benutzen, um Phantasieräume zu produzieren, Freiräume für Phantasie - gegen diesen Imperialismus der Besetzung von Phantasie und der Abtötung von Phantasie durch die vorfabrizierten Klischees und Standards der Medien." "Mich interessiert der Fall Althusser ..." (1981), in *Rotwelsch*, p.177.

The oppression and slow extinction of phantasy is a tendency inherent in any industrial society; "phantasy," as Müller uses the term, is equivalent to "revolutionary energy." See his remarks to this effect in "Gespräch mit Bernard Umbrecht," in *Rotwelsch*, pp.111, 113.

[22] Karl Marx, *Das Kapital*, III, in *Werke. Schriften. Briefe*, ed. Hans-Joachim Lieber, Vol. IV: Ökonomische Schriften, III (Stuttgart: Cotta, 1964), 671-72.

[23] Müller speaks of a synthesis of the two in the essay "'Und vieles wie auf den Schultern eine Last von Scheitern ist zu behalten ...' (Hölderlin)"; in one passage, it is likened to a project of the deconstruction of (presumably bourgeois) ideology:

> Brecht, in einer ersten Diskussion mit Studenten 1948 nach seiner Übersiedlung in die sowjetische Besatzungszone, sprach von Ideologiezertrümmerung als der Zielsetzung seines Theaters für zwanzig Jahre. ... Sein Versuch der Synthese von Realismus und Volkstümlichkeit ist gescheitert. Sein Theater war nicht volkstümlich, als es realistisch, es war nicht mehr realistisch, als es volkstümlich war. (*Rotwelsch*, p.89)

The project of a synthesis is clearly, in Müller's view, the primary concern of the contemporary East German theater:

> Im REICH DER NOTWENDIGKEIT sind Realismus und Volkstümlichkeit zwei Dinge, aber das REICH DER FREIHEIT rückt nicht näher, wenn die Synthese nicht immer neu versucht wird, unter den wachsamen Augen der Brecht-Erben am BERLINER ENSEMBLE oder der Stadtväter in der VOLKSBÜHNE AM LUXEMBURGPLATZ, im ersten Fall vom akademischen Starrkrampf, im zweiten vom Niveausturz bedroht. (*Rotwelsch*, p.91)

[24] *Hamlet* III.ii.360-65.

[25] Federico García Lorca, "Escena del Teniente Coronel de la Guardia Civil," in *Obras completas*, ed. Arturo del Hoyo (Madrid: Aguilar, 1954), pp.254-58.

[26] "'Und vieles wie auf den Schultern eine Last von Scheitern ist zu behalten ...' (Hölderlin)," in *Rotwelsch*, p.88.

[27]"Fragen an Heiner Müller," *Connaissance de la RDA,* No. 12 (1981), p.66.

[28]Cf. Müller's statement in his speech at an international theater colloquium in Budapest in December 1974: "I believe in the feasibility of communism, i.e. in a time when art will cease to be a special vocation. I believe in the possibility of a society in which people will be actors, directors, playwrights among other things. But only *other things.*" "I do not believe in a harmony between theatre and literature," in *The Playwright and the Theatrical Creation,* Proc. of the International Colloquium Budapest, 16-18 December 1974 (Budapest: International Theatre Institute, Hungarian Centre, 1975), p.64.

[29]Thomas Mann, *Doktor Faustus,* in *Gesammelte Werke in zwölf Bänden,* VI (Frankfurt am Main: S. Fischer, 1960), 427.

[30]The split within East German culture, however, is itself one manifestation of a continuous and characteristic split in German literary history:

> Im ganzen hat die deutsche Literatur, anders als zum Beispiel die russische, englische, amerikanische, wenn die Wahrheit der Schönheit zu nahe trat, noch immer ein Auge zugedrückt und sich für die Schönheit entschieden. Über die Gründe ist spätestens seit Marx genug geschrieben worden .... Solange die Gründe fortbestehn, bleiben Realismus und Volkstümlichkeit zwei Dinge. ("Aufforderung zum Erschrecken" [1977], in *Rotwelsch,* p.162)

The split between realism and popular culture, or the everyday life of the people, is in its broadest sense a split between beauty and truth. Another - and, as Müller says, paradigmatic - historical manifestation of this is Weimar Classicism:

> Das Ausbleiben der bürgerlichen Revolution in Deutschland ermöglichte zugleich und erzwang die Weimarer Klassik als Aufhebung der Positionen des Sturm und Drang. Klassik als Revolutionsersatz. Literatur einer besiegten Klasse, Form als Ausgleich, Kultur als Umgangsform mit der Macht und Transport von falschem

Bewusstsein. Goethes bewusste Entscheidung gegen die
hungernden Weber von Apolda für die Jamben der Iphi-
genia ist paradigmatisch. ("Fatzer ± Keuner" [1980],
in *Rotwelsch*, p.140)

[31] Thomas Mann, *Doktor Faustus*, pp.428-29.

[32] Ibid., p.429.

[33] "Miteinander statt oben und unten: Irene Böhme sprach mit
Heiner Müller über die Bearbeitung von 'Horizonte,'" *Sonntag*, 12 Oct. 1969, p.11.

[34] I have been unable to locate the quote in Brecht's published
writings and conversations; it is, in Müller's recollection
(this in a telephone conversation with him in April 1983),
from an unpublished conversation with Manfred Wekwerth. In
the following remarks Müller attributes the quote to a conversation with Peter Palitzsch:

> Er [Brecht] wurde einmal gefragt, ich glaube von
> Palitzsch, ob das, was er macht ... schon episches
> Theater sei. Brecht meinte, episches Theater wäre
> gar nicht möglich, es wäre erst möglich, wenn die
> Perversität aufhöre, aus einem Luxus einen Beruf
> zu machen - die Konstituierung des Theaters aus der
> Trennung von Bühne und Zuschauerraum. Erst wenn das
> aufgehoben ist, jedenfalls tendenziell, dann ist es
> möglich, Theater mit einem Minimum an Dramaturgie,
> also beinahe ohne Dramaturgie, zu machen. Und darum
> geht es jetzt: Ein Theater ohne Anstrengung herzu-
> stellen. ("Der Dramatiker und die Geschichte seiner
> Zeit," *Theater heute*: Jahrbuch 1975, p.121)

Müller refers often to Brecht's concept; see also the discussion "Geschichte und Drama," in *Basis*, 6 (1976), 55,
where Müller speaks of the overcoming of the separation
between audience and actors, resting upon radical economic
and social changes, as being the only possibility for
theater in the future.

[35] "DDR-Dramatiker über Brecht," in *Brecht 1973*, Dokumentation
zur Brecht-Woche der DDR, 9-15 Feb. 1973, ed. Werner Hecht
(Berlin: Henschel, 1973), p.213. Cf. also Müller's statement from an interview in 1977: "Richtig ist eins: Die

Lehrstücktheorie von Brecht ging davon aus, dass es eine Zeit geben wird, in der Theater sich nicht mehr konstituiert aus der Teilung in Publikum und Schauspieler, Zuschauer und Schauspieler. Das heisst, es setzt eigentlich die Aufhebung der Arbeitsteilung voraus. Das ist schon eine sehr kommunistische Utopie. Und alles andere sind Übergänge." "Gespräch mit Bernard Umbrecht," in *Rotwelsch*, p.110.

[36] "DDR-Dramatiker über Brecht," in *Brecht 1973*, p.213. Again, the author is socially obligated to work towards his own obsolescence.

[37] Müller made this point most strikingly in a recent speech in which he attacked the oppressive Eurocentric perspective of the peace movement: "Wenn wir vom Frieden in Europa reden, reden wir von einem Frieden im Krieg. Krieg auf mindestens drei Kontinenten. Der Frieden in Europa ist nie etwas anderes gewesen. So wie der Faschismus eine weissglühende Episode in dem vierhundertjährigen kapitalistischen Weltkrieg war, ein geographischer Lapsus, Genozid in Europa statt, was die Norm war und ist, in Südamerika, Afrika, Asien." "Diskussionsbeitrag auf der 'Berliner Begegnung'" [1981], in *Rotwelsch*, p.199.

[38] "Fragen an Heiner Müller," *Connaissance de la RDA*, No. 12 (1981), pp.63-64.

[39] "Walls" (1981), in *Rotwelsch*, pp.11, 25.

[40] For my information on Latin American authors I draw from the following reference works: *The Penguin Companion to American Literature*, ed. Malcolm Bradbury, Eric Mottram, and Jean Franco (New York: McGraw-Hill, 1971); *The Oxford Companion to Spanish Literature*, ed. Philip Ward (Oxford: The Clarendon Press, 1978); *A Dictionary of Contemporary Latin American Writers*, comp. David William Foster (n.p.: Center for Latin American Studies, Arizona State University, 1975); and the very good essay on Gabriel García Márquez by Dieter Janik, in *Lateinamerikanische Literatur der Gegenwart: In Einzeldarstellungen*, ed. Wolfgang Eitel (Stuttgart: Alfred Kröner, 1978), pp.330-60.

[41] Dieter Janik, "Gabriel García Márquez," p.347.

[42] See Ovid, *Metamorphoses* VI.383-400; Humphries translation, pp.141-42.

[43] "Mich interessiert der Fall Althusser ...," in *Rotwelsch*, pp.176-77. Consider also this comment from the interview "Walls," in *Rotwelsch*, p.26: "The main function of alternative movements in the West is to establish in its midst islands of the Third World. West Berlin has become the third biggest Turkish city in the world. In 10 years, West Germany will be a second Turkish or Greek or Italian state. This is a very positive phenomenon. It will prepare the ground for change."

[44] The "Steckbrief" Müller refers to is Hassan's "POSTmodernISM: A Paracritical Bibliography," which appeared in *New Literary History*, 3, No. 1 (Autumn 1971), 5-30. The seven characteristics or "rubrics," as Hassan terms them, are as follows (I excerpt here from pp.19-21, 24-28 of Hassan's article; cf. the summary presented by Hoffmann, Hornung, and Kunow, "'Modern,' 'Postmodern' and 'Contemporary' as Criteria for the Analysis of 20th Century Literature," pp.34-35):

| MODERNISM | POSTMODERNISM |
|---|---|
| (1) Urbanism | Anarchy and fragmentation; ecological activism; urban crime. |
| (2) Technologism | Runaway technology; new media. |
| (3) "Dehumanization": Elitism | Anti-elitism, anti-authoritarianism; communal, optional, gratuitous, anarchic art. |
| Irony | Radical, self-consuming play: the blank page, silence. |
| Abstraction | New Concreteness: the found object. |
| (4) Primitivism | Beat and Hip; psychedelics. |
| (5) Eroticism | New body consciousness; the homosexual novel, camp/comic pornography. |

| | |
|---|---|
| (6) Antinomianism: pride of art, of the self, defining the conditions of its own grace | The Counter Cultures: SDS, Women's Lib, Chicano Movement, etc.; Zen, mysticism, the occult; apocalyptism as destruction. |
| (7) Experimentalism | Anti-formalism, simultaneism, fusion of forms/media. |

[45] "Der Anschein von Wahl ist ein Vorschein von Freiheit" (96). I read "Vorschein" not as "illusion" as do Jack Zipes and Betty Nance Weber in their translation, but as "appearance" in the sense of first "manifestation." It is possible that Müller draws here from Ernst Bloch's Marxist metaphysics and aesthetics, in which "Vor-Schein" is the objective anticipatory appearance in the process of reality of something that can be realized, through work, in the future.

[46] Jean Baudrillard, *Kool Killer oder Der Aufstand der Zeichen*, trans. Hans-Joachim Metzger (Berlin: Merve, 1978), pp.19-38.

[47] This in an unpublished interview with Sue-Ellen Case. See her "Developments in Post-Brechtian Theater: The Plays of Heiner Müller," Diss. University of California 1981, p.71.

[48] Baudrillard, p.25. The fundamental change in the nature of the city is developed over pp.19-25 of the essay.

[49] Ibid., p.26.

[50] Ibid., p.38.

[51] The name "Comte de Lautréamont" was used only for the first complete edition of *Maldoror* in 1869. The appearance of the first canto in 1868 was anonymous; Ducasse signed his own name to both volumes of *Poésies*. See Chapter II ("Biographical Facts and Surmises") of Wallace Fowlie's *Lautréamont* (New York: Twayne Publishers, 1973), pp.21-33, for a brief presentation of publication and biographical information.

[52] Alex de Jonge, *Nightmare Culture: Lautréamont and "Les Chants de Maldoror"* (New York: St. Martin's Press, 1973), pp.11-16.

[53] The complete quote reads as follows (I give the English translation): "Poetry should be made by all. Not by one. Poor Hugo! Poor Racine! Poor Coppée! Poor Corneille! Poor Boileau! Poor Scarron! Tics, tics, and tics." Lautrémont/Isidore Ducasse, *Poésies and Complete Miscellanea*, ed. and trans. Alexis Lykiard (London: Allison & Busby, 1978), pp. 75, 76.

[54] The best account of Kafka's intention is given by Max Brod, who explains in the Afterword to the first edition of *Der Prozess* his decision to disobey his friend. "Nachwort zur Ersten Ausgabe," *Der Prozess*, by Franz Kafka, ed. Max Brod, 3rd ed. (Frankfurt am Main: S. Fischer; Lizenzausgabe v. New York: Schocken Books, 1946), pp. 315-23. Kafka's orders were explicit and allowed for no exception in their execution:

> Liebster Max, meine letzte Bitte: Alles, was sich in meinem Nachlass (also im Buchkasten, Wäscheschrank, Schreibtisch, zu Hause und im Büro, oder wohin sonst irgend etwas vertragen worden sein sollte und Dir auffällt) an Tagebüchern, Manuskripten, Briefen, fremden und eignen, Gezeichnetem und so weiter findet, restlos und ungelesen zu verbrennen, ebenso alles Geschriebene oder Gezeichnete, das Du oder andre, die Du in meinem Namen darum bitten sollst, haben. Briefe, die man Dir nicht übergeben will, soll man wenigstens selbst zu verbrennen sich verpflichten. (pp. 316-17)

[55] Ibid., p. 315.

[56] Marlowe, *The Tragical History of Doctor Faustus*, Scene xiv, ll. 119-26.

[57] "Home!" (ll. 44-48), in Mayakovsky, *Selected Poetry*, trans. Dorian Rottenberg (Moscow: Foreign Languages Publishing House, n.d.), p. 87.

[58] Mayakovsky, *How Are Verses Made?* trans. G.M. Hyde (London: Jonathan Cape, 1970), p. 15.

[59] As such Mayakovsky exerts a continuing influence on artists and artistic projects in East Germany:

> Schon der Zwang des Materials, dass Bauern auf der
> Bühne sind und in Versen reden, dass Arbeiter in Versen reden, zwingt dazu, die Hochsprache zu zerbrechen, zwingt zu einem Versuch, die Verbindung zu den Dialekten oder zum Jargon zu kriegen mit dem Vers. Das bedeutet schon eine Annäherung an Shakespeare. Und das bedeutet auch, dass man heute, wenn man hier Shakespeare übersetzt, dann macht man das auch als jemand, der Majakowski verarbeitet hat als den ersten grossen Versuch, die Industrie in die Lyrik zu bringen, den Jargon der Industrie und die Sprache der Strasse.

"Shakespeares Stücke sind komplexer als jede Aneignung - man braucht zu verschiedenen Zeiten verschiedene Übersetzungen: Ein Gespräch," *Theater heute,* 16 (July 1975), 35.

[60] Majakowski, *150 Millionen,* Autorisierte Nachdichtung von Johannes R. Becher (Berlin: Malik, 1924; rpt. Königstein Ts.: Athenäum, 1981), p.5. A few lines later appear the statements "Eine Sprechmaschine bin ich" and "Ein Niemand auch hinwiederum / Ist der Verfasser dieses Gedichts." The poem represents a powerful renunciation of the author and of the authority of the individual. The duel of the giants Wilson (Capitalism) and Ivan (Socialism), the Russian hero composed of millions of tiny workers, is at the same time the clash of two aesthetics: that of the decadent, impressionistic "Weltschmerzdichter" and that of the masses, the "Millionen-Chöre" of workers (pp.40-41).

[61] Sartre, Preface, *The Wretched of the Earth,* by Frantz Fanon, trans. Constance Farrington (New York: Grove Press, 1968), p.30.

[62] Müller, "Artaud, die Sprache der Qual ..." (1977), in *Rotwelsch,* p.169.

[63] Hassan, for example, reads Beckett in this way, in Chapter VII ("BECKETT: Imagination Ending"), pp.210-46 of *The Dismemberment of Orpheus:*

> If habits, of which language is the deadliest, deaden, only the "suffering of being" awakens all the faculties

of man. Against the silence of the dead, there is the silence of the agonized living. The latter may be the highest value in Beckett's world, this side of apocalypse. Thus from *The Unnamable,* who is Molloy eons later:

> ... it's to go silent that you need courage, for you'll be punished, for having gone silent, and yet you can't do otherwise than go silent, than be punished for having gone silent.

On this foundation, the impossible art of Beckett rests. (pp.219-220)

[64] Quoted in Hugh Kenner, *Samuel Beckett: A Critical Study* (London: John Calder, 1961), p.30.

[65] Brecht published three scenes of the play in *Versuche,* No. 1 (1930), pp.23-35. The text of three additional scenes, and a summary of the action in eight others, appeared in *Theater heute,* 17 (April 1976), 48-57; and selected individual speeches are quoted in John Milfull, *From Baal to Keuner: The "Second Optimism" of Bertolt Brecht,* Australisch-Neuseeländische Studien zur deutschen Sprache und Literatur, Vol. 5 (Bern, Frankfurt am Main: Herbert Lang, 1974), pp.65-70. Brecht's commentaries on the play are published in *Brechts Modell der Lehrstücke: Zeugnisse, Diskussion, Erfahrung,* ed. Reiner Steinweg (Frankfurt am Main: Suhrkamp, 1976), pp.41-48, 70-78, 173-74, 193. The passage regarding the "neues Tier" does not appear in any of this published material. See Jan Knopf, *Brecht-Handbuch* (Stuttgart: J.B. Metzler; Carl Ernst Poeschel, 1980), pp.351-55, for an account of the history, plot, interpretations, and performances of the play.

[66] See his statements in "DDR-Dramatiker über Brecht," in *Brecht 1973,* pp.212-13; "Der Dramatiker und die Geschichte seiner Zeit," *Theater heute:* Jahrbuch 1975, p.122; and also Müller's essay "Notate zu Fatzer: Einige Überlegungen zu meiner Brecht-Bearbeitung," *Die Zeit,* Overseas Edition, 24 Mar. 1978, pp.9-10.

[67] Müller, "Notate zu Fatzer," p.10.

[68] "'Fatzer', Fassungs-Besprechung vom 25.3.67 (Guy de Chambure, Heiner Müller, Alexander Stillmark)," in Reiner Steinweg, *Das Lehrstück: Brechts Theorie einer politisch-ästhetischen Erziehung* (Stuttgart: J.B. Metzler, 1972), p.254.

[69] "Fatzer ± Keuner," in *Rotwelsch*, p.147.

[70] Benjamin, "Bert Brecht," in *Versuche über Brecht*, ed. Rolf Tiedemann (Frankfurt am Main: Suhrkamp, 1978), p.11; Müller, "Fatzer ± Keuner," in *Rotwelsch*, p.148. Benjamin analyzes Keuner, Baal and Fatzer, and Galy Gay as three major types in Brecht's work.

[71] Müller, "Fatzer ± Keuner," in *Rotwelsch*, p.148.

[72] Müller, *Leben Gundlings Friedrich von Preussen Lessings Schlaf Traum Schrei: Ein Greuelmärchen* (Frankfurt am Main: Verlag der Autoren, 1982), p.43.

[73] "Aufforderung zum Erschrecken," in *Rotwelsch*, pp.162-63. The complete passage, which contains many of the formulas presented in the later essay on postmodernism, is as follows:

> Im ganzen hat die deutsche Literatur, anders als zum Beispiel die russische, englische, amerikanische, wenn die Wahrheit der Schönheit zu nahe trat, noch immer ein Auge zugedrückt und sich für die Schönheit entschieden. Über die Gründe ist spätestens seit Marx genug geschrieben worden, die Folgen sind nicht ausgestanden. Solange die Gründe fortbestehn, bleiben Realismus und Volkstümlichkeit zwei Dinge. Wenn die Literatur auf dem Riss zwischen Umgangs- und Hochsprache besteht statt dass sie mit ihm sich selbst in Frage stellt, kann sie an der Bewegung der Sprache nicht teilnehmen, die sich zuerst in den Jargons vollzieht und nicht auf dem Papier. Literatur nimmt aber an der Geschichte teil, indem sie an der Bewegung der Sprache teilnimmt. In diesem Sinn ist sie EINE ANGELEGENHEIT DES VOLKES (Kafka). Im andern Fall bleibt sie geschichtslos elitär und wird als Kunstgewerbe in das System integriert, das mit der Kulturindustrie an der Betonierung des status quo arbeitet und so Geschichte verhindert.

[74]"Die Kröte auf dem Gasometer," rev. of *Die Vorzüge der Windhühner*, by Günter Grass, *Neue deutsche Literatur*, 5, No. 1 (1957), 160-61; also in *Rotwelsch*, p.127. Cf. Müller, "Mülheimer Rede," *Theater heute*, 20 (October 1979), 14: "Am Verschwinden des Menschen arbeiten viele der besten Gehirne und riesige Industrien. ... Das erhellt die Notwendigkeit der Kunst als Mittel, die Wirklichkeit unmöglich zu machen."

[75]For a good and intelligible discussion of "entropy," see Colin Cherry, *On Human Communication: A Review, a Survey, and a Criticism*, 3rd ed. (Cambridge, Massachusetts: The MIT Press, 1978), pp.214-17.

[76]Müller, "'Viv(r)e la contradiction!' Jacques Poulet s'entretient avec Heiner Müller," *France nouvelle*, 29 Jan. 1979, p.48.

## Chapter II: Leben Gundlings

[1]Müller does not invent, but draws on historical fact. Gundling, who began as a serious and talented scholar, was buried, in accordance with Friedrich Wilhelm's instructions, in a wine cask bearing the inscription: "Hier liegt in seiner Haut, / Halb Schwein, halb Mensch, ein Wunderding." Werner Hegemann, *Das steinerne Berlin: Geschichte der grössten Mietkasernenstadt der Welt* (Berlin: Gustav Kiepenheuer, 1930), p.155; quoted from the 1963 edition in *Spectaculum*, 26 (1977), 292, and in Müller, *Herzstück* (Berlin: Rotbuch, 1983), p.116.

[2]*Leben Gundlings Friedrich von Preussen Lessings Schlaf Traum Schrei: Ein Greuelmärchen*, Theaterbibliothek, 61 (Frankfurt am Main: Verlag der Autoren, 1982), p.7. Subsequent references to the play in this edition will be given in parentheses in the text of the chapter.

[3]Heinrich von Kleist, *Sämtliche Werke und Briefe*, ed. Helmut Sembdner (München: Carl Hanser, 1961), II, 345.

[4]*Hamlet* III.i.150.

[5] Werner Hegemann writes: "Weder mit dem Gut noch mit dem Blut seiner Untertanen ist [Friedrich II] sparsam umgegangen. Goethe's Verehrung für ihn 'erkaltete', weil 'der König seine vortreffliche Armee ganz unnütz aufgeopfert'. Ebenso urteilte Napoleon I. über manche der Schlachten Friedrichs II.: 'Friedrich lieferte seine Bataillone auf die Schlachtbank, wie sie nacheinander kamen, und ohne Aussicht auf Erfolg.' Blutige Kriege und teure Bauten galten damals als erlaubte und wahrhaft königliche *Passionen*." Werner Hegemann, *Das steinerne Berlin*, p.179; also in *Spectaculum*, 26 (1977), 293; and in Müller, *Herzstück*, p.117.

[6] Jakob Grimm and Wilhelm Grimm, *Kinder- und Hausmärchen*, ed. Friedrich von der Leyen (Düsseldorf-Köln: Eugen Diederich, 1962), I, 6-9.

[7] John Bull is intended as a personification of the English nation in the political satire *The History of John Bull* (1713) by John Arbuthnot. Marianne, the name of a secret society formed about 1852 with the purpose of establishing the French Republic, came to signify for Frenchmen the republican form of government. By foreigners it is used as a name for France, as John Bull for England. See *The Oxford Companion to English Literature*, comp. and ed. Paul Harvey, 4th ed., rev. Dorothy Eagle (Oxford: Clarendon Press, 1967), p.516.

[8] Kleist, I, 653.

[9] Cf. Kleist, *Prinz Friedrich von Homburg*, Act IV, Scene i. Natalie tells her uncle: "Das Kriegsgesetz, das weiss ich wohl, soll herrschen, / Jedoch die lieblichen Gefühle auch." Kleist, I, 680.

[10] Friedrich quotes here from Hamlet's speech, II.ii.295-300: "... What a piece of work is man! / how noble in reason! how infinite in faculty! in form and / moving, how express and admirable! in action, how like an / angel! in apprehension, how like a god! the beauty of the / world! the paragon of animals! And yet, to me, what is this / quintessence of dust?"

[11] The Thuringian and Saxonian bedtime prayer is: "Lieber Gott, mach' mich fromm, dass ich in den Himmel komm'!" See *Deutsches Kinderlied und Kinderspiel: Volksüberlieferungen aus allen Landen deutscher Zunge*, ed. Franz Magnus Böhme (Leipzig: Breitkopf und Härtel, 1897), p.315.

[12] Genia Schulz, *Heiner Müller*, p.145, attributes the invention to Schreber, whose name is erroneously given as "Schreiber." Morton Schatzman, *Soul Murder: Persecution in the Family* (New York: Random House, 1973), does not confirm Schreber's responsibility for the invention, but in any case, such a bandage was commonly used to prevent masturbation in the 19th century (pp.118-19). It is unclear whether Schreber used this method on his own two sons. The elder Daniel Gustav eventually committed suicide; Daniel Paul Schreber's *Denkwürdigkeiten eines Nervenkranken* (Leipzig: Oswald Mutze, 1903) has been studied by psychoanalysts and psychiatrists, among them Sigmund Freud and Jacques Lacan, throughout the 20th century and is considered classic evidence of paranoid schizophrenia.

[13] Müller, *Der Auftrag: Erinnerung an eine Revolution* (Frankfurt am Main: Verlag der Autoren, 1981), p.33.

[14] The "Prologue" is published in *Theater heute*, 20 (March 1979), 26.

[15] "My poetry shall consist of attacks, by all means, upon that wild beast, Man, and the Creator, who should never have begotten such vermin!" *Lautréamont's "Maldoror,"* trans. Alexis Lykiard (New York: Thomas Y. Crowell, 1973), p.42.

[16] Césaire, *Discourse on Colonialism*, trans. Joan Pinkham (New York: Monthly Review Press, 1972), pp.46-49.

[17] I quote from the original version, which carries the title "Elegie," given in *Schillers Werke*, Nationalausgabe, ed. Lieselotte Blumenthal and Benno von Wiese, Vol. I, ed. Julius Petersen and Friedrich Beissner (Weimar: Hermann Böhlaus Nachfolger, 1943), pp.260-66.

[18] The line does not stem from Horace, as the text states in a footnote (p.34), but is anonymous. A detailed discussion

of its usage is provided by Herbert von Einem in his commentary to *Goethes Werke,* Hamburger Ausgabe, XI (München: C.H. Beck, 1978), 577-79. "Auch ich in Arkadien" was the motto of both volumes of the first edition of the *Italienische Reise* (1816, 1817), and is frequently found in German literature of the 18th century (quoted, among others, by Wieland, Herder, and Schiller).

[19] *'Tis Pity She's a Whore,* in *The Works of John Ford,* ed. William Gifford, rev. Alexander Dyce (1895; rpt. New York: Russell & Russell, 1965), I, 197-207.

[20] The play is discussed in this respect by Antonin Artaud in the essay "The Theater and the Plague":

> Annabella is captured, convicted of adultery and incest, trampled upon, insulted, dragged by the hair, and we are astonished to discover that far from seeking a means of escape, she provokes her executioner still further and sings out in a kind of obstinate heroism. It is the absolute condition of revolt .... Giovanni, the lover, inspired by the passion of a great poet, puts himself beyond vengeance, beyond crime, by still another crime, one that is indescribably passionate; beyond threats, beyond horror by an even greater horror, one which overthrows at one and the same time law, morality, and all those who dare set themselves up as administrators of justice.

Artaud, *The Theater and its Double,* trans. Mary Caroline Richards (New York: Grove Press, 1958), pp.28-29.

[21] *Der Auftrag,* p.31.

[22] Ibid., p.35.

[23] Müller's subversive criticism of the Enlightenment tradition is lent support by at least one literary scholar. Friedrich Kittler explains the significance of Emilia's death in Lessing's play as follows:

> Der Wunsch der Tochter an den (leiblichen) Vater ist das Gesetz des (idealen) Vaters, das Gesetz des (leiblichen) Vaters der Wunsch der Tochter nach dem

Gesetz (des idealen). Es herrscht vollkommene intersubjektive Reziprozität.

... die reziproken Erwartungserwartungen, die die humanistische Pädagogik lehrt, knüpfen ein unzerreissbares Band, weil sie Gesetz und Wunsch im Subjekt selber legieren und ihm die archaischen Wege des Zorns und der Rebellion versperren. Das ist die Bewandtnis der Psychologisierung. Durch Herstellung von Individuen, die wie Sara [Sampson] und Emilia dem idealen Vater "in" ihrer Psyche auch dann unterstehen, wenn sie vom faktischen Vater getrennt sind, triumphiert die Bürgerfamilie über die Zerreissprobe, die ihr adlige Intriganten und Verführer auferlegen.

Friedrich A. Kittler, "'Erziehung ist Offenbarung': Zur Struktur der Familie in Lessings Dramen," *Jahrbuch der Deutschen Schillergesellschaft,* 21 (1977), 111-37, here pp.131, 133. Kittler analyzes the structure of the bourgeois family of Lessing's plays as a precise system of rules governing intersubjective relationships, with the father as the central authority and guarantor of the order and the continued survival of the family. See also Wolfgang Schaer, *Die Gesellschaft im deutschen bürgerlichen Drama des 18. Jahrhunderts: Grundlagen und Bedrohung im Spiegel der dramatischen Literatur,* Bonner Arbeiten zur deutschen Literatur, Vol. 7 (Bonn: H. Bouvier, 1963): Schaer argues that the new bourgeois morality of the 18th century is expressed in drama within the realm of the family, whose central figure is the father; recognition of and submission to his absolute authority are the basis for moral order.

[24] Lessing, *Werke,* ed. Herbert G. Göpfert et al., II (Darmstadt: Wissenschaftliche Buchgesellschaft, 1971), 276.

[25] Ibid., p.280.

[26] "Schreiben aus Lust an der Katastrophe: Gespräch mit Horst Laube," in *Rotwelsch,* p.183.

[27] "Spartacus," even in the few fragments which remain, sets active revolt above mere "philosophizing":

Der Consul: Ich höre, du philosophierst, Spartacus.
Spartacus: Was ist das? du philosophierst? - Doch ich
erinnre mich - Ihr habt den Menschenverstand in die
Schule verwiesen - um ihn lächerlich machen zu können -
Wo du nicht willst, dass ich philosophieren soll -
Philosophieren - es macht mich lachen - Nun gut - Wir
wollen fechten - Lebwohl - Auf Wiedersehen - wo der
Kampf am hitzigsten wird sein! (Lessing, II, 576)

[28]*Dialektik der Aufklärung*, in Theodor W. Adorno, *Gesammelte Schriften*, ed. Rolf Tiedemann, III (Frankfurt am Main: Suhrkamp, 1981), 19.

[29]Ibid., p.29.

[30]Ibid., pp.32, 45.

[31]Ibid., p.38.

[32]"Geschichte und Drama," *Basis*, 6 (1976), 54.

## Excursus

[1]This section is a modest and partial product of many discussions with Russell Berman on the theory and ideology of German bourgeois drama.

[2]*Theorie des modernen Dramas (1880-1950)* (Frankfurt am Main: Suhrkamp, 1956); see in particular Chapter I, "Das Drama," pp.14-19.

[3]*Hamburgische Dramaturgie*, in Lessing, *Werke*, ed. Herbert G. Göpfert et al., IV (Darmstadt: Wissenschaftliche Buchgesellschaft, 1973). References to the *Hamburgische Dramaturgie* are given by article ("Stück") number in the body of the text.

[4]Hegel, *Werke in zwanzig Bänden*, Vol. XV: *Vorlesungen über die Ästhetik*, III, ed. Eva Moldenhauer and Karl Markus Michel (Frankfurt am Main: Suhrkamp, 1970), p.476. Subsequent references to this edition are given in parentheses in the text.

[5]"[Der Dialog] wurde in der Renaissance, nach Ausschaltung von Prolog, Chor und Epilog, vielleicht zum erstenmal in

der Geschichte des Theaters ... zum alleinigen Bestandteil des dramatischen Gewebes. ... Die Alleinherrschaft des Dialogs, das heisst der zwischenmenschlichen Aussprache im Drama, spiegelt die Tatsache, dass es nur aus der Wiedergabe des zwischenmenschlichen Bezuges besteht, dass es nur kennt, was in dieser Sphäre aufleuchtet." Szondi, p.15.

## Chapter III: Die Hamletmaschine

[1] "'Schreiben aus Schadenfreude ...': Heiner Müller, befragt von Rolf Rüth und Petra Schmitz," *Theater heute,* 23 (April 1982), 3.

[2] *Die Hamletmaschine,* in Müller, *Mauser* (Berlin: Rotbuch, 1978), pp.89-97. All references to this play will be given by page number in parentheses in the body of the chapter.

[3] According to Müller in a personal interview, the settings for Scenes 1 and 5 are based on paintings by the Dutch neo-realist Carel Willink (b. 1900), one depicting the "ruins of Europe," the other a leather easy chair on a beach. Unfortunately I am unable after a necessarily brief search to provide more precise information.

[4] The line Müller quotes appears three times as a refrain in the fifth canto of the poem. T.S. Eliot, *The Complete Poems and Plays, 1909-1950* (New York: Harcourt, Brace & World, 1971), pp.65-66.

[5] In Müller, *Geschichten aus der Produktion 1: Stücke Prosa Gedichte Protokolle* (Berlin: Rotbuch, 1974), p.92.

[6] Richard Weber, "'Ich war, ich bin, ich werde sein!': Versuch, die politische Dimension der Hamletmaschine zu orten," in *Die Hamletmaschine: Heiner Müllers Endspiel,* ed. Theo Girshausen (Köln: Prometh, 1978), p.97, n. 32, attributes the quote to Sartre's *Morts sans Sépulture* (*The Victors*). I am unable to locate the line in Sartre's work.

[7] See Chapter I, p.43.

[8] "An epic, horizontal progression turns into a vertical one. All that is left of Shakespeare's play went into this

scene. The other scenes are variants, seen through different lenses, or through the same lens viewing a different subject matter." Quoted in Carl Weber, "Heiner Müller: The Despair and the Hope," *Performing Arts Journal*, No. 12 (1980), pp.139-40.

[9]"Geschichtsphilosophische Thesen," in Benjamin, *Schriften*, ed. Theodor W. Adorno and Gretel Adorno (Frankfurt am Main: Suhrkamp, 1955), I, 494-506. The Angelus Novus is discussed on p.499.

[10]"Geschichtsphilosophische Thesen," p.503.

[11]Hölderlin, *Sämtliche Werke*, Grosse Stuttgarter Ausgabe, ed. Friedrich Beissner, II (Stuttgart: W. Kohlhammer; J.G. Cottasche Buchhandlung Nachfolger, 1951), 316.

[12]*Germania Tod in Berlin*, in Müller, *Germania Tod in Berlin* (Berlin: Rotbuch, 1977), p.78; *Leben Gundlings* (Frankfurt am Main: Verlag der Autoren, 1982), p.41; "Todesanzeige," in *Germania Tod in Berlin*, p.32.

[13]T.S. Eliot, *The Complete Poems and Plays*, p.68.

[14]
                    Gestern
Haben wir einen Offizier erschossen
Die Tscheka hat ihn eingefangen, ein
Bandit, nach einem Überfall, drei Güter
Wälder und Bauern, vor der Revolution
Sein ganzer Grundbesitz der Hass seitdem. Und
Er sagte, als er an die Wand ging, dass er
Gern in die Hölle geht für seinen Hass
Die Hölle war ihm lieber als der Himmel
Weil er dort seinen Hass behalten kann.
Und als er an der Wand stand, weinte er.
Und willst du wissen, wem er nachgeweint hat.
Den Wölfen, die in seinen Wäldern hausten.
Im Winter manchmal kamen sie ins Dorf
Zerrissen einen Bauern, sagte er
Selber ein Wolf und heulte, bis er starb
Um seine Wölfe.

Müller, *Zement*, in *Geschichten aus der Produktion 2* (Berlin: Rotbuch, 1974), p.79.

[15] In the quote in *Hamletmaschine* one line from the original poem is omitted. The full quotation in context:

> Shakespeare hat *Hamlet* geschrieben, ein Trauerspiel
> Geschichte eines Mannes, der sein Wissen wegwarf
> Sich beugend unter einen dummen Brauch.
> Er hat die Dummheit nicht ausgerottet.
> Wollte er nichts weiter schreiben als einen Steckbrief?
> *Hamlet der Däne Prinz und Wurmfrass stolpernd*
> *Von Loch zu Loch aufs letzte Loch zu lustlos*
> *Im Rücken das Gespenst das ihn gemacht hat*
> *Grün wie Ophelias Fleisch im Wochenbett*
> *Der Horizont die Rüstung dauert länger*
> *Und knapp vorm dritten Hahnenschrei zerreisst*
> *Ein Narr das Schellenkleid des Philosophen*
> *Schlüpft ein beleibter Bluthund in den Panzer.*
> Oder der missverstandene Bertolt Brecht
> Mit grosser Zähigkeit und etwas Hoffnung
> *Mehr als den Bogen spannen konnte auch er nicht*
> Wieviele Strohköpfe überlebten ihn.
> Sein Leben lang suchte er eine Möglichkeit
> Den Nächsten nicht zu töten. Gegen Ende
> Hatte er sie von weitem gesehn
> Halb verdeckt von einem blutigen Nebel.

Müller, *Geschichten aus der Produktion 1*, pp.81-82.

[16] *The Enormous Room* (New York: The Modern Library, 1934).

[17] Lessing's resignatory monologue in the last scene of *Leben Gundlings*, in which he abandons his dream of a national theater, points to the self-destruction required of the heroines of bourgeois drama in their attempt to preserve and fulfill the bourgeois ideal of unassailable individuality, rationality, and freedom: "Ich habe die Hölle der Frauen von unten gesehen: Die Frau am Strick Die Frau mit den aufgeschnittenen Pulsadern Die Frau mit der Überdosis AUF DEN LIPPEN SCHNEE Die Frau mit dem Kopf im Gasherd" (p.41). Ophelia in Scene 2 of *Hamletmaschine*, repeating these lines almost exactly, identifies her oppression unambiguously with the Enlightenment tradition.

[18] "Geschichtsphilosophische Thesen," pp.503-04; *Leben Gundlings*, p.42

[19] An officer of the Cossacks: "Ein Traum ist euer Russland ohne Wölfe. / Mein Schlaf braucht keinen Traum, ich bin ein Wolf"; Einarm: "Und bei den Wölfen, Bruder, wohnt die Freiheit"; Polya (regarding the Cossacks who return to a Soviet Russia): "Die Wölfe haben keine Zähne mehr." Müller, *Zement*, in *Geschichten aus der Produktion 2*, pp.97, 122, 130. See also Note 14 above.

[20] In Carl Weber, "Heiner Müller: The Despair and the Hope," p.137. In a later interview Müller refers to "Journey of the Magi" and extends the Hamlet problematic to include the situation of East German intellectuals who, moving to the West, find themselves caught between two models of society: "T.S. Eliot's text gives a good idea of the feelings of East German intellectuals brought up with an image, with a utopia and now living elsewhere. The utopia never became real but they won't be able to forget it." "Walls," in *Rotwelsch*, pp.22-23; see also p.10. Eliot's text concludes:

> All this was a long time ago, I remember,
> And I would do it again, but set down
> This set down
> This: Were we led all that way for
> Birth or Death? There was a Birth certainly,
> We had evidence and no doubt. I had seen birth and
> death,
> But had thought they were different; this Birth was
> Hard and bitter agony for us, like Death, our death.
> We returned to our places, these Kingdoms,
> But no longer at ease here, in the old dispensation,
> With an alien people clutching their gods.
> I should be glad of another death.

"Journey of the Magi," *The Complete Poems and Plays*, p.69; also included in the transcript of the interview, "Walls," p.23.

[21] *Geschichten aus der Produktion 1*, p.81. See Note 15 above.

[22] Ibid., p.82.

[23] Bonaventura, *Die Nachtwachen*, ed. Wolfgang Paulsen (Stuttgart: Philipp Reclam Jun., 1964, 1974), p.75.

[24] "Mich interessiert der Fall Althusser ...," in *Rotwelsch*, pp.173-74.

[25] Brecht, *Gesammelte Werke in acht Bänden*, ed. Suhrkamp Verlag and Elisabeth Hauptmann (Frankfurt am Main: Suhrkamp, 1967), III, 3014.

[26] Ibid., pp.3016-17. See also the poem "Über Shakespeares Stück 'Hamlet,'" Brecht, IV, 608-09.

[27] Quoted in Carl Weber, "Heiner Müller: The Despair and the Hope," p.138.

[28] The significance of the "second clown" derives possibly from Act V, Scene i of *Hamlet*, in which two clowns dig the grave of Ophelia. The first clown dominates over the second with his stupid-sophistic wit; the second clown must run to "fetch ... a stoup of liquor" for the other.

[29] The worker Barka states in Müller's *Der Bau*: "Mein Lebenslauf ist Brückenbau. Ich bin / Der Ponton zwischen Eiszeit und Kommune." *Geschichten aus der Produktion 1*, p.134. Müller was later asked specifically about the image:

> Girnus: Was aber verstehen Sie unter "Eiszeit"?
> Müller: Den Kapitalismus. ... Die Metapher steht für eine Welt, in der es für Barka nicht möglich war, menschliche Kontakte zu finden ...

"Gespräch mit Heiner Müller," in *Geschichten aus der Produktion 1*, p.141.

[30] *Germania Tod in Berlin*, p.78.

[31] "Viv(r)e la contradiction!" *France nouvelle*, 29 Jan. 1979, p.50.

[32] Müller's short "Elektratext" tells of an Electra who waits twenty years for vengeance. "Zwanzig Jahre lang, Magd unter Mägden im Palast der Mutter, wartet sie auf [Orestes'] Heimkehr." *Theater-Arbeit*, p.119.

[33] Here my interpretation differs from Müller's own: "The final scene is defined by this feeling: that it is too late; the feeling that the revolution can now only exist in a submarine traveling around the globe. Then, in writing

it, I changed this again, so that the revolution, as represented by Ophelia/Electra, is finally silenced, even in the submarine, by the psychiatrists or whatever we assume these men in their white smocks are." Quoted in Carl Weber, "Heiner Müller: The Despair and the Hope," p.140.

[34] Cf. Genia Schulz, *Heiner Müller*, pp.151-52: "Es ist nicht möglich, alle Bedeutungselemente dieses kaum verständlichen Textes anzugeben, oder ihren Zusammenhang stringent zu entwickeln."

[35] "Schreiben aus Schadenfreude ...," *Theater heute*, 23 (April 1982), 3.

[36] Schiller's *Maria Stuart* might serve as an extreme example. The great debate of the two queens builds the exact structural and thematic center of the play.

[37] Quoted in Carl Weber, "Heiner Müller: The Despair and the Hope," p.138.

[38] See my discussion Chapter II, pp.70-71.

[39] Artaud, *Oeuvres complètes*, I (Paris: Editions Gallimard, 1976), 75-76. Müller's "Heiner Müller zu Antonin Artaud" was written for a publication of the German translation, "Der Blutstrahl," trans. Dieter Hülsmanns and Friedolin Reske, in *Stücke der Zwanziger Jahre*, ed. Wolfgang Storch (Frankfurt am Main: Suhrkamp, 1977), pp.133-35; this anthology, which appeared the same year as *Hamletmaschine*, is possibly the source of Müller's acquaintance with Artaud's play. I quote in the original French, since the German translation contains some ambiguities ("son sexe," for example, is given as *"seinem* Geschlecht").

[40] Artaud, *Oeuvres complètes*, II (Paris: Editions Gallimard, 1980), 23. The German translation by Heinz Schwarzinger is also published with Müller's short note and Artaud's "Blutstrahl" in *Stücke der Zwanziger Jahre*, pp.137-38.

[41] "Walls," in *Rotwelsch*, p.43.

[42] "Ich scheiss auf die Ordnung," *Tip*, 1982, Issue No. 7, p.56.

[43] Müller's analysis of the end of the bourgeois intellectual draws upon Michel Foucault's remarks in an interview, "Der

sogenannte Linksintellektuelle," trans. Uli Laukat, *Alternative*, 21 (1978), 74-85. See Müller's statement on Foucault in "Mich interessiert der Fall Althusser ...," in *Alternative*, 24 (1981), 71; reprinted in *Rotwelsch*, p.176.

⁴⁴"Walls," in *Rotwelsch*, pp.12-13.

## Chapter IV: Der Auftrag

¹"Fatzer ± Keuner," in *Rotwelsch*, p.149.

²*Der Auftrag: Erinnerung an eine Revolution*, Theaterbibliothek, 1 (Frankfurt am Main: Verlag der Autoren, 1981). All references will be given in parentheses in the text.

³"Schreiben aus Lust an der Katastrophe: Gespräch mit Horst Laube," in *Rotwelsch*, p.181.

⁴Wirth, "Erinnerung an eine Revolution: sadomasochistisch," *Theater heute*, 22 (February 1981), 6.

⁵*The Wretched of the Earth*, pref. Jean-Paul Sartre, trans. Constance Farrington (New York: Grove Press, 1968), p.315. Müller has pointed out to me the importance of Fanon's *Black Skin, White Masks* (1952) and *The Wretched of the Earth* (1961) for understanding *Der Auftrag*. There has been thus far no discussion of Fanon's ideas in any analysis of the play. Genia Schulz, *Heiner Müller*, p.165, draws only a parenthetical connection: "[Müllers Text] zeigt zudem die Problematik eines Auftrags zum Hass, der nicht gelingen kann, gegenüber dem 'natürlichen' Hass der 'Verdammten dieser Erde' (Frantz Fanon)."

⁶Brecht, *Gesammelte Werke in acht Bänden*, ed. Suhrkamp Verlag and Elisabeth Hauptmann (Frankfurt am Main: Suhrkamp, 1967), I, 633.

⁷See for example Scene 3 of *Die Massnahme*.

⁸Brecht, I, 633.

⁹Müller made the following statement on the "unavoidable" influence of *Dantons Tod* in the writing of *Auftrag*: "Ich habe 'Danton' sicher an vielen Stellen zitiert, parodiert oder travestiert, ohne dass mir das beim Schreiben bewusst

geworden wäre. Es ist schon sehr lange her, seit ich das Stück zum letzten Mal gelesen habe. Aber sicher ist sein Einfluss auf meinen Text unvermeidlich gewesen. Die Ausgangslage von Büchners Stück und die meines eigenen sind sehr ähnlich." Müller, "Schreiben aus Schadenfreude ...," *Theater heute*, 23 (April 1982), 3.

[10] Georg Büchner, *Dantons Tod*, in *Sämtliche Werke und Briefe*, ed. Werner R. Lehmann, I (München: Carl Hanser, 1974), 70.

[11] *Die Hamletmaschine*, in Müller, *Mauser*, p.90.

[12] Brecht, III, 3014-17. See also my discussion of the scene in Chapter III, p.105.

[13] Brecht, III, 3015.

[14] Ibid.

[15] Ibid., p.3017.

[16] Ibid., p.3016.

[17] See for example Act I, Scene ii; Büchner, *Dantons Tod*, pp. 12-16. In Brecht's *Massnahme* also, the (Russian) revolution has not satisfied the basic needs of the people: "Es gibt Unordnung und Mangel, wenig Brot und viel Kampf." Brecht, I, 634.

[18] "Motiv bei A.S.," in Müller, *Germania Tod in Berlin*, p.80. The poem, written in 1958, like the play *Auftrag*, uses motifs from Anna Seghers' "Das Licht auf dem Galgen." Seghers, *Erzählungen* (Neuwied, Berlin: Luchterhand, 1964), II, 169-291.

[19] *Die Hamletmaschine*, p.90.

[20] "Glücksgott," in Müller, *Theater-Arbeit*, p.18. See also Helen Fehervary's discussion of this text on pp.93-95 of "Enlightenment or Entanglement: History and Aesthetics in Bertolt Brecht and Heiner Müller," *New German Critique*, No. 8 (Spring 1976), pp.80-109.

[21] See my discussion in Chapter III, p.100.

[22] "Viv(r)e la contradiction!" *France nouvelle*, 29 Jan. 1979, p.47.

[23] This is Act II, Scene v. Antoine's wife repeats the words of Danton: "Komm ins Bett, Antoine" (10); "Ja Julie, komm, zu Bette!" Büchner, *Dantons Tod*, p.41.

[24] *Mauser*, in Müller, *Mauser*, pp.68-69.

[25] "Der Schrecken die erste Erscheinung des Neuen," in *Rotwelsch*, p.98.

[26] Müller, "Artaud, die Sprache der Qual ...," in *Rotwelsch*, p.169.

[27] *Die Hamletmaschine*, p.97.

[28] Brecht, I, 633-34.

[29] *Black Skin, White Masks*, trans. Charles Lam Markmann (New York: Grove Press, 1967), pp.44-45. For a detailed discussion see Fanon, *The Wretched of the Earth*, pp.38-43.

[30] *The Wretched of the Earth*, p.35. See also p.39: "The look that the native turns on the settler's town is a look of lust, a look of envy; it expresses his dreams of possession - all manner of possession: to sit at the settler's table, to sleep in the settler's bed, with his wife if possible. ... there is no native who does not dream at least once a day of setting himself up in the settler's place." The first ten pages of *The Wretched of the Earth* (pp.35-45) present a stunning analysis of the colonial situation.

[31] *The Wretched of the Earth*, pp.311-16.

[32] *Black Skin, White Masks*, pp.228, 229.

[33] Büchner, *Dantons Tod*, p.33.

[34] Ibid., pp.70-71.

[35] Ibid., p.72.

[36] "Puppen sind wir von unbekannten Gewalten am Draht gezogen; nichts, nichts wir selbst! Die Schwerter, mit denen Geister kämpfen, man sieht nur die Hände nicht, wie im Mährchen." Büchner, *Dantons Tod*, p.41.

[37] Brecht seems to approach Büchner's understanding of masks or roles in *Das Badener Lehrstück vom Einverständnis*.

There man (the young pilot who has crashed) is defined by the office he holds or mission he fulfills for society. "Gesicht" and "Amt" are created and lost together: "sein Gesicht [wurde] / Erzeugt zwischen ihm und uns"; "sein Gesicht / Verlosch mit seinem Amt: / *Er hatte nur eines!*" Brecht, I, 607, 608.

[38] A comparative study of the function of masks or role-playing in Müller and Jean Genet might reveal important insights into Müller's dramaturgical techniques, if not provide evidence of a direct influence. The story of the three revolutionaries in *Der Auftrag* shares with Genet's theater, to state the obvious, the revelation of illusion as reality on a deeper level. In Genet's *The Balcony*, for example, clients of a brothel who act out fantasies of themselves as bishop, judge, and general become these real officials during a revolution. Distinct parallels exist also between Genet's *The Maids* and Müller's *Quartett* (1981), in which the ritualistic role-playing of two allied but rival characters results in the murder of one by the other.

[39] *Mauser*, p.55, et passim.

[40] "Die Revolution ist wie Saturn, sie frisst ihre eignen Kinder." *Dantons Tod*, p.25.

[41] *Die Hamletmaschine*, p.91.

[42] Ibid., p.97.

[43] Ibid., p.91.

[44] "DA DROBEN AUF DEM BERGE / DA WEHET DER WIND / DA SCHLACHTET MARIA / DAS HIMMLISCHE KIND" (18) is a grotesque variation of the lullaby "Wiegenlied im Freien":

> Da oben auf dem Berge,
> Da rauscht der Wind,
> Da sitzet Maria
> Und wieget ihr Kind,
> Sie wiegt es mit ihrer schneeweissen Hand,
> Dazu braucht sie kein Wiegenband.

*Des Knaben Wunderhorn: Alte deutsche Lieder,* comp. L. Achim von Arnim and Clemens Brentano, Vollständige Ausgabe nach dem Text der Erstausgabe von 1806/1808 (München: Winkler, 1962), p.828. A second likely source for Müller's rhyme is the fairy tale "Hänsel und Gretel." When the voice of the witch asks who it is that is eating her house, the children answer, "der Wind, der Wind, / das himmlische Kind." Jakob Grimm and Wilhelm Grimm, Kinder- und Hausmärchen, ed. Friedrich von der Leyen (Düsseldorf-Köln: Eugen Diederich, 1962), I, 233.

[45]*Dantons Tod*, pp.26-27.

[46]To broaden the historical and political significance of the conflict between Danton and Robespierre in the "theater of revolution": Hans-Thies Lehmann notes that the insults they exchange quote from Hitler's own denunciation of Roosevelt. Lehmann, "Dramatische Form und Revolution in Georg Büchners 'Dantons Tod' und Heiner Müllers 'Der Auftrag,'" in *Dantons Tod. Die Trauerarbeit im Schönen: Ein Theaterlesebuch*, ed. Peter von Becker (Frankfurt am Main: Syndikat, 1980), p.111.

[47]Brecht, I, 601.

[48]Ibid., p.602.

[49]Ibid., p.606.

[50]Ibid., p.610.

[51]According to Lehmann, "Dramatische Form und Revolution," p.112, "Nummer Eins" refers to Stalin in Arthur Koestler's *Sonnenfinsternis*.

[52]*Die Hamletmaschine*, p.96.

[53]*Black Skin, White Masks*, pp.192-93.

[54]Brecht, I, 655.

[55]Ibid., p.658.

[56]*Dantons Tod*, p.72.

[57]Brecht, I, 609.

[58]*Black Skin, White Masks*, pp.228, 229, 231.

[59]*Die Hamletmaschine*, p.92.

[60] *The Wretched of the Earth*, pp. 315-16.

[61] Sartre, Pref., *The Wretched of the Earth*, p. 10.

[62] "In den Industriestaaten entstehen immer mehr Enklaven der Dritten Welt. Dass Westberlin die drittgrösste türkische Stadt ist, das finde ich ungeheuer wichtig. ... Die Dritte Welt ist ja nicht nur in Afrika und Lateinamerika, die entsteht in Zürich und in Berlin und in Hamburg, so wie zunächst in New York und in Italien." Müller, "Mich interessiert der Fall Althusser ...," in *Rotwelsch*, pp. 176-77. See also his remarks in "Walls," *Rotwelsch*, pp. 21-22, 26.

[63] Müller, "Schreiben aus Lust an der Katastrophe," in *Rotwelsch*, p. 181.

[64] An interviewer confronted Müller directly on this point: "Damit sagen Sie, dass Revolution notwendig und wiederum fatal von Restauration abgelöst werden muss." Müller responded: "Ja solange es keine Universalgeschichte gibt, wird das so sein. Kann gar nicht anders sein." "Fragen an Heiner Müller," *Connaissance de la RDA*, No. 12 (1981), p. 64.

[65] "Schreiben aus Lust an der Katastrophe," in *Rotwelsch*, p. 181.

[66] "Der Kommunismus ist das Mittlere," Brecht, IV, 504.

## Conclusion

[1] "Deutschland spielt noch immer die Nibelungen," *Der Spiegel*, 9 May 1983, p. 200.

[2] Walter Benjamin, "Der Autor als Produzent," in *Versuche über Brecht*, ed. Rolf Tiedemann (Frankfurt am Main: Suhrkamp, 1978), pp. 101-19. The essay is particularly rich for a discussion of Müller's work. Benjamin writes, for example, "Der Sowjetstaat wird ... [dem Dichter] Aufgaben zuweisen, die es ihm nicht erlauben, den längst verfälschten Reichtum der schöpferischen Persönlichkeit in neuen Meisterwerken zur Schau zu stellen. Eine Erneuerung im Sinn solcher Persönlichkeiten, solcher Werke zu erwarten, ist ein Privileg des Faschismus" (p. 113).

³Adorno, "Der Artist als Statthalter," in *Gesammelte Schriften,* ed. Rolf Tiedemann, II (Frankfurt am Main: Suhrkamp, 1974), 126.

⁴The excellent piece by Hans-Thies Lehmann discusses Müller's concept of history in this context. "Raum-Zeit: Das Entgleiten der Geschichte in der Dramatik Heiner Müllers und im französischen Poststrukturalismus," *Text + Kritik,* No. 73 (January 1982), pp.71-81.

⁵Barthes, "The Death of the Author," in *Image-Music-Text,* trans. Stephen Heath (New York: Hill and Wang, 1977), pp. 143, 146.

⁶Deleuze, "Ein Manifest weniger," in *Kleine Schriften,* trans. K.D. Schacht (Berlin: Merve, 1980), p.64.

⁷Ibid., pp.67-69.

⁸Cf. Helen Fehervary, "Autorschaft, Geschlechtsbewusstsein und Öffentlichkeit: Versuch über Heiner Müllers 'Die Hamletmaschine' und Christa Wolfs 'Kein Ort. Nirgends,'" in *Entwürfe von Frauen in der Literatur des 20. Jahrhunderts,* ed. Irmela von der Lühe, Literatur im historischen Prozess, Neue Folge 5 (Berlin: Argument, 1982), pp.132-53. Fehervary examines the issue of sexuality in *Hamletmaschine* in - the very provocative - terms of an overreaching poetics of authorship and gender.

⁹On the thematic complex of the paternalism/paternality of the son who replaces the father, one might explore the significance of the Oedipus myth in Müller's work, both in terms of the Sophoclean tragedy as a basic dramatic model, and in terms of Deleuze and Guattari's *Anti-Oedipus.*

¹⁰*Rotwelsch,* p.148.

¹¹"Wenn man Stücke schreibt, hat man immer die gleiche Wirkungsabsicht. Die erste Funktion von Dramatik ist Zerstörung. Das kann in verschiedenen Phasen verschiedene Aspekte haben. Nur so kann Dramatik aktiv teilnehmen an einem Umwälzungsprozess, indem sie Ablagerungen zerstört." Müller, "'Die Bauern': Absichten und Erfahrungen mit Stück und Inszenierung," *Material zum Theater,* No. 100, p.40.

[12] "Ich scheiss auf die Ordnung," *Tip*, 1982, Issue No. 7, p.59.

[13] "Der Schrecken die erste Erscheinung des Neuen," in *Rotwelsch*, p.98.

[14] Ibid.

[15] See Chapter I, p.44.

WORKS CONSULTED

## I. WORKS BY HEINER MÜLLER

### A. Collections

1. West German publications

Müller, Heiner. 'Geschichten aus der Produktion 1: Stücke Prosa Gedichte Protokolle.' Texte 1. Berlin: Rotbuch, 1974.
--- 'Geschichten aus der Produktion 2.' Texte 2. Berlin: Rotbuch, 1974.
--- 'Die Umsiedlerin oder Das Leben auf dem Lande.' Texte 3. Berlin: Rotbuch, 1975.
--- 'Theater-Arbeit.' Texte 4. Berlin: Rotbuch, 1975.
--- 'Germania Tod in Berlin.' Texte 5. Berlin: Rotbuch, 1977.
--- 'Mauser.' Texte 6. Berlin: Rotbuch, 1978.
--- 'Rotwelsch.' Berlin: Merve, 1982.
--- 'Herzstück.' Texte 7. Berlin: Rotbuch, 1983.

2. East German publications

--- 'Stücke.' Berlin: Henschel, 1975.
--- 'Die Schlacht/Traktor. Leben Gundlings Friedrich von Preussen Lessings Schlaf Traum Schrei.' Berlin: Henschel, 1977.
--- 'Der Auftrag. Der Bau. Herakles 5.' Berlin: Henschel, 1981.

### B. Singly published works

1. Dramatic texts

Müller, Heiner. 'Der Auftrag: Erinnerung an eine Revolution.' 'Theater heute,' 21 (March 1980), 45-51.

Müller, Heiner. 'Der Auftrag: Erinnerung an eine Revolution.' Theaterbibliothek, 1. Frankfurt am Main: Verlag der Autoren, 1981.
--- 'Cement.' Trans. Helen Fehervary, Sue-Ellen Case, and Marc D. Silberman. New German Critique Publication No. 1. Supplement to Issue No. 16 (Winter 1979).
--- 'The Hamletmachine.' Trans. Carl Weber. 'Performing Arts Journal,' No. 12 (1980), pp.141-46.
--- 'Herzstück.' 'Text + Kritik,' No. 73 (January 1982), p.1.
--- 'The Horatian.' Trans. Marc D. Silberman, Helen Fehervary, and Guntram Weber. 'The Minnesota Review,' NS 6 (Spring 1976), 43-50.
--- 'Leben Gundlings Friedrich von Preussen Lessings Schlaf Traum Schrei.' 'Spectaculum,' 26 (1977), 149-67; "Materialien," 290-95.
--- 'Leben Gundlings Friedrich von Preussen Lessings Schlaf Traum Schrei: Ein Greuelmärchen.' Mit einer Anmerkung u. einem Vorspiel zur Frankfurter Aufführung. 'Theater heute,' 20 (March 1979), 26-33.
--- 'Leben Gundlings Friedrich von Preussen Lessings Schlaf Traum Schrei: Ein Greuelmärchen.' Theaterbibliothek, 61. Frankfurt am Main: Verlag der Autoren, 1982.
--- 'Macbeth. Nach Shakespeare.' Theaterbibliothek, 34. Frankfurt am Main: Verlag der Autoren, 1981.
--- "Philoktet 1979: Drama mit Ballet (Entwurf)." 'Die Zeit,' Overseas Edition, 5 Jan. 1979, p.9.
--- "Quadriga." In 'Die Hamletmaschine: Heiner Müllers Endspiel.' Ed. Theo Girshausen. Köln: Prometh, 1978, pp.155-56.
--- 'Quartett. Nach Choderlos de Laclos.' 'Theater heute,' 22 (July 1981), 46-51.
--- 'Quartett.' Theaterbibliothek, 51. Frankfurt am Main: Verlag der Autoren, 1981.
--- 'Sophokles. Ödipus, Tyrann. Nach Hölderlin.' 'Neue Texte: Almanach für deutsche Literatur,' Fall 1967. Berlin, Weimar: Aufbau, 1967, pp.272-316.
--- 'Sophokles. Ödipus Tyrann. Nach Hölderlin.' Berlin, Weimar: Aufbau, 1969.
--- 'Verkommenes Ufer Medeamaterial Landschaft mit Argonauten.' 'Alternative,' 25 (1982), 178-85.

Müller, Heiner, and Hagen Stahl. 'Zehn Tage, die die Welt erschütterten: Szenen aus der Oktoberrevolution nach Aufzeichnungen John Reeds.' Leipzig: VEB Friedrich Hofmeister, 1958.

2. Lyric texts

--- "Dt 64." 'Forum,' 18, No. 11 (1964), 2-3.
--- "Epigramme über Lyrik." 'Neue deutsche Literatur,' 4, No. 8 (1956), 160.
--- "Fragen für Lehrer." 'Forum,' 17, No. 13 (1963), 15.
--- "Winterschlacht 1963." 'Forum,' 17, No. 6 (1963), 6-7.
--- "Wohin?" 'Neue deutsche Literatur,' 3, No. 2 (1955), 98.

3. Prose texts

--- "Drei Parabeln." 'Sonntag,' 30 Aug. 1953, p.8.
--- "Das eiserne Kreuz." 'Neue deutsche Literatur,' 4, No. 1 (1956), 75-76.
--- "Das Loch im Strumpf." 'Sonntag,' 28 June 1953.
--- "Parabeln." 'Sonntag,' 15 Apr. 1951.
--- "Der seltsame Vorbeimarsch." 'Sonntag,' 26 Apr. 1953.
--- "Das Volk ist in Bewegung." 'Sonntag,' 16 Dec. 1951.

4. Speeches and essays

--- "Absage." 'Theater heute,' 19 (April 1978), 10.
--- "Author's Note." In 'Cement.' Trans. Helen Fehervary, Sue-Ellen Case, and Marc D. Silberman. New German Critique Publication No. 1. Supplement to Issue No. 16 (Winter 1979), p.67.
--- "Author's Preface" to 'The Horatian.' Trans Marc D. Silberman, Helen Fehervary, and Guntram Weber. 'The Minnesota Review,' NS 6 (Spring 1976), 42.
--- "Befreiung ist eben auch heute noch Arbeit." 'Tribüne,' 11 Apr. 1975, p.11.

Müller, Heiner. "Blut ist im Schuh oder Das Rätsel der Freiheit: für Pina Bausch." 'Theater heute': Jahrbuch 1981, pp.34-35.
--- "Brecht gebrauchen, ohne ihn zu kritisieren, ist Verrat." 'Theater heute': Jahrbuch 1980, pp.134-35.
--- "Ein Brief." 'Theater heute': Jahrbuch 1977, p.93.
--- "Die Einsamkeit des Films." In 'Syberbergs Hitler-Film.' Arbeitshefte Film, 1. Ed. Klaus Eder. München: Carl Hanser, 1980, pp.81-82.
--- "'Et beaucoup de choses comme sur les épaules un fardeau de l'échec sont à conserver' (Hölderlin)." 'Le Monde,' 5 Apr. 1979, p.18.
--- "Heiner Müller on Verse." In 'Cement.' Trans. Helen Fehervary, Sue-Ellen Case, and Marc D. Silberman. New German Critique Publication No. 1. Supplement to Issue No. 16 (Winter 1979), p.69.
--- "Heiner Müller zu Antonin Artaud." In 'Stücke der Zwanziger Jahre.' Ed. Wolfgang Storch. Frankfurt am Main: Suhrkamp, 1977, p.132.
--- "I do not believe in a harmony between theatre and literature." In 'The Playwright and the Theatrical Creation.' Proc. of the International Colloquium Budapest. 16-18 December 1974. Budapest: International Theatre Institute, Hungarian Centre, 1975, pp.63-64.
--- "Ich wollte lieber Goliath sein. (Hommage à Chaplin ...)" 'Die Zeit,' Overseas Edition, 13 Jan. 1978, p.18.
--- "Keuner ± Fatzer." 'Brecht-Jahrbuch 1980.' Ed. Reinhold Grimm and Jost Hermand. Frankfurt am Main: Suhrkamp, 1981, pp.14-21.
--- "Mülheimer Rede." 'Theater heute,' 20 (October 1979), 14.
--- "Notate zu Fatzer: Einige Überlegungen zu meiner Brecht-Bearbeitung." 'Die Zeit,' Overseas Edition, 24 Mar. 1978, pp.9-10.
--- "Reflections on Post-Modernism." Trans. Jack Zipes and Betty Nance Weber. 'New German Critique,' No. 16 (Winter 1979), pp.55-57.
--- "Der Schrecken, die erste Erscheinung des Neuen: Zu einer Diskussion über Postmodernismus in New York." 'Theater heute,' 20 (March 1979), 1.

Müller, Heiner. "Zum Beispiel Paul Dessau." 'Sinn und Form,' 31 (1979), 1150-51.
--- "Zwischenbemerkung." 'Neue deutsche Literatur,' 7, No. 1 (1959), 120-21.

5. Interviews and discussions

"Brecht, Kleist und deutsche Realität: Aus einem Gespräch mit Karge, Langhoff und Heiner Müller." 'Theater heute,' 19 (April 1978), 15.
Case, Sue-Ellen. "Notes on Directing 'Cement.'" New German Critique Publication No. 1. Supplement to Issue No. 16 (Winter 1979), pp.71-80.
"DDR-Dramatiker über Brecht." Akademie der Künste der DDR/ Berliner Ensemble Podiumsgespräch. In 'Brecht 1973.' Dokumentation, Brecht-Woche der DDR. 9-15 Feb. 1973. Ed. Werner Hecht. Berlin: Henschel, 1973, pp.197-230.
"'Fatzer,' Fassungs-Besprechung vom 25.3.67 (Guy de Chambure, Heiner Müller, Alexander Stillmark)." In Reiner Steinweg, 'Das Lehrstück: Brechts Theorie einer politisch-ästhetischen Erziehung.' Stuttgart: J.B. Metzler, 1972, pp.254-55.
"Gespräch über 'Ödipus, Tyrann.'" In Heiner Müller, 'Sophokles. Ödipus Tyrann. Nach Hölderlin.' Berlin, Weimar: Aufbau, 1969, pp.93-176.
Henrichs, Benjamin. "Die zum Lächeln nicht Zwingbaren: Zu 'Macbeth': eine verspätete Polemik, eine verunglückte Inszenierung, ein Interview." 'Die Zeit,' Overseas Edition, 31 May 1974, p.11.
Linzer, Martin. "Messer der Meister von morgen? Autoren lasen auf den Werkstatt-Tagen." 'Theater der Zeit,' 35, No. 7 (1980), 12-13.
Müller, Heiner. "'Die Bauern': Absichten und Erfahrungen mit Stück und Inszenierung." 'Material zum Theater,' No. 100, pp.37-46.
--- "'Deutschland spielt noch immer die Nibelungen': DDR-Dramatiker Heiner Müller über seine Theaterarbeit zwischen Ost und West." 'Der Spiegel,' 9 May 1983, pp.196-207.

Müller Heiner. "'Die Differenz nicht wegmogeln': Anmerkungen zur Inszenierung seines 'Lohndrückers' an der Berliner Schaubühne." 'Nürnberger Nachrichten,' 4 Sept. 1974, p.15.

--- "Der Dramatiker und die Geschichte seiner Zeit: Ein Gespräch zwischen Horst Laube und Heiner Müller." 'Theater heute': Jahrbuch 1975, pp.119-23.

--- "Drei Fragen." In 'Theaterbuch 1.' Ed. Horst Laube and Brigitte Landes. München: Carl Hanser, 1978, pp.259-60.

--- "Ermunterung im heutigen Klassenkampf: ND-Gespräch mit dem Dramatiker Heiner Müller zur Uraufführung von 'Zement' am Berliner Ensemble." 'Neues Deutschland,' 10 Oct. 1973, p.4.

--- "Fragen an Heiner Müller." 'Connaissance de la RDA,' No. 12 (1981), pp.63-67.

--- "Fragespiel." In 'Theaterbuch 1.' Ed. Horst Laube and Brigitte Landes. München: Carl Hanser, 1978, pp.260-62.

--- "Geschichte und Drama: Ein Gespräch mit Heiner Müller." 'Basis: Jahrbuch für deutsche Gegenwartsliteratur,' 6 (1976), 48-64.

--- "Gespräche mit Heiner Müller." 'Europäische Ideen,' No. 13 (1975), pp.1-11.

--- "Hat Heiner Müller bisher gelogen?" In 'Theaterbuch 1.' Ed. Horst Laube and Brigitte Landes. München: Carl Hanser, 1978, p.259.

--- "Heute abend: 'Zement'. Uraufführung eines neuen Stückes im Berliner Ensemble." 'Berliner Zeitung,' 12 Oct. 1973, p.6.

--- "Ich scheiss auf die Ordnung." 'Tip,' 1982, Issue No. 7, pp.50-59.

--- "Mich interessiert der Fall Althusser ..." Gesprächsprotokoll. 'Alternative,' 24 (1981), 70-72.

--- "Miteinander statt oben und unten: Irene Böhme sprach mit Heiner Müller über die Bearbeitung von 'Horizonte.'" 'Sonntag,' 12 Oct. 1969, p.11.

--- "Nerven haben, Durchstehen, Abwarten." Aus dem Gespräch mit Horst Laube, "Der Dramatiker und die Geschichte seiner Zeit." In 'Theaterbuch 1.' Ed. Horst Laube and Brigitte Landes. München: Carl Hanser, 1978, pp.235-41.

Müller, Heiner. "Schreiben aus Lust an der Katastrophe." In 'Die Hamletmaschine.' Frankfurt am Main: Schauspiel Frankfurt, 1980, pp.5-13.
--- "'Schreiben aus Schadenfreude ...': Heiner Müller, befragt von Rolf Rüth und Petra Schmitz." 'Theater heute,' 23 (April 1982), 1-3.
--- "'Viv(r)e la contradiction!' Jacques Poulet s'entretient avec Heiner Müller." 'France nouvelle,' 29 Jan. 1979, pp.43-50.
--- "The Walls of History." 'Semiotexte,' 4, No. 2 (1982), 36-76.
"Ödipus Tyrann im Streitgespräch." 'Theater der Zeit,' 22, No. 24 (1967), 10-12.
"Shakespeare in heutiger Übersetzung: Ein Gespräch mit Maik Hamburger, Heiner Müller und Klaus Tragelehn." 'Theater der Zeit,' 20, No. 7 (1970), 7-11.
"Shakespeares Stücke sind komplexer als jede Aneignung - man braucht zu verschiedenen Zeiten verschiedene Übersetzungen: Ein Gespräch." 'Theater heute,' 16 (July 1975), 32-37.
Weber, Carl. "Heiner Müller: The Despair and the Hope." 'Performing Arts Journal,' No. 12 (1980), pp.135-40.

6. Reviews and journalistic articles

Müller Heiner. "'Begeistert von Berlin': Kritische Anmerkungen zu einer Anthologie." Rev. of 'Begeistert von Berlin' (Aufbau-Verlag). 'Sonntag,' 22 Mar. 1953, p.4.
--- "Der Bienenstock." Rev. of 'Der Bienenstock,' 2 vols., by Anna Seghers. 'Sonntag,' 31 May 1953, p.4.
--- "Der chinesische Gorki: Zu den Erzählungen von Lu Hsün." 'Sonntag,' 20 Sept. 1953, p.4.
--- "Die Dichtung muss sich stellen ...: Bemerkungen zu einem Gedichtband von Paul Wiens." Rev. of 'Beredte Welt.' 'Sonntag,' 22 Nov. 1953, p.7.
--- "'Fragen eines lesenden Arbeiters': Zu einigen Briefen an Johannes R. Becher." 'Sonntag,' 9 May 1954.
--- "Gekläff aus Stuttgart." Reply to "Zur Literatur in Ostdeutschland - gesehen mit westdeutschen Augen,"

by Herbert Lestiboudois, in 'Die Kultur' [Stuttgart], 15 June 1954. 'Sonntag,' 3 Oct. 1954, p.6.

--- "Das Gesetz: Zum 50. Geburtstag von Peter Huchel." 'Sonntag,' 5 Apr. 1953, p.4.

--- Rev. of 'Der Graf und die Zirkusreiterin,' by Kálmán Mikszáth. 'Sonntag,' 16 Oct. 1955, p.8.

--- "Gut gemeint und schlecht gemacht: Zu einer Anthologie des Insel-Verlages." Rev. of 'Auf der Schwelle,' ed. F.A. Hünich. 'Sonntag,' 23 Aug. 1953, p.5.

--- Rev. of 'Heimaterde,' by Michailo Stelmach. 'Sonntag,' 30 Oct. 1955.

--- "Individuum und Gesellschaft." Rev. of 'Jüdisches Largo,' by Martin Gregor. 'Neue deutsche Literatur,' 5, No. 1 (1957), 140-41.

--- "Die Kröte auf dem Gasometer." Rev. of 'Die Vorzüge der Windhühner,' by Günter Grass. 'Neue deutsche Literatur,' 5, No. 1 (1957), 160-61.

--- "Nicht für 'Eisenbahner': Kritische Bemerkungen zu einem Heimatbuch." Rev. of 'Das Fischland,' by Käthe Miethe. 'Sonntag,' 7 Mar. 1954, p.8.

--- "Novellen aus unserer Zeit." Rev. of 'Das gelbe Kreuz,' by Boris Djacenko. 'Neue deutsche Literatur,' 2, No. 3 (1954), 146-47.

--- "'Die Pfeffermühle': Ein Leipziger Kabarett im Berliner Theater der Freundschaft." 'Sonntag,' 13 June 1954, p.5.

--- "Poesie und Phrase: Bemerkungen zu einer Anthologie." Rev. of 'Anthologie neuer deutscher Lyrik' (Weimar: Thüringer Volksverlag). 'Sonntag,' 18 July 1954.

--- "Probleme der Laienkunst: Bemerkungen zur Arbeit des Laienensembles, die während des II. Deutschlandtreffens in Berlin auftraten." 'Sonntag,' 13 June 1954, p.5.

--- "Sieg des Realismus." Rev. of 'Was einem Siege gleichkommt' (an anthology of Hungarian short prose). 'Neue deutsche Literatur,' 1, No. 11 (1953), 161-63.

--- "Die Unbesiegten." Rev. of 'Dein unbekannter Bruder,' by Willi Bredel. 'Neue deutsche Literatur,' 1, No. 5 (1953), 198-200.

--- "'... und das ist mein Vaterland': Über den literarischen Wettbewerb zum II. Deutschlandtreffen." 'Sonntag,' 30 May 1954.

Müller Heiner. "Vom Bauernjungen zum Schriftsteller: Besuch bei Ehm Welk." 'Sonntag,' 29 Aug. 1954.
--- "Wie es bleibt, ist es nicht." Rev. of 'Kargo,' by Thomas Brasch. 'Der Spiegel,' 12 Sept. 1977, pp. 212-15.
--- "Wir wollen unsre Kraft dem Leben weihn: Eindrücke von den Wettbewerben der Solistengruppen und Volkskunstensembles in Berlin." 'Sonntag,' 19 July 1953.
--- "Der Wurm in der Brücke oder Ein Säule steht selten allein." Reply to a review by De H. of 'Anthologie 56' (Verlag Neues Leben), 'Die Union' [Dresden], 28 Feb. 1957. 'Neue deutsche Literatur,' 5, No. 4 (1957), 162-63.

## II. WORKS ON HEINER MÜLLER

### A. Scholarly works

Bathrick, David, and Andreas Huyssen. "Producing Revolution: Heiner Müller's 'Mauser' as Learning Play." 'New German Critique,' No. 8 (Spring 1976), pp.110-21.
Bertram, Christian. "Im Auftrag ohne Auftrag." 'Theater heute,' 21 (March 1980), 43-44.
--- "Machine Morte oder Der entfesselte Wahnsinn: Heiner Müller's 'Hamletmaschine.'" 'Spectaculum,' 33 (1980), 308-11.
Case, Sue-Ellen. "Developments in Post-Brechtian Political Theater: The Plays of Heiner Müller." Diss. University of California 1981.
--- "From Bertolt Brecht to Heiner Müller." 'Performing Arts Journal,' No. 19 (1983), pp.94-102.
--- "Notes on Directing 'Cement.'" New German Critique Publication No. 1. Supplement to Issue No. 16 (Winter 1979), pp.71-80.
Charbon, Rémy. "'Denn das Schöne bedeutet das mögliche Ende der Schrecken': Versuch über Heiner Müller und das Theater der DDR in der Epoche des Neuen ökonomischen Systems." 'Wirkendes Wort,' 30 (1980), 149-77.

Fehervary, Helen. "Autorschaft, Geschlechtsbewusstsein und
 Öffentlichkeit: Versuch über Heiner Müllers 'Die Ham-
 letmaschine' und Christa Wolfs 'Kein Ort. Nirgends.'"
 In 'Entwürfe von Frauen in der Literatur des 20.
 Jahrhunderts.' Ed. Irmela von der Lühe. Literatur
 im historischen Prozess, Neue Folge 5. Berlin: Argu-
 ment, 1982, pp.132-53.
--- "Enlightenment or Entanglement: History and Aesthetics
 in Bertolt Brecht and Heiner Müller." 'New German
 Critique,' No. 8 (Spring 1976), pp.80-109.
--- introd. 'The Horatian.' By Heiner Müller. Trans. Marc
 D. Silberman, Helen Fehervary, and Guntram Weber.
 'The Minnesota Review,' NS 6 (Spring 1976), 40-42.
Fiebach, Joachim. "Nachwort." 'Die Schlacht/Traktor. Leben
 Gundlings Friedrich von Preussen Lessings Schlaf
 Traum Schrei.' By Heiner Müller. Berlin: Henschel,
 1977, pp.112-38.
Girshausen, Theo, ed. 'Die Hamletmaschine: Heiner Müllers
 Endspiel.' Köln: Prometh, 1978.
--- "Subjekt und Geschichte: Aspekte zur Neudefinition
 von Geschichte als ästhetischem Gegenstand in den
 Stücken Heiner Müllers." In 'Die Hamletmaschine:
 Heiner Müllers Endspiel.' Ed. Theo Girshausen. Köln:
 Prometh, 1978, pp.104-27.
--- "Vom Umgang mit Nietzsche in der Hamletmaschine:
 Anmerkungen zur Technik des literarischen Zitats bei
 Heiner Müller." In 'Die Hamletmaschine: Heiner Müllers
 Endspiel.' Ed. Theo Girshausen. Köln: Prometh, 1978,
 pp.98-103.
--- Burkhard Schmiester, and Richard Weber. "Kommunismus
 oder Barbarei: Ein Gespräch über Politik in der Ham-
 letmaschine." In 'Die Hamletmaschine: Heiner Müllers
 Endspiel.' Ed. Theo Girshausen. Köln: Prometh, 1978,
 pp.25-45.
Grimm, Reinhold. "Georg Büchner and the Modern Concept of
 Revolt." 'Studi Tedeschi,' 21, No. 2 (1978), 7-66.
Hörnigk, Frank. "Erinnerung an Revolutionen: Zu Entwicklungs-
 tendenzen in der Dramatik Heiner Müllers, Peter
 Hacks' und Volker Brauns am Ende der siebziger Jahre."
 In 'Tendenzen und Beispiele: Zur DDR-Literatur in den
 siebziger Jahren.' Ed. Hans Kaufmann. Leipzig: Philipp
 Reclam jun., 1981, pp.148-84.

Iversen, Fritz, and Norbert Servos. "Sprengsätze: Geschichte und Diskontinuität in den Stücken Heiner Müllers und der Theorie Walter Benjamins." In 'Die Hamletmaschine: Heiner Müllers Endspiel.' Ed. Theo Girshausen. Köln: Prometh, 1978, pp.128-38.

Laska, Martin. "Inszenierungstabelle der Stücke Heiner Müllers." 'Text + Kritik,' No. 73 (January 1982), pp.82-87.

Laube, Horst. "(Zerreissung der Fotographie des Autors)." In 'Theaterbuch 1.' Ed. Horst Laube and Brigitte Landes. München: Carl Hanser, 1978, pp.243-45.

Lehmann, Hans-Thies. "Dramatische Form und Revolution in Georg Büchners 'Dantons Tod' und Heiner Müllers 'Der Auftrag.'" In 'Dantons Tod. Die Trauerarbeit im Schönen: Ein Theaterlesebuch.' Ed. Peter von Becker. Frankfurt am Main: Syndikat, 1980, pp.106-21.

--- "Raum-Zeit: Das Entgleiten der Geschichte in der Dramatik Heiner Müllers und im französischen Poststrukturalismus." 'Text + Kritik,' No. 73 (January 1982), pp.71-81.

Mäde, Hans Dieter. "Die Neufassung." 'Neue deutsche Literatur,' 7, No. 1 (1959), 122-27.

Mangel, Rüdiger, and Georg Wieghaus. "Abgrenzung und Teilhabe: Thesen zu Heiner Müllers Position im Literaturprozess der DDR." 'Text + Kritik,' No. 73 (January 1982), pp.32-44.

Rischbieter, Henning. "Zwei Stücke über deutsche Geschichte: Hinweise und Überlegungen." 'Theater heute': Jahrbuch 1977, pp.92-95.

Rohmer, Rolf. "Nachwort." 'Stücke.' By Heiner Müller. Berlin: Henschel, 1975, pp.390-99.

Schmiester, Burkhard. "Ein Fragment gegen Strohköpfe: Oder was die 'Hamletmaschine' bewirken kann." In 'Die Hamletmaschine: Heiner Müllers Endspiel.' Ed. Theo Girshausen. Köln: Prometh, 1978, pp.156-63.

Schulz, Genia. "Abschied von Morgen: Zu den Frauengestalten im Werk Heiner Müllers." 'Text + Kritik,' No. 73 (January 1982), pp.58-70.

--- 'Heiner Müller.' Sammlung Metzler, 197. Stuttgart: J.B. Metzler, 1980.

--- "Something is Rotten in this Age of Hope: Heiner Müllers Blick auf die (deutsche) Geschichte." 'Merkur,' 33 (1979), 468-80.

Schulz, Genia, and Hans-Thies Lehmann. "Es ist ein eigentümlicher Apparat: Versuch über Heiner Müllers 'Hamletmaschine.'" 'Theater heute,' 20 (October 1979), 11-14.

Schweikert, Uwe. "Die entfesselte Kassandra: Ein Versuch über Heiner Müller." 'Frankfurter Rundschau,' 30 Aug. 1980.

Silberman, Marc. 'Heiner Müller.' Forschungsberichte zur DDR-Literatur, Vol. 2. Ed. Gerd Labroisse. Amsterdam: Rodopi, 1980.

Töteberg, Michael. "Vorgeschichte eines Autors: Über Heiner Müllers Anfänge: Journalistische Arbeiten, frühe Lyrik." 'Text + Kritik,' No. 73 (January 1982), pp.2-9.

Umbrecht, Bernard. "Fin de mission: Sur la dernière pièce, 'der Auftrag' de Heiner Müller." 'Connaissance de la RDA,' No. 12 (1981), pp.69-79.

Vassan, Florian. "Der Tod des Körpers in der Geschichte: Tod, Sexualität und Arbeit bei Heiner Müller." 'Text + Kritik,' No. 73 (January 1982), pp.45-57.

Vormweg, Heinrich. "Sprache - die Heimat der Bilder: Vorschläge zur Annäherung an Heiner Müller." 'Text + Kritik,' No. 73 (January 1982), pp.20-31.

Weber, Carl. "Heiner Müller: The Despair and the Hope." 'Performing Arts Journal,' No. 12 (1980), pp.135-40.

Weber, Richard. "'Ich war, ich bin, ich werde sein!': Versuch, die politische Dimension der Hamletmaschine zu orten." In 'Die Hamletmaschine: Heiner Müllers Endspiel.' Ed. Theo Girshausen. Köln: Prometh, 1978, pp.86-97.

Wieghaus, Georg. 'Heiner Müller.' Autorenbücher, 25. Ed. Heinz Ludwig Arnold and Ernst-Peter Wieckenberg. München: C.H. Beck; Verlag Edition Text und Kritik, 1981.

Wirth, Andrzej. "Vom Dialog zum Diskurs: Versuch einer Synthese der nachbrechtschen Theaterkonzepte." 'Theater heute,' 21 (January 1980), 16-19.

Wittstock, Uwe. "Auswahlbibliographie zu Heiner Müller." 'Text + Kritik,' No. 73 (January 1982), pp.91-95.

--- "Die schnellen Wirkungen sind nicht die neuen: Ein Porträt des Dramatikers Heiner Müller." 'Text + Kritik,' No. 73 (January 1982), pp.10-19.

Zaum, Ulrich. "Zwischen Dichtung, Bekenntnis und bürgerlicher Avantgarde: Bemerkungen zu Etappen der Rezeption

Heiner Müllers in der BRD." In 'Die Hamletmaschine: Heiner Müllers Endspiel.' Ed. Theo Girshausen. Köln: Prometh, 1978, pp.79-85.

## B. Theater reviews

Allemann, Urs. "Berlin (DDR). Der Säufer als Utopist: Heiner Müller 'Die Bauern' uraufgeführt." 'Theater heute,' 17 (August 1976), 10-13.

Berg, Jan. "Mehrdeutig, doch nicht beliebig. Ausgerechnet, doch nicht einlinig: Die Theatersprache der 'Macbeth'-Inszenierung." 'Theater heute,' 23 (December 1982), 24-25.

Erdmann, Michael. "Die Heimatlosigkeit der Wollust: Heiner Müllers 'Auftrag' in Frankfurt und sein neuer Text 'Quartett.'" 'Theater heute,' 22 (July 1981), 42-45.

Henrichs, Benjamin. "Die zum Lächeln nicht Zwingbaren: Zu 'Macbeth': eine verspätete Polemik, eine verunglückte Inszenierung, ein Interview." 'Die Zeit,' Overseas Edition, 31 May 1974, p.11.

Lehmann, Hans-Thies. "Das Ende der Macht - auf dem Theater: Heiner Müllers 'Macbeth' - Text 1972: Inszenierung 1982." 'Theater heute,' 23 (December 1982), 16-24.

Linzer, Martin. "Der Auftrag bleibt gültig: Heiner Müller - Uraufführung im 3. Stock der Volksbühne." 'Theater der Zeit,' 36, No. 1 (1981), 34-35.

Müller, Christoph. "Die Deutschen und ihr Krieg: Neue Versuche mit Heiner Müllers 'Schlacht' in Basel und Mannheim." 'Theater heute,' 17 (December 1976), 16-18.

Navratil, Carl M. "Budapest. Vielfalt der Mittel, Einfalt der Wirkung: Aufführungsbeschreibung: Heiner Müllers 'Zement.'" 'Theater heute,' 17 (August 1976), 14-17.

Rischbieter, Henning. "Hamburg. 'Fatzer', fatal: Brechts Fragmente, von Heiner Müller montiert." 'Theater heute,' 19 (April 1978), 9-11.

--- "Nazizeit auf dem Theater. Tötungs-Reigen: 'Die Schlacht' von Heiner Müller in Berlin und Hamburg." 'Theater heute,' 16 (December 1975), 6-14.

--- "Nur heilloser Schrecken? Heiner Müllers 'Germania Tod in Berlin' an den Münchner Kammerspielen." 'Theater heute,' 19 (June 1978), 7-11.

Rischbieter, Henning. "Unter der schwarzen Sonne der Folter: Stücke von Heiner Müller in Frankfurt und Paris." 'Theater heute,' 20 (March 1979), 35-41.

--- "Die Wörter + Die Zeichen: Heiner Müller, Nina Ritter und Erich Wonder inszenieren Heiner Müllers 'Auftrag' in Bochum." 'Theater heute,' 23 (April 1982), 7-12.

Rühle, Günther. "Die Traktierung des Heiner Müller: 'Mauser' in Köln, 'Hamletmaschine' in Frankfurt - zwei Fälle und viele Fragen." 'Theater heute,' 21 (June 1980), 18-22.

Stoessel, Marleen. "Bochum: Mit Dolchen Reden." 'Theater heute,' 23 (June 1982), 2-4.

Wirth, Andrzej. "Erinnerung an eine Revolution: sadomasochistisch: Heiner Müller inszeniert seinen Text 'Der Auftrag' in Ostberlin." 'Theater heute,' 22 (February 1981), 6-8.

## III. OTHER PRIMARY WORKS

A. Literary works

Artaud, Antonin. "Le Jet de Sang." In 'Oeuvres complètes.' Vol. I. Paris: Editions Gallimard, 1976, pp. 70-76.

Beckett, Samuel. 'Endgame: A Play in One Act.' Trans. Samuel Beckett. New York: Grove Press, 1958.

Bonaventura. 'Die Nachtwachen.' Ed. Wolfgang Paulsen. Stuttgart: Philipp Reclam Jun., 1964, 1974.

Brecht, Bertolt. 'Gesammelte Werke in acht Bänden.' Ed. Suhrkamp Verlag and Elisabeth Hauptmann. Frankfurt am Main: Suhrkamp, 1967.

--- "Geschichten aus der Revolution." In 'Versuche,' No. 7 (1933), pp. 79-81.

--- "Der Untergang des Egoisten Fatzer." 'Theater heute,' 17 (April 1976), 48-57.

Büchner, Georg. 'Sämtliche Werke und Briefe.' Historisch-kritische Ausgabe. Ed. Werner R. Lehmann. Vol. I. München: Carl Hanser, 1974.

Césaire, Aimé. 'Cahier d'un Retour au Pays Natal.' Introd. "Un grand Poète noir" by André Breton. Trans. Lionel Abel and Ivan Goll. New York: Brentano's, 1947.

Conrad, Joseph. 'Heart of Darkness.' Ed. Robert Kimbrough. 2nd ed. New York: W.W. Norton, 1971.

Cummings, E.E. 'The Enormous Room.' New York: The Modern Library, 1934.

'Des Knaben Wunderhorn: Alte Deutsche Lieder.' Comp. L. Achim von Arnim and Clemens Brentano. Vollständige Ausgabe nach dem Text der Erstausgabe von 1806-1808. München: Winkler, 1962.

'Deutsches Kinderlied und Kinderspiel: Volksüberlieferungen aus allen Landen deutscher Zunge.' Ed. Franz Magnus Böhme. Leipzig: Breitkopf und Härtel, 1897.

Eliot, T.S. 'The Complete Poems and Plays, 1909-1950.' New York: Harcourt, Brace & World, 1971.

Ford, John. ''Tis Pity She's a Whore.' In 'The Works of John Ford.' Ed. William Gifford, rev. Alexander Dyce. 1895; rpt. New York: Russell & Russell, 1965. I, 107-208.

García Lorca, Federico. "Escena del Teniente Coronel de la Guardia Civil." In 'Obras completas.' Ed. Arturo del Hoyo. Madrid: Aguilar, 1954, pp.254-58.

Genet, Jean. 'The Balcony.' Trans. Bernard Frechtman. In 'Seven Plays of the Modern Theater.' Introd. Harold Clurman. New York: Grove Press, 1962, pp.269-370.

--- 'The Blacks: A Clown Show.' Trans. Bernard Frechtman. New York: Grove Press, 1960.

--- 'The Maids.' Introd. Jean-Paul Sartre. In 'The Maids and Deathwatch.' Trans. Bernard Frechtman. New York: Grove Press, 1954, 1961.

--- 'Querelle.' Trans. Anselm Holle. New York: Grove Press, 1974.

Goethe, Johann Wolfgang. 'Werke.' Hamburger Ausgabe in 14 Bänden. Ed. Erich Trunz. Vol. XI: Autobiographische Schriften, III. München: C.H. Beck, 1978.

Grimm, Jakob, and Wilhelm Grimm. 'Kinder- und Hausmärchen.' Ed. Friedrich von der Leyen. 2 vols. Düsseldorf-Köln: Eugen Diederich, 1962.

Heym, Georg. 'Dichtungen und Schriften.' Ed. Karl Ludwig Schneider. Hamburg, München: Heinrich Ellermann, 1964. Vol. I: Lyrik.

Hölderlin, Friedrich. 'Sämtliche Werke.' Grosse Stuttgarter Ausgabe. Ed. Friedrich Beissner. Vol. II. Stuttgart:

W. Kohlhammer; J.G. Cottasche Buchhandlung Nachfolger, 1951.
Kafka, Franz. 'Der Prozess: Roman.' Ed. Max Brod. 3rd ed. Frankfurt am Main: S. Fischer; Lizenzausgabe v. New York: Schocken Books, 1946.
--- 'Tagebücher 1910-1923.' Ed. Max Brod. Frankfurt am Main: S. Fischer; Lizenzausgabe v. New York: Schocken Books, 1948-1949.
Kleist, Heinrich von. 'Sämtliche Werke und Briefe.' Ed. Helmut Sembdner. 2 vols. München: Carl Hanser, 1961.
'Lautréamont's "Maldoror."' Trans. Alexis Lykiard. New York: Thomas Y. Crowell, 1973.
Lautréamont (Isidore Ducasse). 'Poésies and Complete Miscellanea.' With English and French texts. Ed. and trans. Alexis Lykiard. London: Allison & Busby, 1978.
Lessing, Gotthold Ephraim. 'Werke.' Ed. Herbert G. Göpfert et al. Vol. II. Darmstadt: Wissenschaftliche Buchgesellschaft, 1971.
Mann, Thomas. 'Gesammelte Werke in zwölf Bänden.' Vol. VI: 'Doktor Faustus: Das Leben des Deutschen Tonsetzers Adrian Leverkühn erzählt von einem Freunde.' Frankfurt am Main: S. Fischer, 1960.
Marlowe, Christopher. 'The Complete Works.' Ed. Fredson Bowers. London: Cambridge Univ. Press, 1973. Vol. I.
Mayakovsky, Vladimir. 'Selected Poetry.' Trans. Dorian Rottenberg. Moscow: Foreign Languages Publishing House, n.d.
--- '150 Millionen.' Trans. Johannes R. Becher. Berlin: Malik, 1924; rpt. Königstein Ts., München: Athenäum, 1981.
Ovid. 'Metamorphoses.' Trans. Rolfe Humphries. Bloomington, Indiana: Indiana Univ. Press, 1955.
Racine, Jean. 'Complete Plays.' Trans. Samuel Solomon. 2 vols. New York: Random House, 1967.
Rimbaud, Arthur. 'Oeuvres complètes.' Ed. Rolland de Reneville and Jules Mouquet. Bibliothèque de la Pléiade, 68. Tours: Editions Gallimard, 1963.
Sartre, Jean-Paul. 'Nausea.' Trans. Lloyd Alexander. Introd. Hayden Carruth. New York: New Directions, 1964.
--- 'The Victors.' Trans. Lionel Abel. In 'Three Plays.' New York: Alfred A. Knopf, 1949, pp.197-272.

Schiller, Friedrich. 'Schillers Werke.' Nationalausgabe.
  Ed. Lieselotte Blumenthal and Benno von Wiese. Vol.
  I. Ed. Julius Petersen and Friedrich Beissner. Weimar: Hermann Böhlaus Nachfolger, 1943.
Seghers, Anna. "Das Licht auf dem Galgen." In 'Erzählungen.'
  Neuwied, Berlin: Luchterhand, 1964. II, 169-291.
Shakespeare, William. 'Hamlet.' New Variorum Edition. Ed.
  Horace Howard Furness. 2 vols. 10th ed., 1877; rpt.
  New York: Dover Publications, 1963.
--- 'King Richard III.' Arden Edition. Ed. Antony Hammond. London, New York: Methuen, 1981.
--- 'Macbeth.' New Variorum Edition. Ed. Horace Howard Furness, Jr. 5th ed., 1873; rpt. New York: Dover Publications, 1963.
Strauss, Johann, and Richard Genee. 'Die Fledermaus.' English and German text. Boston: Oliver Ditson, n.d.
'Stücke der Zwanziger Jahre.' Ed. Wolfgang Storch. Frankfurt am Main: Suhrkamp, 1977.
Trakl, Georg. 'Dichtungen und Briefe.' Historisch-kritische Ausgabe. Ed. Walther Killy and Hans Szklenar. 2 vols. Salzburg: Otto Müller, 1969.

B. Theoretical works

Adorno, Theodor W. "Der Artist als Statthalter." In 'Gesammelte Schriften.' Ed. Rolf Tiedemann. Vol. II. Frankfurt am Main: Suhrkamp, 1974, pp.114-26.
Artaud, Antonin. "Manifeste pour un théâtre avorté." In 'Oeuvres complètes.' Vol. II. Paris: Editions Gallimard, 1980, pp.22-25.
--- 'Selected Writings.' Ed. and introd. Susan Sontag. Trans. Helen Weaver. New York: Farrar, Straus and Giroux, 1976.
--- 'The Theater and its Double.' Trans. Mary Caroline Richards. New York: Grove Press, 1958.
Barthes, Roland. 'Image-Music-Text.' Selected and trans. Stephen Heath. New York: Hill and Wang, 1977.
Baudrillard, Jean. 'Kool Killer oder Der Aufstand der Zeichen.' Trans. Hans-Joachim Metzger. Berlin: Merve, 1978.

Benjamin, Walter. "Geschichtsphilosophische Thesen." In 'Schriften.' Ed. Theodor W. Adorno and Gretel Adorno. Frankfurt am Main: Suhrkamp, 1955. I, 494-506.
--- 'Versuche über Brecht.' Ed. Rolf Tiedemann. Frankfurt am Main: Suhrkamp, 1978.
Césaire, Aimé. 'Discourse on Colonialism.' Trans. Joan Pinkham. New York: Monthly Review Press, 1972.
--- "Isidore Ducasse Comte de Lautréamont: La poésie de Lautréamont belle comme un décret d'expropriation." 'Tropiques,' No. 6-7 (February 1943), pp.10-15.
Deleuze, Gilles. "Ein Manifest weniger." In 'Kleine Schriften.' Trans. K.D. Schacht. Berlin: Merve, 1980, pp.37-74.
--- and Félix Guattari. 'Kafka: Für eine kleine Literatur.' Trans. Burkhart Kroeber. Frankfurt am Main: Suhrkamp, 1976.
Fanon, Frantz. 'Black Skin, White Masks.' Trans. Charles Lam Markmann. New York: Grove Press, 1967.
--- 'The Wretched of the Earth.' Pref. Jean-Paul Sartre. Trans. Constance Farrington. New York: Grove Press, 1968.
Foucault, Michel. 'Madness and Civilization: A History of Insanity in the Age of Reason.' Trans. Richard Howard. New York: Random House, 1973.
--- "Der sogenannte Linksintellektuelle." Trans. Uli Laukat. 'Alternative,' 21 (1978), 74-85.
Hegel, G.W.F. 'Werke in zwanzig Bänden.' Vol. XV: 'Vorlesungen über die Ästhetik,' III. Ed. Eva Moldenhauer and Karl Markus Michel. Frankfurt am Main: Suhrkamp, 1970.
Horkheimer, Max, and Theodor W. Adorno. 'Dialektik der Aufklärung.' In Theodor W. Adorno, 'Gesammelte Schriften.' Ed. Rolf Tiedemann. Vol. III. Frankfurt am Main: Suhrkamp, 1981.
Lessing, Gotthold Ephraim. 'Briefe, die neueste Literatur betreffend 1759-1765.' In 'Werke.' Ed. Herbert G. Göpfert et al. Vol. V. Darmstadt: Wissenschaftliche Buchgesellschaft, 1973, pp.30-329.
--- 'Hamburgische Dramaturgie.' In 'Werke.' Ed Herbert G. Göpfert et al. Vol. IV. Darmstadt: Wissenschaftliche Buchgesellschaft, 1973, pp.229-720.

Marx, Karl. 'Werke. Schriften. Briefe.' Ed. Hans-Joachim Lieber. Vol. VI: Ökonomische Schriften, III: 'Das Kapital: Kritik der politischen Ökonomie,' III. Ed. Hans-Joachim Lieber and Benedikt Kautsky. Stuttgart: Cotta, 1964.
--- and Friedrich Engels. 'Die deutsche Ideologie.' In Karl Marx, 'Werke. Schriften.' Ed. Hans-Joachim Lieber. Vol. II: Frühe Schriften, II. Ed. Hans-Joachim Lieber and Peter Furth. Stuttgart: Cotta, 1971, pp.5-655.
--- and Friedrich Engels. 'The Marx-Engels Reader.' Ed. Robert C. Tucker. New York: W.W. Norton, 1972.
--- and Friedrich Engels. 'On Literature and Art: A Selection of Writings.' Ed. Lee Baxandall and Stefan Morawski. Documents on Marxist Aesthetics, Vol. 1. New York: International General, 1973.
Mayakovsky, Vladimir. 'How are Verses Made?' Trans. G.M. Hyde. London: Jonathan Cape, 1970.
Nietzsche, Friedrich. 'Die Geburt der Tragödie.' In 'Nietzsches Werke.' Kritische Gesamtausgabe. Ed. Giorgio Colli and Mazzino Montinari. Vol. III-1. Berlin, New York: Walter de Gruyter, 1972.

## IV. OTHER SECONDARY WORKS

Bolte, Johannes, and Georg Polivka. 'Anmerkungen zu den Kinder- u. Hausmärchen der Brüder Grimm.' 5 vols. Hildesheim: Georg Olms, 1963.
'Brechts Modell der Lehrstücke: Zeugnisse, Diskussion, Erfahrung.' Ed. Reiner Steinweg. Frankfurt am Main: Suhrkamp, 1976.
Bürger, Peter. "The Significance of the Avant-Garde for Contemporary Aesthetics: A Reply to Jürgen Habermas." 'New German Critique,' No. 22 (Winter 1981), pp. 19-22.
--- 'Theorie der Avantgarde.' Frankfurt am Main: Suhrkamp, 1974.
Case, Sue-Ellen. "Der Zwang zum Modell und zur Metapher: Tendenzen und Widersprüche im DDR-Theater." 'Theater heute,' 21 (October 1980), 8-14.

Cherry, Colin. 'On Human Communication: A Review, a Survey, and a Criticism.' 3rd ed. Cambridge, Massachusetts: The MIT Press, 1978.

de Jonge, Alex. 'Nightmare Culture: Lautréamont and "Les Chants de Maldoror."' New York: St. Martin's Press, 1973.

Descombes, Vincent. 'Modern French Philosophy.' Trans. L. Scott-Fox and J.M. Harding. Cambridge: Cambridge Univ. Press, 1980.

'Dokumente zur Kunst-, Literatur- und Kulturpolitik der SED.' Ed. Elimar Schubbe. Stuttgart: Seewald, 1972.

Fowlie, Wallace. 'Lautréamont.' New York: Twayne Publishers, 1973.

'Grundbegriffe des Marxismus: Eine lexikalische Einführung.' Ed. Iring Fetscher. Hamburg: Hoffmann und Campe, 1976.

Guthke, Karl S. 'Das deutsche bürgerliche Trauerspiel.' Stuttgart: J.B. Metzler, 1972.

Habermas, Jürgen. "Die Moderne - ein unvollendetes Projekt." 'Die Zeit,' Overseas Edition, 26 Sept. 1980, pp. 17-18.

--- "Modernity versus Postmodernity." 'New German Critique,' No. 22 (Winter 1981), pp.3-14.

Hassan, Ihab. 'The Dismemberment of Orpheus: Toward a Postmodern Literature.' 2nd ed. Madison, Wisconsin: Univ. of Wisconsin Press, 1982.

--- "POSTmodernISM: A Paracritical Bibliography." 'New Literary History,' 3, No. 1 (Autumn 1971), 5-30. Rpt. in Ihab Hassan, 'Paracriticisms: Seven Speculations of the Times.' Urbana, Illinois: Univ. of Illinois Press, 1975, pp.39-58.

--- "The Question of Postmodernism." 'Performing Arts Journal,' No. 16 (1981), pp.30-37.

Hegemann, Werner. 'Das steinerne Berlin: Geschichte der grössten Mietkasernenstadt der Welt.' Berlin: Gustav Kiepenheuer, 1930.

Hermand, Jost. "Das Gute-Neue und das Schlechte-Neue: Wandlungen der Modernismus-Debatte in der DDR seit 1956." In 'Literatur und Literaturtheorie in der DDR.' Ed. Peter Uwe Hohendahl and Patricia Herminghouse. Frankfurt am Main: Suhrkamp, 1976, pp.73-99.

Hoffmann, Gerhard, Alfred Hornung, and Rüdiger Kunow. "'Modern,' 'Postmodern' and 'Contemporary' as Criteria for the Analysis of 20th Century Literature." 'Amerikastudien/American Studies,' 22, No. 1 (1977), 19-46.

Huyssen, Andreas. "The Search for Tradition: Avant-Garde and Postmodernism in the 1970s." 'New German Critique,' No. 22 (Winter 1981), pp.23-40.

Janik, Dieter. "Gabriel García Márquez." In 'Lateinamerikanische Literatur der Gegenwart in Einzeldarstellungen.' Ed. Wolfgang Eitel. Stuttgart: Alfred Kröner, 1978, pp.330-60.

Kenner, Hugh. 'Samuel Beckett: A Critical Study.' London: John Calder, 1961.

Kittler, Friedrich A. "'Erziehung ist Offenbarung': Zur Struktur der Familie in Lessings Dramen." 'Jahrbuch der Deutschen Schillergesellschaft,' 21 (1977), 111-37.

Knopf, Jan. 'Brecht-Handbuch.' Stuttgart: J.B. Metzler; Carl Ernst Poeschel, 1980.

Köhler, Michael. "'Postmodernismus': Ein begriffsgeschichtlicher Überblick." 'Amerikastudien/American Studies,' 22, No. 1 (1977), 8-18.

Lifshitz, Mikhail. 'The Philosophy of Art of Karl Marx.' Trans. Ralph B. Winn. London: Pluto Press, 1973.

Milfull, John. 'From Baal to Keuner: The "Second Optimism" of Bertolt Brecht.' Australisch-Neuseeländische Studien zur deutschen Sprache und Literatur, Vol. 5. Ed. Gerhard Schulz and John A. Asher. Bern, Frankfurt am Main: Herbert Lang, 1974.

Sanders, Ed. 'The Family: The Story of Charles Manson's Dune Buggy Attack Battalion.' New York: E.P. Dutton, 1971.

Schaer, Wolfgang. 'Die Gesellschaft im deutschen bürgerlichen Drama des 18. Jahrhunderts: Grundlagen und Bedrohung im Spiegel der dramatischen Literatur.' Bonner Arbeiten zur deutschen Literatur, Vol. 7. Ed. Benno von Wiese. Bonn: H. Bouvier, 1963.

Schatzman, Morton. 'Soul Murder: Persecution in the Family.' New York: Random House, 1973.

St. Aubyn, F.C. 'Arthur Rimbaud.' Boston: Twayne Publishers, 1975.

Starkie, Enid. 'Arthur Rimbaud.' London: Faber and Faber, 1938.

Szondi, Peter. 'Die Theorie des bürgerlichen Trauerspiels im 18. Jahrhundert: Der Kaufmann, der Hausvater und der Hofmeister.' Studienausgabe der Vorlesungen, Vol. 1. Frankfurt am Main: Suhrkamp, 1973.

--- 'Theorie des modernen Dramas (1880-1950).' Frankfurt am Main: Suhrkamp, 1956.

# NEW YORK UNIVERSITY OTTENDORFER SERIES, NEUE FOLGE

- Bd. 1 Rosenbauer, Brecht und der Behaviorismus. 102 Seiten, 1970.
- Bd. 2 Zipes, The Great Refusal, Studies of the Romantic Hero in German and American Literature. 158 Seiten, 1970.
- Bd. 3 Hughes, Mythos und Geschichtsoptimismus in Thomas Manns Joseph Romanen. 116 Seiten, 1975.
- Bd. 4 Salloch, Peter Weiss' «Die Ermittlung». Zur Struktur des Dokumentartheaters. 170 Seiten, 1972.
- Bd. 5 Peter/Grathoff/Hayes/Loose, Ideologiekritische Studien zur Literatur, Essays I. 260 Seiten, 1972.
- Bd. 6 Seitz, Johann Fischarts Geschichtsklitterung zur Prosastruktur und zum grobianischen Motivkomplex. 252 Seiten, 1974.
- Bd. 7 Vaget/Barnouw, Thomas Mann-Studien zu Fragen der Rezeption. 158 Seiten, 1975.
- Bd. 8 Baron/Mühsam/Heidesieck/Grimm/Theisz, Ideologiekritische Studien zur Literatur. Essays II. 158 Seiten, 1975.
- Bd. 9 Silbermann, Literature of the Working World. A Study of the Industrial Novel in East Germany. 118 Seiten, 1976.
- Bd. 10 Rosellini, Thomas Müntzer im deutschen Drama. Verteufelung, Apotheose und Kritik. 176 Seiten, 1978.
- Bd. 11 Antosik, The Question of Elites. An Essay on the Cultural Elitism of Nietzsche, George and Hesse. 204 Seiten, 1978.
- Bd. 12 Becker, A War of Fools. The Letters of Obscure Men: A Study of the Satire and the Satirized. 190 Seiten, 1981.
- Bd. 13 Van Cleve, Herlequin Besieged. The Reception of Comedy in Germany during the Early Enlightenment. 203 Seiten, 1980.
- Bd. 14 McKnight, The Novels of Johann Karl Wezel. Satire, Realism and Social Criticism in Late 18th Century Literature. 311 Seiten, 1981.
- Bd. 15 Stern, Gegenbild, Reihenfolge, Sprung. An Essay on Related Figures of Argument in Walter Benjamin. 121 Seiten, 1982.
- Bd. 16 Poore, German-American Socialist Literature, 1865–1900. 225 Seiten, 1982.
- Bd. 17 Berman, Between Fontane and Tucholsky: Literary Criticism and the Public Sphere in Imperial Germany. 175 Seiten, 1983.
- Bd. 18 Blevins, Franz Xaver Kroetz: The Emergence of a Political Playwright. 295 Seiten, 1983.
- Bd. 19 Grimm, Texturen – Essays und anderes zu Hans Magnus Enzensberger. 236 Seiten, 1984.
- Bd. 20 Reutershan, Clara Zetkin und Brot und Rosen. Literaturpolitische Konflikte zwischen Partei und Frauenbewegung in der deutschen Vorkriegssozialdemokratie. 264 Seiten, 1985.

Die Bände 1, 2, 4, 5 und 6 sind direkt beim Athenäum-Verlag in Frankfurt/M. zu beziehen. Alle übrigen, sowie die später erscheinenden Bände werden durch den Verlag Peter Lang AG, Bern hergestellt und ausgeliefert.